Data Sources
for
Business and Market Analysis

by

Nathalie D. Frank

Second Edition

The Scarecrow Press, Inc.
Metuchen, N.J.   1969

SBN 8108-0261-9

The first edition was issued under the title:
Market Analysis; handbook of current data sources.

To

My Mother

who lent heart and hand
to a seemingly endless task

Table of Contents

	Page
Introduction	11
Marketing Information and Its Retrieval	13
The Climate	13
The Person	14
The Information	14
The Source	15
The Search	18
Compendia and Market Data Guides	21
General	21
Market Data	23
Federal Statistical Program	27
General Organization	27
Methodology Reports and Manuals	29
Advisory Bodies	36
Bureau of the Census Publications	40
Special Publications	41
Major Censuses and Current Reports	42
Agriculture	42
Current Reports	45
Business	46
Special Reports	50
Combined Reports	50
Current Reports	52
Combined	52
Retail Trade	52
Services	53
Wholesale Trade	53
Commercial Fisheries	53
Manufactures	54
Special Reports	55
Current Reports	57
Mineral Industries	62
Transportation	63
Governments	65
Current Reports	68
Population and Housing	69
Combined Reports	74
Guides to 1960 Censuses	75
Current Reports	75

Bureau of the Census Publications   Page
    Current Reports (cont.)

Population	75
Housing	77
Construction Statistics	77
Foreign Trade Statistics	79
Summaries	81
Detailed Export Reports	81
Detailed Import Reports	84
Geographic Reports	86
Other Federal Sources	88
Executive Office of the President	88
The President	88
Council of Economic Advisers	89
Bureau of the Budget	89
Committees and Commissions	90
The Congress	90
Joint Economic Committee	91
Department of Agriculture	93
Agricultural Economics	94
Statistical Reporting Service	95
Economic Research Service	96
Consumer and Marketing Service	101
Other Units	101
Department of Commerce	103
Business and Defense Services Administration	103
Office of Business Economics	107
Bureau of International Commerce	109
Other Units	112
Department of Health, Education and Welfare	115
Public Health Service	115
Office of Education	118
Social Security Administration	119
Department of Housing and Urban Development	120
Federal Housing Administration	120
Renewal Assistance Administration	121
Department of the Interior	121
Bureau of Mines	121
Fish and Wildlife Service	123
Other Units	124
Department of Labor	127
Bureau of Labor Statistics	127
Prices and Cost of Living	128
Consumer Prices	128
Primary Market Prices	129
Employment and Labor Force	129
Consumer Expenditures	131
Special Reports	135
Guides to BLS Publications	137
Office of Manpower Policy, Evaluation and Research	137
Bureau of Employment Security	137
Women's Bureau	138

Department of Transportation 139
   Federal Aviation Administration 139
   Federal Highway Administration 139
   United States Coast Guard 140
Department of the Treasury 141
   Fiscal Service 141
   Internal Revenue Service 141
   Other Units 143
Board of Governors of the Federal Reserve System 143
   Banking and Finance 144
   Consumer Credit and Finances 145
   Federal Reserve Banks 146
Federal Trade Commission 147
United States Tariff Commission 148
Securities and Exchange Commission 149
Small Business Administration 150
Post Office Department 150
National Science Foundation 150
Other Agencies 151

Regional and Local Sources--Official and Quasi-official 155
   Governments 155
     State 156
     Local 157
   Chambers of Commerce 158
   Other 159
   Guides to Sources 160
     Regional 160
     State 161
       Omnibus Guides 161
       Single-State Guides 162
       Topical Guides 163
     Local 165
       Omnibus Guides 165
       Single-Area Guides 166
       Topical Guides 168

University Programs 169
   Private Grant Projects 169
   Continuing Programs and Publications 170
   Institutes 171
   Theses and Dissertations 171
   Bureaus of Business Research 171
   Guides to Projects and Publications 180
     Guides to University Research 180
     Guides to Theses and Dissertations 180
       Comprehensive 180
       Topical 181
         Marketing 181
         Other 182
     Guides to Business Bureaus 182

	Page
Research Institutions	184
Professional and Trade Associations	192
Professional Societies	192
Marketing	192
General	192
Industry Oriented	192
Allied Disciplines	194
Trade Associations	196
"Facts and Figures"	197
Statistical Releases	197
Operating Cost Studies	197
Special Reports and Analyses	198
Administrative Publications	198
Directories	198
Services and Field Research	200
Services for Marketing and Market Research	200
Consumer Marketing Services	201
Industrial Marketing Services	205
Individual Industry and Product Services	206
Business, Economic and Statistical Services	209
Financial Services	212
Other Services	213
Guides to Services and Field Research	214
Published Services	214
Firms and Individuals	214
Foreign	216
Advertising Media	218
Newspapers and Newspaper Supplements	219
Consumer Magazines	222
Marketing Guides	222
Surveys	225
Digests and Fact Sheets	226
Farm Publications	227
Trade Papers	228
Air Media	233
Guides to Media Sources	234
Business Firms	237
Product and Company Information	237
Product Literature	237
Corporate Literature	238
Advisory Literature	239
Industry Information	239
Advisory	239
Statistical	240
Marketing	241
Business Conditions	243
National	243
Regional/Local	244

	Page
Services	244
Guides to Business Firm Sources	245
Directories and Mailing Lists	247
Directories	247
Telephone Directories	247
City Directories	248
Biographical Directories	248
Business Directories	249
Products	250
Plants	252
Companies	253
Bibliographies and Guides	255
Comprehensive	255
Specialized	256
Mailing Lists	258
Periodicals	261
Tables of Contents	262
Professional Journals	262
Business Magazines	263
Newsletters	264
National Affairs	264
Individual Industries	265
Trade Publications	267
Advertising and Marketing	267
Other Industries	268
Directories of Periodicals	269
Abstracts and Indexes	272
Abstracts	272
Marketing Abstracts	273
General Business and Industry "Abstracts"	274
Individual Industry Abstracts	274
Allied Discipline Abstracts	275
Inter-disciplinary Abstracts	276
Indexes	276
Marketing	277
Business Press	278
Technical Press	279
Statistics	279
Government Data	280
Individual Industries	281
Information Centers and Specialists	284
Libraries	284
Field Offices of Federal Agencies	286
Directories of Information Centers and Specialists	290
Comprehensive	290
Federal Sources	292
State and Local Sources	293
Associations	293

Information Centers and Specialists (cont.)   Page
            Media   294
            Consultants   294

Research Aids   296
   Bibliographies and Guides   296
      Marketing   297
         Topical   298
      Government Publications   300
      General Business   301
         Topical   301
            Finance   302
            Metallurgy   303
            Transportation   303
            Statistics   304
            Packaging   304
   Catalogs and Checklists   304
      Comprehensive   305
      Special Purpose   305
         Media   305
         Federal Publications   305
         State Publications   309
   Current Press   310

Appendix--State Statistical Abstracts   314

Index   323

x

Introduction

Many changes have marked research tools and researchers since the publication, in 1954, of the compiler's modest guide to sources of marketing information. Foreseen then were the trends toward a data explosion and the need for expertise among researchers in locating available facts. The initial edition of the present handbook was an attempt to offer assistance to those caught between the two. The acceleration of both trends and the emergence of new developments have prompted the present revision.

The federal government still constitutes the largest single source of accessible business data. Recently, however, there has been a notable rise in activity in the statistical programs and publications at the state and local levels. The use of computers has prompted greater standardization and systematization of data, the tapping of previously inaccessible information resources and the rise of data banks sponsored by private services as well as by government agencies. Among the new sources, input-output analysis and warehouse withdrawal data distinguished themselves by their sudden appearance and speedy acceptance by industry. Whereas a few years ago much attention was directed to the search for facts, present effort is equally concerned with marshalling available intelligence into information systems as a base for business decisions and action. Basically, the typical sources of secondary data have remained the same. Their output, however, has grown in quantity and detail. In many instances it has assumed the elusive form of tape and punchcard.

Faced with these complexities and under pressure of the omnipresent factual climate, the student, the researcher and the practitioner are showing a greater awareness that for every question there is an answer--somewhere. The purpose of this guide, therefore, is to provide a broad reservoir of documentation from which

11

each can draw understanding and direction as the individual need arises.

Because current, continuing information plays a primary role in business decisions, emphasis in this edition, as in the last, has been placed on original sources of quantitative data and on continuing keys to business facts. No attempt has been made to produce a definitive bibliography. Individual references have been selected on the basis of their general usefulness in researching economic conditions, business trends, and consumer and industrial markets. Excluded are the tools of advertising and media research. Publications characteristic of individual industries have been included as illustrative examples. Others of like nature can be located through the bibliographies and guides suggested throughout the text.

The arrangement by type of source, rather than by topic, has been retained to aid the user in identifying the major suppliers of information with the nature of their product. Such orientation, although not infallible, transcends the vagaries of specific programs and publications and provides more lasting guidelines to the origins of business data and, more importantly, to their underlying, unpublished strata.

Nathalie D. Frank

New York

November 1968

MARKETING INFORMATION
AND ITS RETRIEVAL

The value of information to management lies in its accessibility and use. Since the capacity of the human mind to store knowledge is limited, sound decision and effective action rest on the assembly of pertinent facts quickly and economically.

To solve the problem of accessibility many organizations have established special units staffed with professionals whose sole responsibility is the systematic accumulation, organization, and intramural dissemination of information applicable to current activities and long-range programs. Despite the proliferation of such information centers, published facts, particularly, still present an acute problem of inaccessibility to many marketing men. Thus, researchers lacking organized facilities would benefit appreciably from a personal program of regular scanning, selection and acquisition of source materials bearing directly upon immediate projects and foreseeable interests.

THE CLIMATE

Successful retrieval of available facts, either from an organized collection or from their scattered origins, depends not only on the individual but also to a large extent upon the intellectual climate within which he functions. Speaking from the vanguard of the information retrieval movement one of its leading exponents, Calvin N. Mooers, states: "...for many people it is more painful and troublesome to have information than not to have it. ...On the other hand, there are situations where the diligent finding and use of information is stressed and rewarded..."[1]

Either approach may be detected in the posing of the question to one's self and to others. Under optimum conditions the searcher participates in the discussion of plans, goals, underlying assumptions, and end uses of the desired facts. He is briefed directly, thoroughly and, if need be, continuously. Written requests for unrelated specifics produce, at best, "echo" results which many times are not representative of pertinent data available. Similarly, seepage and misinterpretation of purpose and direction accompany the transmittal of an information call from person to person. Direct communication, on the other hand, engages the judgment, perception and experience of the searcher. It hardly fails to produce related data and helpful intelligence. More often than not it precludes wasted effort and disappointing results.

THE PERSON

To achieve success, however, the fact-finder, on his part, must contribute certain personal characteristics, knowledge, and search techniques.

Idle browsing is the antithesis of the purposeful search. Concentrated, critical scanning with a sense of direction can be learned. More often, however, it is the sign of a naturally inquisitive and imaginative, as well as of a disciplined mind productively at work. These characteristics together with initiative, perseverance, understanding and insight are fundamental to the application of knowledge and sound techniques.

Knowledge necessary to the successful search seldom lies in total recall of specific facts or specialized publications. More valuable is a broad acquaintance with the characteristics and behavior of information and its sources.

THE INFORMATION

Familiarity with marketing facts, their types and nature, indicates that not all useful information is quantitative. Statements of experience and opinion, either individual or collective, offer a multitude of case histories, trends, forecasts, guesstimates and analyses to the solution of marketing problems.

Quantified and systematized, facts become statistics. Some

represent the results of single research efforts.   Others are collected and compiled continuously, and issued regularly with varying
frequency.   Benchmark data published by the federal government
furnish the greatest amount of general purpose detail and serve as
a basic reference.   These are updated and supplemented by a large
number of current statistics issued at more frequent intervals.

Nor do all the answers lie in published or recorded fact.
An expert's voiced knowledge, experience and opinion rank high as
information, particularly in those areas which lack research effort
or formal documentation.

THE SOURCE

So transient and mutable are information sources that knowledge, even of standard works past and present, quickly becomes
obsolete.   Moreover, the advent of the computer has given rise to
a new and even more elusive source.   Data banks, on punchcard
and tape, and other stores of unpublished facts are growing in number and size at an accelerated rate.   And, although there are book
catalogs and periodical indexes, a data bank directory has yet to be
compiled.

Current awareness of data collecting and producing sources,
therefore, is more important than "knowledge."   For continuous updating both must rely on certain aids and on a method of evaluating current sources and their output.   Guides, bibliographies, catalogs, checklists, as well as the literature of specific subjects and
industries provide current orientation and a basis for judging the
adequacy of each source.   This may be done principally in terms
of its authoritativeness, scope and timeliness.

Much of the validity of information rests on the authority of
the source: the status and background of the individual or organization providing the information; methods of collection and compilation; proximity of the source to the actual fact.

Primary sources, or those which originate the data, are
preferable to secondary sources, or those which republish information produced by others.   Many sources are secondary in their en-

tirety. A large number are primary for some information and secondary for other. Although often helpful because of their selection and arrangement, secondary sources frequently lack valuable explanatory
material, detail, recency and proper documentation. On the other
hand, precise identification of cited data, preferably in complete
bibliographic form, enhances their usefulness as secondary sources
and as guides to primary sources.

The adequacy of a source for any given purpose also depends
on its scope and timeliness. The coverage, nature, detail and pre-
ciseness of information are best judged from a study of its prefatory
text, definitions and annotations. Recency and frequency of publication are the main indicators of timeliness. Particularly important for
statistical data, it is the critical factor in the selection and use of a
statistical source. Nor does recency of publication insure the location of only the latest information. Advance or preliminary releases,
for example, often carry greater detail as well as revisions of data
previously published in final form.

Since the survey method is widely used in the production of
current marketing data, noted here for further reference are a
number of promulgated standards used in the mounting of field research and in the evaluation of its results.

AMERICAN Marketing Association. Criteria to Assist Users of
Marketing Research... Chicago: American Marketing Association,
1962. 21 p.   (A 1)

> "...a guide primarily for the buyer of research, covering both
> methodological and ethical considerations. ... Emphasis is on
> the survey method..."

ADVERTISING Research Foundation. Criteria for Marketing and Advertising Research. New York: Advertising Research Foundation,
1963. [16] p.   (A 2)

> Developed by a subcommittee of the Research Committee of the
> American Association of Advertising Agencies, this checklist is
> intended primarily to test the validity of quantitative consumer
> studies.

AMERICAN Association of Advertising Agencies. How Advertising
Agencies Evaluate Various Types of Newspaper Research.

New York: American Association of Advertising Agencies, 1962.
19 p.   (A 3)

   Outlines the most prevalent types of newspaper research (market
   and advertising) from the viewpoint of acceptable methodology
   and usefulness. Suggests improvements for current studies and
   a program for future research effort.

---How Advertising Agencies Evaluate Various Types of Radio Research.
New York: American Association of Advertising Agencies, 1963.
20 p.   (A 4)

   Similar to the above. Touches briefly on market data produced by
   the medium.

---How Advertising Agencies Evaluate Various Types of Research Issued by Television Stations, Networks, and Representatives. New
York: American Association of Advertising Agencies, 1966. 7 p.

                                                                         (A 5)

   Includes various types of marketing information with suggestions
   for improving it.

 ---Recommended Breakdowns for Consumer Media Data, revised Sept.
1965. New York: American Association of Advertising Agencies [1965]
[6] p.   (A 6)

   Outlines desirable standard breakdowns for demographic characteristics to be used as a guide in data collecting and tabulating.
   Although formulated specifically for surveys of consumer media
   audiences in anticipation of increased computerization of media
   analysis, these definitions are presented as applicable in any research to be done which relates to demographic characteristics.

ASSOCIATION of National Advertisers, Inc. A Check List for
Evaluating Marketing Research Studies for Advertising Executives.
New York: Association of National Advertisers, Inc. , 1950, reprint-
ed May 1961. [4] p.   (A 7)

   Presents basic points for appraising market, media and similar
   studies.

---Full Disclosure Form for Business Paper Research. New York:

Association of National Advertisers, Inc. , 1966. 6 p.   (A 8)

Prepared under the guidance of the American Business Press, this form "is offered for use by all business paper publishers in an effort to upgrade advertising and marketing research through full disclosure of research methodology."

INDUSTRIAL Advertising Research Institute. Yardsticks for Evaluating Industrial Advertising Research. Princeton, N. J.: Industrial Advertising Research Institute, 15 Chambers St. , 1954. 11 p. (A 9)

These criteria, intended as a guide for industrial advertising managers, are equally applicable to market survey results.

THE SEARCH

Many a search for information is frustrated not so much by the obscurity of the fact as by the lack of systematic application of search techniques.

Proper orientation should be followed by an analysis and definition of the problem. Complex projects need to be particularized and outlined. This may be done from the project's overall strategy or guided by an intramural or published model, marketing plan. Such a procedure highlights the areas requiring information.

Habitual reliance on memory is often a shortcut to overlooking new data, new sources, even new features of standard works. When undertaking a project it is advisable to review the types and nature of marketing facts, their origin and sources. A thorough check of pertinent catalogs, guidelists and other bibliographic tools produces a current list of research materials. This, if coded to the outline preferably as culled, creates a working plan with which to expedite the assembly of necessary sources and give direction to the search.

Further application of the search technique may vary with the problem, the individual and the source. A few basic principles, however, are universally applicable. A number of these are cited here to serve as a guide to more productive effort.

Consult the specific, primary source.

If unfamiliar with the original source, refer to secondary sources, compendia, indexes and other bibliographic tools for guidance to the primary source.

Start with the most recent source and work back to insure accuracy and recency, particularly of statistical data.

Use the index, if one is available, checking under all terms from the most specific through the most general. Follow through on all cross references and page references.

Tables of contents are available in works which are not indexed. Mark likely references throughout and consult each in turn. A thorough check of related data often reveals unexpected detail.

Consult the introductory text for terminology and methodology; footnotes for scope and bibliographic citation; the front and back of the work for errata, addenda, appendices. In case of continuing doubt consult the technical personnel of the issuing body.

Weigh each fact against the needs and goals of the project.

Watch for trends; for related, supplementary, contradictory facts; for data which can be correlated, juxtaposed, projected.

Recheck the original outline and work plan with persons concerned for policy and implications of supplementary or substitute information.

Check each source through for all necessary facts before turning to the next.

Note all sources consulted.

Note all further sources to be consulted as they suggest themselves.

Take notes or abstract data systematically, preferably verbatim, and in adequate detail.

Identify each fact citing the source in full bibliographic form: author, title, edition, publication date (month, day and year where applicable) page number, table number, and column number, if need be.

From time to time, published sources fail to provide some or any of the needed information. Asking the man who knows is a delicate task and is best undertaken from a position of knowledge based on a thorough search. It is important to be specific and, insofar as possible, to supply him with the intended context for the required information. The expert's specialty is the obscure fact which, in itself, often contains broad implications, limitations and complexities. Nothing discourages his cooperation more effectively than an offhand request, muffled in secretiveness, for the obvious or for the limitless generality.

Although the principles highlighted here are familiar to many, it is surprising how often they are overlooked under the pressure of an immediate information need. The primary purpose for setting them forth, therefore, is not only to provide orientation and a critical approach to the sources which follow but also to assist the literature search past the more common pitfalls to more frequent achievement of optimum results.

Notes

(1) Mooers, Calvin N. Mooers' Law: or, Why Some Retrieval Systems are Used and Others Are Not. American Documentation, vol. 11, no. 3, July 1960, p. ⌊204.⌋

COMPENDIA AND

MARKET DATA GUIDES

A number of publications present within small compass a
large selection of basic economic and marketing data. Some are compiled from a multitude of original sources and arranged for ease of
access and ready reference. A few are also primary sources of
data not published elsewhere.

GENERAL

U. S. Bureau of the Census. Statistical Abstract of the United
States. Washington, D. C.: Government Printing Office. Annual.

(B 1)

This basic reference work summarizes current and historical
data provided by some 200 government and private agencies.
Its documented tables and charts are an excellent reference
guide to more current and detailed data available. ..... A
special feature of the 1967 edition is a section, "Metropolitan
Area Statistics." It presents in two tables a broad selection
of statistics for each standard metropolitan statistical area and
for state economic areas in New England. Reprints of this section are available from the Government Printing Office. ....
The following supplements provide historical and geographical
scope.

---Historical Statistics of the United States, Colonial Times to
1957 ... (A Statistical Abstract Supplement). Washington, D. C.:
Government Printing Office, 1960. xi, 789 p.   (B 2)

Compiled in cooperation with the Social Science Research
Council, this volume presents more than 8,000 statistical
series covering all major phases of business, economics,

21

government and social development.

> HISTORICAL Statistics of the United States, Colonial Times to
> 1957; Continuation to 1962 and Revisions. Washington, D. C.:
> Government Printing Office, 1965. 158 p. Supplement to and
> keyed for use with the basic volume listed above.

---County and City Data Book, 1967. (A Statistical Abstract supplement). Washington, D. C.: Government Printing Office, 1967.
713 p.   (B 3)

> Most of the data presented are from the latest censuses of
> agriculture, business, governments, housing, manufactures,
> mineral industries, and population. Also included are
> statistics of other governmental and private agencies. Statis-
> tical items number 144 for each county, 148 for each incorpora-
> ted city with 25,000 inhabitants or more. Some data are also
> given for regions, divisions, states, and standard metropolitan
> statistical areas.

---Congressional District Data Book (Districts of the 88th Congress).
(A Statistical Abstract Supplement). Washington, D. C.: Government Printing Office [1963] xliii, 560 p. maps.   (B 4)

> Second of a new series. Summarizes, by districts, data from
> the most recent censuses, certain governmental and private
> institutions. Updated by state supplements for those states
> which redistrict prior to publication of new edition.

U. S. Office of Business Economics. Business Statistics. (A supplement to the Survey of Current Business). Washington, D. C.:
Government Printing Office. Biennial.   (B 5)

> Compilation of historical data, with descriptive notes and
> source references, for series published currently in the
> Survey of Current Business.

---Survey of Current Business. Washington, D. C.: Government
Printing Office. Monthly with weekly statistical supplement. (B 6)

> Each issue of this official journal of the Office of Business
> Economics, carries over 2,000 statistical series including

gross national product, national income, prices, orders, inventories, employment, earnings, a wide variety of industrial data and other business indicators; feature articles; analyses of economic developments. The May 1967 issue presented the first estimates of a new series - total and per capita personal income in standard metropolitan statistical areas. January or February issue is the "Annual Review Number;" July issue is the "National Income Number" which shows personal income and expenditures.

U. S. Bureau of the Census. Long Term Economic Growth, 1860-1965. (Series ES4). Washington, D. C.: Government Printing Office, 1966, 259 p. Charts, tables.   (B 7)

Statistical compendium for the study of long term economic trends. Data categories: aggregate output, input and productivity; processes related to economic growth; regional and industry trends; international comparisons; growth rate triangles.

---Business Conditions Digest. (Series ES1). Washington, D. C.: Government Printing Office. Monthly.   (B 8)

A compilation of leading economic statistical series arranged for convenient analysis of business cycles.

ECONOMIC Almanac . . . New York: The Macmillan Co. Irregular.
(B 9)

A statistical compendium presenting economic and industry information for the nation. Compiled by the National Industrial Conference Board from its own and other authoritative sources.

MARKET DATA

SALES Management. Survey of Buying Power. New York: Sales Management, Inc. Annual.   (BA 1)

Published as the June 10th issue of the magazine. Each edition, based on latest available benchmarks, carries the following data for states, cities, counties and metropolitan

areas: population; total retail, food, drug, general merchandise and other outlet sales;   effective buying income; buying
power and quality indexes. Introductory chapters present potential uses for and case histories of the application of these
statistics.

The November 10th issue, currently titled Marketing on
the Move, contains projections for various market factors,
including population, effective buying income and retail sales
projections for metropolitan areas. Contents of the issue vary
from year to year. A large volume of data, published and
unpublished, is available on IBM cards, from Market Statistics,
Inc. at a nominal cost.

---Survey of Newspaper Markets. New York: Sales Management,
Inc. Annual.   (BA 2)
Begun in 1963 and published as the first February issue of the
magazine. Market potentials in terms of population, effective
buying income, retail sales (total and for five store groups --
food, general merchandise, furniture-appliance, automotive,
drug) and per cent household coverage are given for all newspaper markets delineated on the basis of circulation penetration.

---Survey of Television Markets. New York: Sales Management.
Inc. Annual.
                                                              (BA 3)
Inaugurated in 1963 and published as the first August issue of
the magazine. Market data similar to that above, estimates
of television homes, and average daily total circulation are
given for television markets arranged by state and by rank
order.

STANDARD Rate & Data Service, Inc. [Consumer Market Data]
Skokie, Ill.: Standard Rate & Data Service, Inc.   (BA 4)
A series of statistical analyses presented in the appropriate
editions each of which covers a specific advertising medium.

On a complete or selective basis, also available in computer deck or tape form. For states, counties and cities gives the following estimates based on the latest official statistics: population, households, consumer spendable income, retail sales for seven types of outlets, car registrations; standard metropolitan statistical area rankings for each of the preceding categories; farm population, gross farm income and income by farm product category, total farms, Negro population projections for metropolitan areas and certain southern counties. Pertinent editions provide additional farm market statistics.

EDITOR & Publisher. Market Guide. New York: The Editor & Publisher Co. , Inc. Annual   (BA 5)
    Arranged by state and city. For each city gives principal industries, number and sales of retail outlets, population and housing data, automobile registrations, and other data for market analysis.

RAND McNally Commercial Atlas and Marketing Guide. New York, etc.: Rand McNally & Co. Annual   (BA 6)
    Maps and statistics on retail sales, agriculture, manufactures, population, bank deposits, automobile registrations and other market data. Zip Code numbers for places with and without post offices. Unique source of city and town population figures not available elsewhere.

        Useful compendia of special market information appear occasionally in the literature of specific subject fields or are issued by the sources grouped in the following chapters. One example is listed below. Similar compilations will undoubtedly multiply with the increasing output of statistical data and the growing concern for factual bases in marketing management.

U. S. Bureau of Labor Statistics. The Negroes in the United States, Their Economic and Social Situation. (Bulletin 1511). Washington, D. C.: Government Printing Office, 1966.

241 p.

Detailed statistics on population distribution, employment, income distribution, area and occupational groupings, housing characteristics.

FEDERAL
STATISTICAL PROGRAM
GENERAL ORGANIZATION

The greatest single supply of research data originates in the agencies of the federal government. These the Office of Statistical Standards of the Bureau of the Budget classifies into three groups according to the predominant nature of their chief statistical programs:

Administrative or regulatory agencies which collect statistics as a by-product of their operations or to implement their programs and to provide a factual basis for their policies.

Fact-producing agencies whose primary function is the collection and dissemination of statistics for general use.

Analytic and research agencies whose statistical importance lies in the interpretation and analysis of data collected by other sources both governmental and private.

Since some agencies support more than one type of program the categories are not mutually exclusive.

Interagency coordination of federal statistical activities is vested in the Bureau of the Budget which is part of the Executive Office of the President. Through its Office of Statistical Standards, the Bureau promotes the integration and balanced development of federal statistical programs; encourages uniformity in statistical standards and techniques; reviews all reporting forms; and, on the international level, acts as central liaison for the federal government in all statistical matters.

27

The Bureau's chart, The Federal Statistical System,
is revised periodically and serves as an excellent organization guide
to the federal statistical complex. Fuller understanding of its functions, activities and product may be obtained from the following:

U. S. Bureau of the Budget. Statistical Services of the
United States Government. Washington, D. C.: Govern-
ment Printing Office. Irregular.   (C 1)

> Defines the organization, principles and practices of the
> federal statistical system. The Federal Statistical
> System chart is included as an insert. Descriptions of the
> major social and economic statistical programs are grouped
> by subject and provide a guide to past and current data output.
> Tabulates for each agency its area of statistical responsibility,
> principal periodic statistical publications, and selected special
> studies. The publications list is issued in interim editions
> and the whole updated by information in the Bureau's
> STATISTICAL REPORTER (see C 2).

---Statistical Reporter. Washington, D. C.: Government Printing
Office. Monthly.   (C 2)

> Prepared primarily as an exchange of information among
> government employees engaged in statistical and research ac-
> tivities, it offers feature articles and timely news notes on
> new statistical programs and publications; major agency
> changes; personnel appointments to federal statistical pro-
> grams. Semiannual index by name of agency.

U. S. Joint Economic Committee. A Federal Statistics Program for the 1960's; a study prepared for the Subcommittee on Economic Statistics ... by the Office of
Statistical Standards, Bureau of the Budget, October
15, 1962. (Joint Committee Print, 87th Congress, 2nd Session).
Washington, D. C.: Government Printing Office, 1962. vi, 69 p.
                                                                    (C 3)

U. S. General Services Administration. U. S. GOVERNMENT

Brief guide to federal statistics programs. Published as a basis for public discussion. Enumerates specific improvements recently made and currently under way, as well as directions for future development.

HAUSER, Philip M. and Leonard, William R. , eds. Government Statistics for Business Use, 2nd ed. New York: Wiley; London: Chapman & Hall, 1956. xx, 440 p.   (C 4)

Authored by a group of specialists, arranged by subject, and well indexed, this work explains the statistical series of the federal government and their practical application in business.

U. S. General Services Administration. U. S. Government Organization Manual. Washington, D. C. : Government Printing Office. Annual.   (C 5)

This official handbook of the federal government provides reasonably detailed and current information on the organization, functions, activities and major publications of the legislative, judicial and executive branches. A supplementary section covers abolished and transferred agencies and functions, as well as quasi-official agencies and selected international and bilateral organizations.

METHODOLOGY REPORTS AND MANUALS

The origin and techniques of preparation are of major importance in the proper interpretation and effective use of statistical data.

Federal government sources excel in providing explicit definitions, methodology statements and manuals. A number of generally applicable procedures and classification schemes have been developed by the Office of Statistical Standards. Others, more specialized, have been formulated by the individual agencies in conjunction with their specific programs. Among the latter, some are issued separately, others as reports in the series to which they pertain. When such individual publications are lacking, primary sources for the particular statistical series carry ample annotations and references to pertinent explanatory materials available.

At intervals, evaluative studies appear which explore the scope and adequacy of basic data, governmental and private. Improvements in statistics are constantly being proposed, studied, and effected by the federal agencies concerned. Much of this work is done on an interagency level and in cooperation with industry as, for example, the Department of the Interior's program to provide improved petroleum statistics.

From the many separately published manuals and methodology reports the following were selected as most useful in the interpretation and application of some of the general purpose business statistics.

ROBINSON, Patrick J. , et al. Standard Industrial Classification for Effective Marketing Analysis. Cambridge, Mass.: Marketing Science Institute, Nov. 1967. ii, 42 p.   (CA 1)
> Explains the SIC and its applications in industrial market analysis.

U. S. Bureau of the Budget. Standard Industrial Classification Manual, 1967. Washington, D. C.: Government Printing Office, 1967. xii, 615 p.   (CA 2)
> Presents complete numerical scheme with alphabetical indexes, definitions and conversion tables for the 1957 and 1967 editions. Widely used by government and private sources in classifying statistical data for business establishments by type of activity. Similar classification schemes for commodities have been developed by the Budget and Census Bureaus for identifying products and product groups.

---Standard Enterprise Classification. Washington, D. C.: Bureau of the Budget, 1963, 23 p.   (CA 3)
> An adaptation of the Standard Industrial Classification for use in collecting and presenting data relating to enterprises.

U. S. Bureau of the Census. Industry Classification and Sec-
tor Measures of Industrial Production, by James W.
McKie.(Working paper, no. 20). Washington, D. C. : Bureau of the
Census, 1965. 12, p.   (CA 4)

> Manufacturing division of the Standard Industrial Classifica-
> tion evaluated, particularly in respect to the requirements of
> users of economic data.

---International Standard Industrial Classification and the U. S.
Standard Industrial Classification (A Comparison with Particular
Application to the Bureau of the Census).(Technical paper, no. 14).
Washington, D. C. : Government Printing Office, 1965. 25 p.
                                                                (CA 5)

> Compares the 1957 SIC as amended January 1963 with the
> 1958 edition of the United Nations' INTERNATIONAL STAND-
> ARD INDUSTRIAL CLASSIFICATION OF ALL ECONOMIC AC-
> TIVITIES.

U. S. Bureau of the Budget. Standard Metropolitan Statistical Areas. [Washington, D. C. : Government Printing Office]
1967. viii, 56 p.   (CA 6)

> Gives criteria used in establishing SMSA's; their names,
> definitions, and 1960 population; names and definitions of
> Standard Consolidated Areas.

U. S. Bureau of the Census. Congressional District Identification
of Counties and Selected Places (Districts of the 90th Congress).
(Geographic reports, GE-10, no. 4). Washington, D. C. : Government Printing Office, December 1966. 65 p.   (CA 7)

The following reports represent some of the basic methodology publications stemming from the statistical programs of individual agencies.

U. S. Department of Agriculture
MAJOR Statistical Series

of the U. S. Department of Agriculture -- How They are Constructed and Used. (Agriculture Handbook no. 118). Washington, D. C.:
Government Printing Office, 1957-1960. 10 vols.   (CA 8)

U. S. Bureau of the Census

A large part of the Census Bureau's methodology appears in
the footnotes and introductory texts of its statistical publications.
More detailed explanations are issued in a variety of forms. Statistical program guides and manual-type information of general interest appear as separate publications. Major censuses generate manual-type publications as well as detailed, technical methodology reports. The former appear either separately or as numbered parts
of a particular census. The latter are issued in a series covering
sampling, data-collection forms and procedures,data processing
quality control.

All such reports, including those issued in its series of
TECHNICAL PAPERS and WORKING PAPERS, can be located
through the Bureau's catalog of publications.

THE COMPILATION of Manufacturing Statistics [by] Frank
A. Hanna. Washington, D. C.: Government Printing Office, 1959.
xiv, 233 p.   (CA 9)
> Describes the Bureau's industrial statistics program from
> planning stages through tabulation and distribution of results.

CENSUS Tract Manual, 5th ed. Washington, D. C.: Government
Printing Office, 1966. 85 p.   (CA 10)
> Describes the delineation of component areas, the nature of
> census tracts, and how tract data are used.

1960 CENSUS of Population: Alphabetical Index of Occupations and
Industries. Washington, D. C.: Government Printing Office, 1960,
xxiv, 649 p. looseleaf.   (CA 11)
> Titles are listed alphabetically with their occupation and in-
> dustry codes. Used in classifying returns from demographic

schedules. This and its companion volume listed below are
issued with each population census. Both are useful in inter-
preting decennial and current occupation data.

1960 CENSUS of Population: Classified Index of Occupations and Industries. Washington, D. C.: Government Printing Office, 1960. xx, 383 p.   (CA 12)
    Classified list of occupations and industries showing titles
    included in each group. Intercensal editions prepared when
    necessary.

U. S. Censuses of Population and Housing, 1960: Geographic
Identification Code Scheme. (Series PHC (2)). Washington, D. C.:
Bureau of the Census, 1961. 51 reports.   (CA 13)
    One part for each state and the District of Columbia, and a
    compilation of these parts into one publication for the entire
    United States. Identifies all political and statistical subdivi-
    sions for which data from the 1960 population and housing
    censuses are tabulated.
U. S. Censuses of Population and Housing, 1960: Census County
Division Boundary Descriptions. (Series PHC (3)). Washington,
D. C.: Government Printing Office, 1962. 18 reports.   (CA 14)
    Reports for the 18 states where census county divisions were
    established. These delineations, used for reporting census
    statistics, are listed alphabetically by county within each state.

UNITED States Census of Agriculture, 1959, and Related Surveys:
Principal Data-Collection Forms and Procedures. [Washington,
D. C.: Government Printing Office, 1962] iv, 104 p.   (CA 15)

1960 CENSUSES of Population and Housing: Procedural History.
Washington, D. C.: Government Printing Office, 1966. 393 p.
                                                               (CA 16)
    Comprehensive report on methodology applied from the plan-
    ning and pretesting stages through the tabulation and publica-
    tion of the final reports.

EVALUATION and Research Program of the U. S. Censuses of
Population and Housing, 1960. (Series ER60). Washington, D. C.:
Government Printing Office [1963]   (CA 17)

> A series of reports on procedures, forms, accuracy of
> coverage, content, response variance, and processing.

U. S. Bureau of Labor Statistics

In addition to the comprehensive handbook listed below,
methodology reports on the Bureau of Labor Statistics' statistical
series are published regularly in the MONTHLY LABOR REVIEW.

HANDBOOK of Methods for Surveys and Studies. (Bulletin no. 1458).
Washington, D. C.: Government Printing Office, 1967. 238 p.

(CA 18)

> Provides answers to questions most often asked about BLS
> statistics. Explains techniques and procedures under the fol-
> lowing headings: background and description of surveys; data
> sources and collection methods; sampling and estimating pro-
> cedures; analysis and presentation; uses and limitations.

U. S. Bureau of Employment Security

DIRECTORY of Important Labor Areas. Washington, D. C.: Bureau
of Employment Security. Irregular.   (CA 19)

> Delineation of geographical boundaries and an alphabetical in-
> dex of counties or parts of counties constituting these areas.

DICTIONARY of Occupational Titles, 3rd ed. Washington D. C.:
Government Printing Office, 1965-1967. 2 vols.; supplements.(CA 20)

> Standard reference for job definitions and occupational classifi-
> cation.
> Vol. I, Definitions of Titles. Defines and identifies
> by code number some 23,000 separate occupations.
> Vol. II, Occupational Classification and Industry
> Index. Presents jobs in two arrangements: 1) in numerical
> order according to some combination of work field, purpose,

material, product, subject matter, generic term, and/or
industry; 2) according to some combination of required education, vocational preparation, aptitudes, interests, tempera-
ments and physical demands. Also lists titles by industry.
Selected Characteristics of Occupations (Physical Demands,
Working Conditions, Training Time); a supplement ...
1966. 280 p.
Suffix Codes for Jobs Defined in the Dictionary ... Feb.
1967, 265 p.
Provides 3-digit suffix codes to be substituted for job titles
for easier machine processing, statistical reporting and tabulating.

EMPLOYMENT Security Research Methods, Handbook Series ...
Washington, D. C.: Bureau of Employment Security, 1958-
Irregular.   (CA 21)
A series of manuals presenting techniques and methods for
estimating area employment and unemployment, developing
labor information for small areas, defining labor market
areas and similar subjects.

U. S. Board of Governors of the Federal Reserve System

MEASURES of Industrial Production and Final Demand.
(Staff Economic Studies, no. 24). Washington, D. C.: Board of
Governors of the Federal Reserve System, Jan. 1967.   (CA 22)
This conference paper updates the description and analysis of
market groupings of the industrial production index and presents the improvements and new features provided by the revision of the index.

Interesting because of its different approach is the following report:

U. S. Bureau of Mines. A METHOD of Analyzing Demand
for Mineral Commodities: A Case Study of Salt [by]

Richard Stevenson Watt. (Bureau of Mines Information Circular
8057). Washington, D. C.: Bureau of Mines, 1962. ii, 35 p.
charts, tables.   (CA 23)

This case study presents one of the Bureau's methods for
analyzing and projecting the demand for any industrial raw
material.

ADVISORY BODIES

Because of the increasing reliance of business, public organizations and government itself on the quantitative data emanating
from federal agencies, interest and pressure for better statistics
have been steadily mounting from both public and private sources.
Special studies of federal statistical programs and data have been
conducted from time to time by Congressional committees and by consulting bodies appointed by the Executive Office of the President and
individual government agencies.

Within the legislative branch the Subcommittee on Economic
Statistics and its parent, the Joint Economic Committee, charged
with guiding the Congress in economic policies and programs, have
had a continuing interest in all tools of economic analysis. From
time to time public hearings are held inviting comment, from data
producers and users, on statistical series -- usually those guiding
Congressional action of the moment. The resultant reports not only indicate the direction and area of mutual action but also provide
an insight into the comparability, methodology and applicability of
such data. A complete list of these publications appears in the
Committee's catalog.

In 1959 a Subcommittee on Census and Statistics was appointed within the House Committee on Post Office and Civil Service.
Among its programs is the reduction of paperwork and costs en-
tailed in furnishing statistical reports to the government; an evaluation of existing transportation statistics and data requirements in
this field; the study of the most desirable frequency and scope of
the censuses of population and housing. Its survey of federal data
compilation activities and contracts is published biennially.

Government agencies, too, have long actively sought advice as well as cooperation from the business community on a continuing basis. Inadequacies in the collection or compilation of statistical data may be brought to the attention of government officials either directly or through the many governmental, professional and trade association committees charged with such liaison duties.

The Office of Statistical Standards of the Bureau of the Budget, in view of its primary function, is a central point of referral for reporting managements as well as for researchers. It may be approached directly or, for example, through The Advisory Council on Federal Reports. This organization is supported by leading national trade associations and, through more than 20 committees, it "channels to the Bureau of the Budget, the advice and recommendations of business on statistical, reporting and record-keeping problems confronting business."

Many federal agencies also enjoy the services of special advisory committees of varying functions and on numerous levels. In May 1967 the Department of Commerce announced the formation of the National Marketing Advisory Committee. It is composed of marketing specialists from business, industry and education. Its official liaison is the Department's Office of Marketing and Services. Although the Committee's program ranges from the promotion of graduate education in marketing to the application of marketing techniques in the solution of social problems, some attention is due to be focused on marketing research, statistics and publications.

A large number of advisory committees consult with government bureaus on their statistical programs and methods exclusively. This is done either on a continuing basis or at the planning stage of special statistical projects. As an illustrative sample the following are cited from the Bureau of the Census roster:

Census Advisory Committee on State and Local Government Statistics, established in 1948, is comprised of individuals especially qualified to counsel the Bureau on the various aspects of its statistics program relating to state and local governments. It is used by the Bureau in determining program objectives and serves in keeping it current on the availability of statistical information on state and local governments, as well as their data needs.

Technical Advisory Committee for the 1960 Population Census, was organized in 1956. Its members, drawn from governmental and private organizations, advised the Bureau on important technical aspects of the 18th decennial Census of Population. It has given consideration to the scope and quality of CENSUS data and to the tabulation and publication programs.

Census Advisory Committee on Construction Statistics, formed in 1960, provides advice on various aspects of the construction statistics program, which was transferred to the Bureau of the Census in 1959. It offers informed opinion on items such as what data are needed, how the data are used, and how users react to it. In addition, consideration is given to proposed revisions and to solutions of any reporting problems.

Census Advisory Committee on Housing Statistics was established in 1961 to assist in the development of the technical aspects of programs which will be of maximum value to local, national, public and private users.

Some liaison bodies are maintained by professional associations:

Census Advisory Committee of the American Statistical Association has been in existence since 1919. It advises the Bureau on overall program content and on specialized technical matters. In recent years, it has been particularly active in the long range program planning efforts of the Bureau.

In November 1964, the Social Science Research Council appointed a Committee on Areas for Social and Economic Statistics to review the criteria which define standard metropolitan statistical areas.

Census Advisory Committee of the American Marketing Association, established in 1946, provides the Bureau with counsel on those aspects of its program which entail data for marketing use. It has also been assisting the Bureau in its review of the business statistics program.

Census Advisory Committee of the American Economic Association, organized in 1960, advises the Bureau on its economic statistics program. It acts as a sounding board against which to test the Bureau's program proposals, to gain insight on how the data might be used, and to obtain general information on the formulation of inquiries to be made.

The Federal Statistics Users' Conference, and independent organization, acts as a spokesman for the "consumer." Through meetings, committees and publications, it provides its business, farm, labor and nonprofit research organization members a means of evaluating the usefulness of federal statistical programs and voicing their statistical needs.

The increasing flow of statistical information from the federal government is creating greater utilization and a growing awareness of this fact supply. To their mutual advantage, these trends indicate a broadening interchange between the federal statistical authorities and businessmen.

BUREAU OF THE CENSUS

PUBLICATIONS

The Bureau of the Census is the largest statistical service agency of the federal government. In one year it averaged nine reports every working day. Its current major censuses alone provide over 130,000 pages of closely printed data (1). It is also the principal source of market and business statistics.

The Bureau's benchmark and current publications are listed below. A considerable amount of data collected, however, do not find their way into printed reports. Unpublished information is often available free. Special studies compiled upon request are furnished on a cost basis. The Bureau lists the latter in a special section of its catalog and has been describing its unpublished resources in a new series of bulletins:

DATA Access Descriptions. Washington, D. C.: Bureau of the
Census. Irregular. (D 1)
    Describes unpublished data available and planned for tape or
    punchcard publication.

In addition, the Bureau provides statistical services to other agencies. Results of data processing and factfinding surveys are either turned over to the originating agency for analysis and distribution or published by the Bureau in cooperation with the agency concerned. Such reports of general market measurement interest have been included here rather than with the publications of the cooperating agency.

The statistical core of market research is supplied by the seven major censuses compiled by the Bureau at regular intervals. Publication schedules outlining the contents and distribution dates

of preliminary, advance and final reports are available upon request
from the Bureau.   Press releases highlighting facts of popular interest are issued from time to time and often appreciably antedate
the publication of the final report. These are listed in the Business
Service Checklist. (See QB 13). Since occasional reports based
on major censuses are issued without prior announcement, it is also
necessary to consult the Bureau's CATALOG to insure completeness.

The Bureau also maintains a continuing program of statistical
surveys whose periodic reports may be used to update some of the
benchmark data.   For this reason such reports are grouped here immediately after the censuses which they supplement.

Special Publications

Several special publications issued by the Bureau of the Census are included among the compendia in an earlier chapter.   The
reports listed here are more specialized.

COUNTY Business Patterns.   Washington, D. C. : Government Printing Office.   Annual.   (D 2)

Published in 53 reports; subsequently reissued in bound form.
State reports and a United States summary provide statistics
for nonfarm commercial and industrial activities and nonprofit
membership organizations reported under the Federal Insurance Contributions Act. Data presented by 2-digit and 4-
digit SIC groups for states, counties and standard metropolitan
statistical areas show the number of employees, taxable payrolls, total reporting units, and number of reporting units by
employee-size class.

U. S. Commodity Exports and Imports as Related to Output . . .
(Series ES2). Washington, D. C. : Government Printing Office. Annual.   (D 3)

Contains export-output data for some 1,010 comparable commodity classifications, and import-output data for 670 commodities at various levels of detail. Classification of U. S.
exports and imports by 5-digit and 4-digit groups permits the

correlation of these statistics with a large volume of domestic
industry data similarly classified.

Major Censuses and Current Reports

The listing below   of major censuses is limited to main titles
of final reports and is not complete in all cases since some were
in process at the time of writing.

Major Censuses: Agriculture

The first agriculture census was taken in 1840 in conjunction
with the sixth decennial census and was included in each decennial
census thereafter through 1950. It is now conducted in October of
every fifth year ending in 4 and 9. For years ending in 9, censuses
of irrigation and drainage are added.

CENSUS of Agriculture, 1964.   Washington, D. C.: Government
Printing Office, 1967 - (In process)   (DA 1)
    Planned in three volumes:
    Volume I, Counties.   53 reports.
    Volume II, General Report: Statistics by Subject. 11 reports.
    Volume III, [1965 Sample Survey of Agriculture]
    The first two volumes parallel in contents the first two vol-
    umes of the 1959 census listed below in toto to indicate the
    full scope of these benchmark data, including irrigation and
    drainage which were not scheduled for survey in 1964.

CENSUS of Agriculture, 1959. Washington, D. C.: Government
Printing Office, 1961-63. 5 vols.
    Volume I, Counties.   54 reports. One report for each
    state and outlying area.   Statistics on number of farms, farm
    characteristics, acreage, uses of land, land-use practices,
    irrigation, facilities and equipment, labor, expenditures, com-
    mercial fertilizer use, livestock, crops, value of farm prod-
    ucts, etc.

Volume II, General Report: Statistics by Subjects.
1,556 p.

Contains the following chapters previously issued separately:

Introduction

I   Farms and Land in Farms

II   Age, Residence, Years on Farm, Work Off Farm

III   Farm Facilities, Farm Equipment

IV   Farm Labor, Use of Fertilizer, Farm Expenditures,
      Cash Rent

V   Size of Farm

VI   Livestock and Livestock Products

VII   Field Crops and Vegetables

VIII Fruits and Nuts, Horticultural Specialties, and Forest
      Products

IX   Value of Farm Products

X   Color, Race, and Tenure of Farm Operator

XI   Economic Class of Farm

XII   Type of Farm

Volume III, The United States: Irrigation of Agricultural
Lands. 432 p.

Data for the 17 western states and Louisiana and for the conterminous United States, by drainage basins, on number of
establishments, water conveyed, area served   number of farm
water users served, number of enterprises by size and type of
organization, water sources, and area irrigated. Also includes
data on land irrigated and acres and production of crops on
irrigated land in the 18 conterminous states and Hawaii.

Volume IV, The United States: Drainage of Agricultural
Lands. 387 p.

Data by states and counties and for the conterminous United
States on the number, area, and construction costs of drainage works.

Volume V, Special Reports.

Part 1, Special Census of Horticultural Specialties.
601 p.

Number and kinds of operations; gross receipts and/or gross
sales; sales of individual nursery products, flower seed, vegetables grown under glass, bulb crops, and propagated mush-
rooms; number of container-grown plants; inventory of selected growing stock; employment; structures and equipment.

Part 2, Irrigation in Humid Areas. 173 p.

1960 data for 30 eastern states showing acres irrigated, number of constructed ponds and reservoirs, source and method
of applying water, type of .pumping power, acreage of individual crops irrigated and frequency of irrigation, by states
and counties.

Part 3, Ranking Agricultural Counties. 100 p.

Statistics for selected items of inventory and agricultural production for the leading counties in the United States.

Part 4, Farm Mortgage, Debt and Farm Taxes. 117 p.

A cooperative report by the Economic Research Service of the
Department of Agriculture and the Bureau of the Census. 1960
data by states on taxes on farms and ranches, mortgaged
farms, mortgage debt, amount of interest paid, etc.

Part 5, 1960 Sample Survey of Agriculture. 62 p.

Statistics by economic class and type of farms, income of
farm families from off-farm sources, value of farm products
sold, cash farm operating expenses, number of selected type
of farm equipment and acres on which used, wheel tractors by
year of manufacture and kind of fuel used, construction for
new buildings, number of farmers having contracts with dealers, processors, and others for the production and marketing
of 15 farm products; real estate and non-real estate debt of
farm operators and landlords.

Part 6, A Graphic Summary of Agriculture, 1959. 3
reports.

Prepared cooperatively by the Economic Research Service of
the Department of Agriculture and the Bureau of the Census.

These graphic reports cover uses being made of agricultural land, the extent and nature of the various forms of tenure, and changes and developments in agricultural resources and production.

CENSUS of Agriculture, 1959: Farm Census Shows Big Changes in Poultry Industry. Washington, D. C.: Bureau of the Census, 1961. 6 p.   (DA 2)
Final figures from the 1959 census, for divisions and states, on farms reporting chickens four months old and over.

Agriculture -- Current Reports
The Bureau's current agricultural statistics are limited to periodic reports on cotton ginnings and production.

COTTON Ginnings: Washington, D. C.: Bureau of the Census.
                                                            (DA 10)

---Report on Cotton Ginnings by States. (Series A10)
Issued as of 11 dates during the July to January season including an end-of-season (March) report. An additional final report is issued in May of each year.

---Report on Cotton Ginnings by Counties. (Series A20) 6/season.

CONSOLIDATED Cotton Report. Washington, D. C.: Bureau of the Census. 5/yr.   (DA 11)

COTTON Production in the United States ... Washington, D. C.: Government Printing Office. Annual   (DA 12)
Includes state and county data on production and ginnings of cotton, number of gins.

COTTON Production and Distribution ... Washington, D. C.:
                                                            (DA 13)

Government Printing Office.   Annual.

Much of the domestic data presented by state;   world data by
country.

Major Censuses: Business

Currently the business census is taken every fifth year ending
in 2 and 7. Published data cover each of the three trades: retail,
wholesale, and selected services. For the first time since 1939, the
construction industry is to be included in the business census scheduled to cover the year 1967. Information, obtained by mail, will report on contract construction, subdividing and developing, and opera-
tive or merchant builders, as well as on all types of subcontractors
or specialty contractors. Data will be provided on establishments,
employees, payrolls, receipts, costs of materials, payments to other
contractors, capital expenditures and other items.

CENSUS of Business, 1963.   Washington, D. C.: Government Printing Office, 1966-67. 7 vols. (17 books)   (DB 1)
Volume I, Retail Trade Summary Statistics:
Part 1, U. S. Summary ...
Sales size data for the United States, states, and standard metropolitan statistical areas; data also for the United States by employment-size groups and legal forms of organization.
Employment size data for the United States, states, and standard
metropolitan statistical areas.
Single units and multiunits data on firm-size groups by kinds
of business for the United States, states, and standard metropolitan statistical areas and, for the United States, by legal
forms of organization.
Legal form of organization data on 5 legal-form groups and
92 kinds of business for the United States and on 4 legal-form
groups and 27 kinds of business for each state.
Parts 2-5, Merchandise Line Sales ...
First updating of these statistics since 1948. Sales and estab-

lishment data by 25 broad merchandise lines for geographic divisions, states, standard metropolitan statistical areas, and areas outside standard metropolitan statistical areas.

Volume II, Retail Trade Area Statistics ... Parts 1-3.

Data for each state, the District of Columbia, the Virgin Islands and Guam: number of establishments, sales, payroll, employment, and number of proprietors of unincorporated businesses for the state and standard metropolitan statistical areas, by 95 kinds of business; for counties and cities with 500 establishments or more, by varied kind-of-business detail; and for counties and cities of 2,500 inhabitants or more, by 11 major kind-of-business groups.

Volume III, Major Retail Center Statistics ... Parts 1-2.

Presents data for 116 standard metropolitan statistical areas and a United States summary. Data are also shown for central business districts in cities having 100,000 inhabitants or more and for other major retail centers in standard metropolitan statistical areas covered. Statistics are for retail stores, hotels, motels, motion picture theaters, on number of establishments, sales or receipts, employment and payrolls.

Volume IV, Wholesale Trade Summary Statistics. Part 1, U. S. Summary ...

Sales size, employment size, single units and multiunits information on wholesale establishments or firms for the United States, geographic divisions, states, and standard metropolitan statistical areas.

Receivables and bad-debt losses of merchant wholesalers by kinds of business for the United States and standard metropolitan statistical areas.

Sales by class of customer (retailer, repair shop, industrial user, wholesaler, etc.) and by kind of business for the United

States and standard metropolitan statistical areas. Warehouse and storage space, including cold storage and grain bin space, for the United States, geographic divisions, states, and standard metropolitan statistical areas.

For petroleum bulk stations and terminals gives: data, as of April 1, 1962, on the number of establishments, storage capacity, inventories, method of receiving bulk products, and plant power source; data, for the year 1961, on gallonage sales by product; and 1963 data for states and counties, on dollar sales, for the year, and number of establishments, dollar inventories, and storage capacity as of December 31.

Part 2, Commodity Line Sales and Miscellaneous Subjects; Public Warehousing.

Sales of wholesale establishments by commodity lines or product classes for the United States, geographic divisions, selected states, and the 15 standard metropolitan statistical areas with the largest dollar volume of wholesale trade. Public warehousing data on establishments, revenue, payroll, space, for the United States, regions, divisions, and states with summary totals for standard metropolitan statistical areas with 250,000 inhabitants or more.

Volume V, Wholesale Trade Area Statistics.
Reports for each state, the District of Columbia, the Virgin Islands and Guam, statistics on the number of establishments, sales, payroll, and number of proprietors of unincorporated businesses for the state, standard metropolitan statistical areas, and counties with 100 establishments or more, by a maximum of 57 kinds of business and varied types of operation; and for counties and cities of 5,000 inhabitants or more, by merchant wholesalers and combined for all other operating types.

Volume VI, Selected Services Summary Statistics.
Data by receipts-size groups and kinds of business for the United States, states, and standard metropolitan statistical areas.

Data by employment-size groups and kinds of business for the
United States, states and standard metropolitan statistical areas.
Single units and multiunits information on the number of firms
and establishments by firm size and kind of business for the

United States, states.
Legal form of organization data by kind of business for the
United States and states.
Hotels, motor hotels, and motels data on operations.
Laundries, cleaning plants, related services data on operations,
receipts size, receipts by source and by type of work performed, employment size, single units and multiunits, legal
form of organization - and cleaning and dyeing plants, by type
of solvent used.
Motion picture data on operations of regular and outdoor motion picture producers, distributors, theaters, and allied service
establishments.

Volume VII, Selected Services Area Statistics.
Parts 1-3.
Reports for each state, the District of Columbia, the United
States, the Virgin Islands, and Guam, the number of establishments, receipts, payroll, employment, and number of proprietors of unincorporated businesses for the state and standard
metropolitan statistical areas, for counties and cities with
1,000 establishments or more, by 110 kinds of business; for
all other standard metropolitan statistical areas and for counties and cities with 500 to 999 establishments, by 45 kinds of
business; for counties and cities with 200 to 499 establishments, by 13 kinds of business; and for all counties and for each
city of 2,500 inhabitants or more, by 7 major kinds-of-busi-
ness groups.

CENSUS of Business of Puerto Rico, 1963: Retail, Wholesale,

and Selected Services. (BC63-PR). Washington, D. C. :

Government Printing Office, 1965, 300 p.   (DB2)

> Conducted jointly by the Puerto Rico Planning Board, the
> Government of the Commonwealth of Puerto Rico, and the
> U. S. Bureau of the Census. Includes data by kind of busi-
> ness and geographic area for wholesale, retail, and selected
> services on number of establishments, sales or receipts, per-
> sonnel, payroll, legal form of organization, class of customer,
> employment size, etc.

Business -- Special Reports

CENSUS of Business, 1963: Retail Trade. (BC63(S) RS). Wash-

ington, D. C. : Bureau of the Census, 1967. 3 reports.   (DB 3)

> Leased Departments. 23 p.
> Retail and Wholesale Cooperatives. 77 p.
> Gasoline Service Stations and Liquified Petroleum
> (LP) Gas Dealers. 104 p.

MEASURES of Value Produced In and By Merchant Whole-

saling Firms: 1963. Washington, D. C. : Government Print-

ing Office, 1965. 34 p.   (DB 4)

> Prepared in connection with the 1963 CENSUS OF BUSINESS.
> Total operating receipts, gross margin, value added, net in-
> come produced at market prices and at factor cost, and pay-
> roll are presented in detail by kind of business, by size of
> firm, and by legal form of organization.

Business -- Combined Reports

> The following reports are based on the CENSUSES OF BUSI-
NESS, MANUFACTURES, AND MINERAL INDUSTRIES. Due to the
economic aspects of the data presented, they are listed here.

CENSUSES of Business, Manufactures, Mineral Industries,

1963. (Series EC63). Washington, D. C. : Government Printing Of-

fice, 1965. 2 reports.   (DB 5)

Guam. 23 p.

Virgin Islands.   25 p.

Data on establishments, sales or receipts, payroll, and personnel, by industry division and kind of business within the
scope of the three censuses.

ENTERPRISE Statistics, 1963. (ES-3). Washington, D. C.:
Government Printing Office.   3 reports. (Planned)   (DB 6)

Establishment data retabulated to show the significant patterns
in terms of the size of individual enterprises, industrial diversification, and other structural characteristics.

Part 1, General Report on Industrial Organization.

Feb. 1968. 340 p.

Establishment data showing the economic characteristics of the
owning companies.   Statistics for various enterprise-establish-
ment relationships shown by type of company organization, by
company size, and by industry classification, as well as cross-
tabulations indicating industrial diversification and regional
distribution of the companies and their establishments.

Part 2, Central Administrative Offices and Auxiliaries.

May 1968. 126 p.

Characteristics of establishments which perform various cen-
tralized management functions for their firms and various support services to the operating establishments of their firms.
Data for central administrative offices and auxiliaries presented by industry classification of the operating establishments
served in 1963, by type of service function performed, by
employment size, by geographic location, and by industry category and employment-size characteristics of the owning companies.

Part 3, Link of Census and IRS Corporation Data.

Comparison of the enterprise and establishment data with the
financial statistics of the owning companies as extracted from
their tax returns by the Internal Revenue Service.

COMPANY Statistics on Research and Development.

(Planned) (DB 7)

Will present cost of research and development by industry and other company data.

Business -- Current Reports

Current data on distribution and services, based on sample surveys, are issued in a series of weekly, monthly and annual reports.

Business -- Current Reports: Combined

CURRENT Business Reports: Capital Expenditures, 1963. Washington, D. C.: Government Printing Office, August 1965. 13 p.

(DB 10)

For retail trade, merchant wholesalers and selected services, shows type of expenditure by selected kinds of business and capital expenditures of establishments operated by corporations.

See also County Business Patterns (D 2).

Business -- Current Reports: Retail Trade

CURRENT Retail Trade Reports. Washington, D. C.: Government Printing Office. (DB 11)

Weekly Retail Sales.

For historical data in compact form: Final Weekly Sales Estimates: 1962 to 1967. (BR10-67S). March 25, 1968. 13 p.

Advance Monthly Retail Sales.

Monthly Retail Trade.

Retail sales estimates and accounts receivable, by kind of business, for geographic regions, divisions and selected states, standard metropolitan statistical areas and standard consolidated areas. Department store sales are given for some 200 SMSA's, selected standard consolidated areas, cities, central business districts and miscellaneous areas. The latter table also issued separately (see DB 12).

Retail Trade. Annual.

Sales, year-end inventories and accounts receivable by kinds
of business for geographic regions, 15 large states, five
SMSA's, 2 standard consolidated areas.

SPECIAL Current Business Reports: Monthly Department Store Sales
in Selected Areas. Washington, D. C.: Bureau of the Census. Monthly.   (DB 12)
Separate release of department store data published in the
MONTHLY RETAIL TRADE report (see DB 11).

Business -- Current Reports: Services

CURRENT Selected Services Report: Monthly Selected
Services Receipts. Washington, D. C.: Bureau of the Census.
Estimated monthly receipts for hotels, motels, camps and
other lodging places; personal services; business services;
automobile repair, automobile services; miscellaneous repair
services; motion pictures and amusement and recreation services, except motion pictures.

Business -- Current Reports: Wholesale Trade

MONTHLY Wholesale Trade Report: Sales and Inventories. Washington, D. C.: Bureau of the Census. Monthly.   (DB 14)
Presents sales, inventory trends and stock-sales ratios of
merchant wholesalers. Sales and inventory trends for the
United States are shown for about 70 kinds of business and for
14 kinds of business for geographic divisions.

Major Censuses: Commercial Fisheries

CENSUS of Commercial Fisheries, 1963. (FC63-1). Washington,
D. C.: Government Printing Office, 1966. 25 p.   (DC 1)
Conducted in cooperation with the Bureau of Commercial
Fisheries, Department of the Interior, this is the first census

of this industry taken since 1908. Data on operators, employment, gross receipts; fishing regions, primary catch, fishing
gear; vessel size, cost, year purchased or built. Operator and
vessel data by geographic division and state.

Major Censuses: Manufactures

After World War II the manufactures census was taken for
the years 1947, 1954, 1958 and 1963. Current plans call for this
census to be conducted every fifth year ending in 2 and 7. First reports of the 1967 census (e. g. DD5) were issued in early 1968.

CENSUS of Manufactures, 1963. Washington, D. C.: Government
Printing Office, 1967. 3 vols.   (DD 1)
   Volume I, Summary and Subject Statistics. 1,025 p.
   In addition to a general summary by states and SMSA's, this
   volume presents data on size of establishments; type of organization; manufacturers' inventories by type of industry,
   geographic divisions and states; expenditures for new plant
   and new equipment by industry, geographic divisions and states;
   power equipment in manufacturing industries as of December
   31, 1962 by major industry group for divisions, states and
   SMSA's; selected materials consumed by industry, geographic
   divisions and states; and water used in manufacturing by industry by state. Also included are two tables from the special
   report entitled, CONCENTRATION RATIOS IN MANUFACTUR-
   ING INDUSTRY, 1963, as well as data on manufacturing activity in government establishments; shipments of defense-
   oriented industries; and the origin of exports of manufactured
   products.

   Volume II, Industry Statistics.
   Part 1, Major Groups 20 to 28, 1300 p.
   Part 2, Major Groups 29 to 39 and 19. 1,574 p.
   Data for 430 manufacturing industries on quantity and value
   of products shipped and materials consumed; cost of fuels and

electric energy; capital expenditures; inventories; employment; payrolls; man-hours; value added by manufacture;
horsepower of power equipment; number of establishments and
number of companies. Data are shown for the United States,
geographic regions and states, employment-size class of
establishment, and for degree of primary product specialization. Separate summary chapters are also shown for each of
the major industry groups.

Volume III, Area Statistics. 1,288 p.
General statistics (number of establishments, employment,
payrolls, value added by manufacture, and capital expenditures) are presented for each state, the District of Columbia,
selected standard metropolitan statistical areas, and counties,
by industry groups and important individual industries. Total
for all manufacturing is shown for all counties and for cities
of 10,000 inhabitants or more.
Volume IV, Indexes of Production. 183 p.
Produced in cooperation with the Board of Governors of
the Federal Reserve System. Presents measures of
change in manufacturing output from 1954 to 1958 and 1958
to 1963 with historical comparisons.

CENSUS of Manufactures of Puetro Rico, 1963. (MC63-PR).
Washington, D. C.: Government Printing Office, 1965. 201 p.

(DD 2)

Conducted jointly by the Puerto Rico Planning Board, the
Government of the Commonwealth of Puerto Rico, and the
U. S. Bureau of the Census. Findings include statistics of
manufacturing activity by industry and geographic area on value
added by manufacture, employment, payrolls, inventories,
capital expenditures, etc.

See also DB 5, DB 6.

Manufactures -- Special Reports

The above volumes are supplemented by the following miscellaneous series of reports:

CENSUS of Manufactures, 1963. (MC63(S)). Washington, D. C.:
Government Printing Office. (In process)   (DD 3)
> Series of supplementary reports. Those which were incorporated in the bound volumes are excluded here.
> Location of Manufacturing Plants by Industry, County, and Employment Size. (MC63(S)-3). 1966. 9 reports.
> For each 4-digit SIC industry group provides statistics on number of plants in each county by employment size. Counties are shown in the state of location; state order is by geographic division.
> Location of Manufacturing Plants by County, Industry, and Employment Size. (MC63(S)-4). 1966. 9 reports.
> For each county within a state, the number of plants in each industry is shown by employment size.
> 1963 Establishment Statistics by Company Employment Size. (MC63(S)-7). 1967. 96 p.

CONCENTRATION Ratios in Manufacturing Industry, 1963.
Washington, D. C.: Government Printing Office, 1966-1968.
2 pts. , Suppl.   (DD 4)
> Prepared at the request of the Subcommittee on Antitrust and Monopoly of the Senate Committee on the Judiciary. Shows rank and share of industry by the largest manufacturers on the basis of value added, value of shipments in each industry, and value of shipments of each class of products accounted for by the largest companies.

CENSUS of Manufactures, 1963: Alphabetic List of Manufactured Products. Washington, D. C.: Government Printing Office, 1964. 103 p.   (DD 5)
> Shows 5-digit SIC code for each product.

---Numerical List of Manufactured Products. Washington,
D. C.: Government Printing Office, 1964. 393 p.

> Products are listed by their 7-digit SIC code within their re-
> spective 5-digit product classes, 4-digit industries, and 2-
> digit major industry groups. Also tabulates the tie-in between
> the 1963 CENSUS OF MANUFACTURES and CURRENT INDUS-
> TRIAL REPORTS product detail. New editions of both volumes
> from the 1967 census were issued in early 1968.

Manufactures -- Current Reports

Intercensal data on manufacturing activity appear in the following basic reports.

ANNUAL Survey of Manufactures. (M...(AS)). Washington, D. C.:
Bureau of the Census. Annual (except census years).   (DD 10)

> Irregular number of reports are issued for each series year
> prior to bound volume. Based on a scientific sample of some
> 60,000 manufacturing establishments, these surveys are con-
> ducted for intercensal years. Provides general statistics on
> employment, man-hours, payrolls and labor costs not included
> in payrolls, value added by manufacture, capital expenditures,
> cost of materials, and value of products shipped for industry
> groups and industries; value of shipments for more than 1,000
> classes of manufactured products; value of manufacturers' in-
> ventories; fuels and electric energy used, by major industry
> groups, and by divisions and states; expenditures for new
> plant and new equipment for major industry groups and states;
> book value of fixed assets and rental payments for building and
> equipment for major industry groups and states; statistics for
> states, standard metropolitan statistical areas and large in-
> dustrial counties.

---Acquisitions and Disposals of Manufacturing Facilities, 1959-1962,
Part 1. (M62(AS)-S1(Part 1)). Washington, D. C.: Bureau of the
Census, 1965. 32 p.   (DD 10a)

Second report in a series being developed as a by-product of
the ANNUAL SURVEY OF MANUFACTURES.   Data given by
type of acquisition and by year; by industry and size-class of
acquiring company and acquired facility; and by the 200 largest
manufacturing companies.

COUNTY Business Patterns (D2).

CURRENT Industrial Reports. (Series M...). Washington,
D. C.: Bureau of the Census. Monthly; Quarterly; Semiannual;
Annual.   (DD 11)

Information at factory level on inventories, production, and
shipments for 5,000 products published in the report series
listed below.   Each series is identified by a number which consists of the letter M to designate "manufactures" (followed by A
for annual, two digits to identify major SIC group, and further
alphabetic designation as a more specific identification within the
2-digit group.   Those issued jointly with the Business and
Defense Services Administration are identified by the letters
BDSAF. All monthly and quarterly series include annual summaries.

All Manufacturing Industries

Manufacturers' Export Sales and Orders. (M4-A).
    Monthly.
Manufacturers' Shipments, Inventories, and Orders
    (M3-1). Monthly.

Processed Foods

Flour Milling Products. (M20A). Monthly.
Confectionery, Including Chocolate Products. (M20C).
    Monthly.
Fats and Oils (Preliminary): Oil Seed Crushings. (M20-J).
    Monthly.
Fats and Oils (Preliminary): Production Consump-
    tion, and Stocks. (M20K). Monthly.
Salad Dressing, Mayonnaise, and Related Products.
    (MA-20F).   Annual

Textile Mill Products

Woven Fabrics: Production, Inventories, and Unfilled Orders. (M22A). Monthly.

Consumption on the Woolen and Worsted Systems. (M22D). Monthly.

Woolen and Worsted Machinery Activity. (MA-22E). Annual.

Stocks of Wool and Related Fiber. (MA-22M). Annual.

Spun Yarn for Sale. (M22F). Annual.

Shipments of Knit Cloth. (M22K). Quarterly.

Tufted Textile Products. (M22L). Semiannual.

Cotton, Man-made Fiber Staple, and Linters: Consumption and Stocks, and Spindle Activity (Preliminary). (M22P). Monthly.

Rugs, Carpets, and Carpeting. (MA-22Q). Annual.

Cotton, Silk, and Man-made Fiber Woven Goods Finished. (MA-22S). Annual.

Cotton Broad-woven Goods. (M22T.1). Quarterly.

Man-made Fiber Broad-woven Goods (M22T.2). Quarterly.

Wool Broad-woven Goods. (M22T.3). Quarterly.

Tire Cord and Tire Cord Fabrics. (M22T.4). Quarterly.

Nonwoven Textiles. (MA-22T.5). Annual.

Apparel and Leather

Apparel. (MA-23A). Annual.

Women's, Misses' and Juniors' Apparel. (M23H). Monthly.

Men's Apparel. (M23B). Monthly.

Knit Underwear and Nightwear. (M23C). Quarterly.

Gloves and Mittens. (MA-23D). Annual.

Brassieres, Corsets, and Allied Garments. (MA-23J). Annual.

Sheets, Pillowcases, and Towels. (MA-23X). Annual.

Shoes and Slippers. (M31A). Monthly.

Luggage, Briefcases, and Personal Leather Goods. (M31E). Monthly.

Lumber, Furniture, and Paper Products

Hardwood Plywood. (MA-24F). Annual.

Softwood Plywood. (MA-24H). Annual.

Particleboard. (MA-24L). Annual.

Lumber Production and Mill Stocks. (MA-24T). Annual.

Household Furniture and Bedding Products. (MA-25D).
   Annual.

Mattresses and Bedsprings. (M25E). Monthly.

Office Furniture. (MA-25H). Annual.

Pulp, Paper, and Board. (M26A). Monthly.

Converted Flexible Packaging Products. (M26F).
   Monthly.

Chemicals, Rubber and Plastics

Inorganic Chemicals and Gases. (M28A). Monthly.

Superphosphate and Other Phosphatic Fertilizer Materials.
   (M28D). Monthly.

Paint, Varnish, and Lacquer. (M28F). Monthly.

Pharmaceutical Preparations, Except Biologicals. (MA-28G).
   Annual.

Asphalt and Tar Roofing and Siding Products. (M29A).
   Monthly.

Rubber: Supply and Distribution for the U. S. (M30A).
   Monthly.

Shipments of Selected Plastic Products. (MA-30D).
   Annual.

Plastic Bottles. (M30E). Monthly.

Stone, Clay, and Glass Products

Refractories. (M32C). Quarterly.

Clay Construction Products. (M32D). Monthly.

Consumer, Scientific, Technical, and Industrial Glassware.
   (MA-32E). Annual.

Glass Containers. (M32G). Monthly.

Fibrous Glass. (MA-32J). Annual

Flat Glass. (M32A). Quarterly.

Primary Metals

Iron and Steel Castings. (M33A). Monthly.

Steel Mill Products. (MA-33B). Annual.

Inventories of Steel Mill Shapes. (M33-3). Monthly.

Commercial Steel Forgings. (MA-33C). Annual.

Nonferrous Castings. (M33E). Monthly.

Magnesium Mill Products. (MA-33G). Annual.

Inventories of Brass and Wire Mill Shapes. (M33K).
Monthly.

Insulated Wire and Cable. (MA-33L). Monthly.

Copper-Base Mill and Foundry Products. (BDSAF-84).
Quarterly.

Titanium Ingot and Mill Products. (BDSAF-263).
Monthly.

Intermediate Metal Products

Metal Cans. (M34D). Monthly.

Plumbing Fixtures. (M34E). Quarterly.

Steel Power Boilers. (MA-34G). Annual.

Closures for Containers. (M34H). Monthly.

Steel Shipping Barrels, Drums and Pails. (M34K).
Monthly.

Heating and Cooking Equipment. (M34N). Monthly.

Aluminum Foil Converted. (BDSAF-765). Annual.

Machinery and Equipment

Farm Machinery and Equipment. (M35A). Quarterly.

Typewriters. (M35C). Monthly.

Office, Computing and Accounting Machines. (MA-35R).
Annual.

Construction Machinery. (M35D). Quarterly.

Mining Machinery and Equipment. (MA35F). Annual.

Fans, Blowers, and Unit Heaters. (M35H). Quarterly.

Internal Combustion Engines. (MA-35L). Annual.

Refrigeration Equipment. (MA-35M). Annual.

Pumps and Compressors. (MA-35P). Annual.

Tractors, Except Garden Tractors. (M35S). Monthly.

Vending Machines. (MA-35U). Annual.

Metalworking Machinery. (M35W). Quarterly.

Switchgear, Switchboard Apparatus, Relays, and Industrial
  Controls. (MA-36A). Annual.

Electric Lamps. (M36B). Quarterly.

Flourescent Lamp Ballasts. (M36C). Quarterly.

Electric Housewares and Fans. (MA-36E). Annual.

Motors and Generators. (MA-36H). Annual.

Wiring Devices and Supplies. (MA-36K). Annual.

Electric Lighting Fixtures. (MA-36L). Annual.

Home Radio Receivers and Television Sets; Automobile Radios,
  Phonograph and Record Player Attachments. (MA-36M).
  Annual.

Selected Electronic and Associated Products. (MA-36N).
  Annual.

Backlog of Orders for Aerospace Companies. (M37D).
  Quarterly.

Aircraft Propellers. (MA-37E). Annual.

Complete Aircraft and Aircraft Engines. (M37G).
  Monthly.

Truck Trailers. (M37L). Monthly.

Selected Instruments and Related Products. (MA-38B).
  Annual.

Atomic Energy Products. (MA-38Q). Annual.

Communication Equipment. (BDSAF-363B). Annual.

Motorized Fire Apparatus. (BDSAF-504A). Annual.

Major Censuses: Mineral Industries

The Census of Mineral Industries, first taken in 1840, was
conducted at about ten-year intervals during the next century. It was
taken for the years 1954, 1958, and 1963. Like business and manufactures, it is now to be conducted every fifth year ending in 2 and 7.

CENSUS of Mineral Industries, 1963. Washington, D. C.: Government Printing Office, 1967, 2 vols.   (DE 1)

Volume I, Summary and Industry Statistics. 955 p.

Presents data on the following subjects: size of establishments; type of organization; employment and related statistics; type of operation; fuels, electric energy, and selected supplies used; power equipment in mineral industries. and water use in mineral industries. Statistics for each of 50 mineral industries and 14 subindustries: number of companies; number of establishments; employment, man-hours, payrolls; value added in mining; quantity and value of products shipped and supplies used; quantity and cost of fuels and electric energy purchased as well as the quantities of fuels produced and consumed; cost of contract work; cost of purchased machinery; capital expenditures; and horsepower of equipment. Selected comparable figures are included for earlier years. Detailed statistics are shown by geographic region and state and by type of operation. Selected statistics are shown by size of establishment, by ratio of output to man-hours, and by ratio of payroll to value added in mining.

Volume II, Area Statistics.   705 p.
This volume presents for each state (except Delaware, Maryland, and the District of Columbia which are combined) figures for each of the 50 mining industries, insofar as they have operations in the state, and for 2- and 3-digit industry groups by type of operation and county. Statistics are shown for the following items: value of shipments; value added by mining; employment, payrolls, man-hours; capital expenditures; costs of supplies; purchased machinery installed; and number of establishments. Selected product statistics are also included.

See also DB5, DB6.

Some data on a current basis appear in County Business Patterns (D2) and in the publications of the Bureau of Mines.

Major Censuses: Transportation
The first national census of transportation ever taken in the

United States covers the year 1963. Data collected and published were limited to those not available from other government agencies, regulatory bodies or private organizations. It is planned to conduct such a census every five years in the years ending in 2 and 7.

CENSUS of Transportation, 1963. Washington, D. C.: Government Printing Office, 1966-67. 4 vols. (DF 1)

Volume I, Passenger Transportation Survey. 111 p.
National travel data are shown for trips, travelers, and traveler nights, by such characteristics as means of transportation, purpose, duration, distance and region of origin and destination of trip, size of party, and lodgings used. Also presented are data on travel frequency of households and persons by socio-economic status factors and travel characteristics listed above. On home-to-work travel, data are furnished on such items as means of transportation, distance to work, time required to get to work, availability of public transportation, and selected socio-economic status characteristics of workers.

Volume II, Truck Inventory and Use Survey. 704 p.
Data based on a probability sample of trucks in the 50 states and the District of Columbia on the characteristics and uses of the nation's truck resources. Data in most tables are expressed in percent distributions and cover various characteristics related to annual mileage, annual use, annual vehicle miles, area of operation, body type, driver man-hours, load length or capacity, maintenance responsibility, major use, production area, size class, truck fleets, number of trucks, type of fuel used, weekly use, year of model. Advance reports were issued for each state, District of Columbia and the nine geographic divisions.

Volume III, Commodity Transportation Survey.
Parts 1 and 2, Commodity Groups. 479 p.
Data on the flow of commodities classified in terms of the

transportation commodity classification system (TCC). Detailed statistics for the 2-, 3-, 4-, and 5-digit TCC levels on tons of shipments by means of transport and commodity, distance and commodity, weight and commodity; ton-miles of shipments by means of transport and commodity, weight and commodity. Also, tables for selected individual 3-digit groups on tons of shipments by means of transport, region of origin, and distance shipped; geographic divisions of origin and destination; means of transport and weight of shipment; geographic division of destination and origin. For the same groups, ton-miles of shipments are shown by geographic division of destination and origin; geographic division of origin and destination; means of transport and weight of shipment.

Parts 3 and 4, Shipper Groups and Production
Areas. 569 p.
Shipper data show tons and ton-miles of commodities shipped by manufacturing establishments in each of 24 major shipper groups defined on the 4-digit SIC level, classified by means of transport, length of haul, geographic division of origin and destination, commodity, and size of plant.
Production area data show the flow of commodities from manufacturing plants located in each of 25 production areas (each area consists of one or a cluster of standard metropolitan statistical areas). Data are shown for tons and ton-miles of commodities shipped classified by weight, means of transport, length of haul, and destination.

Volume IV, Motor Carrier Survey. 30 p.
Data on the operation of bus carriers and "for hire" truck carriers not subject to the regulations of the Interstate Commerce Commission. Subjects covered, some by geographic division, include form of ownership, expenses, operating revenues, and principal type of service.

Major Censuses: Governments

The Bureau's governments program relates to the characteristics and functions of state and local governments. During the period
1850 to 1942, the governments census was taken at approximately ten-
year intervals, providing more complete and detailed information on
state and local governments than is reported on a current basis. After
1942 it was taken in 1957 and 1962 and is planned to continue quinqu-
ennially for the years ending in 2 and 7.

CENSUS of Governments, 1967. Washington, D. C.: Government
Printing Office, 1967-   (In process)   (DG 1)
Planned in seven volumes parallel in contents to the seven
volumes of the 1962 census detailed below.

CENSUS of Governments, 1962. Washington, D. C.:   Government
Printing Office, 1963-1965.   7 vols.
Volume I, Governmental Organization. v, 376 p.
Numbers of governmental units and dependent school systems;
national and state data on county, municipal and township governments by population size; statistics on school districts and
other school systems; parallel detail on local governments in
standard metropolitan areas and their component counties.
Summary description of local governments and school systems,
their fiscal powers and governing bodies.

Volume II, Taxable Property Values. iv, 160 p.
Valuations set for local taxation; assessed valuations by state
and county and for individual cities of 300,000 or more inhabitants; estimated distribution for each state of taxable realty by
use class, with separate figures for metropolitan areas; real
estate sales; etc.

Volume III, Compendium of Public Employment. v, 536 p.
Public civilian employment as of October 1962. Detailed data
concerning state and local government employees and payrolls
by states, SMSA's, and summary data for other counties and
municipalities.

Volume IV, Governmental Finances.

No. 1: Finances of School Districts. iv, 58 p.

Revenue, expenditure, debt, and financial assets of school districts. Also statistics by states.

No. 2: Finances of County Governments. iv, 196 p.

Revenue, expenditure, debt, and financial assets of county governments shown nationally and state-by-state.

No. 3: Finances of Municipalities and Township Governments. 291 p.

Revenue, expenditure, debt, and financial assets are presented for individual municipalities and townships, by population-size groups, by states.

No. 4: Compendium of Government Finances.
621 p.

Nationwide totals for the federal government, states, and local governments by type of government; related figures for state and local governments by states, including for numerous local government items a breakdown by type of government. Data given separately for local governments within metropolitan areas and for counties.

Volume V, Local Government in Metropolitan Areas.
705 p.

Data on numbers of local governments by type and size, local government employment, and local government finances for SMSA's and for their component counties.

Volume VI, Topical Studies.

No. 1:   Employee Retirement Systems of State and Local Governments. iv, 53 p.

No. 2:   State Payments to Local Governments. iv, 109 p.

No. 3:   State Reports on State and Local Government Finances. iv, 51 p.

No. 4:   Historical Statistics on Governmental Finances
            and Employment. 132 p.

No. 5:   Graphic Summary. 57 p.

Volume VII, State Reports. 52 reports.

Set of separate reports for each state, District of Columbia
and Puerto Rico giving findings on governmental structure and
numbers, public employment and state and local government
finances.

Governments -- Current Reports

Current governments data concern primarily public finance
and employment and are reported in the following series:

GOVERNMENTAL Finances ... (GF). Washington, D. C.: Government Printing Office. 6 annual reports.   (DG 1(

This series of reports presents fiscal data for the United
States, states, cities, and selected standard metropolitan
statistical areas and their component counties.

GOVERNMENT Employment ... (GE). Washington, D. C.: Government Printing Office. 2 annual reports.   (DG 1

Report devoted to city employment presents employment and
payroll data in summary and for individual cities and townships of 50,000 inhabitants or more.

The public employment report shows employment and payrolls of states and local governments by type of government
and by function.

QUARTERLY Tax Reports: Quarterly Summary of State and Local
Tax Revenue. (GT). Washington, D. C.: Bureau of the Census.
Quarterly.   (DG 1

National totals of state and local tax revenues by level of
government and type of tax; property tax collections in 200
major county areas; collections of selected state taxes, by

states.

QUARTERLY Public Construction Reports: Construction Expenditures of State and Local Governments. (GC). Washington, D. C.: Bureau of the Census. Quarterly.   (DG 13)
    Nationwide figures on construction expenditures of state and local governments, by level of government and by function.

STATE and Local Government Special Studies. (G-SS). Washington, D. C.: Bureau of the Census. Irregular.   (DG 14)
    Continuing series presenting miscellaneous data.

Major Censuses: Population and Housing

    The census of population has been taken every ten years in the years ending in 0. The latest, the 18th, was conducted as of April 1, 1960.

CENSUS of Population, 1960. Washington, D. C.: Government Printing Office, 1960-   3 vols.   (DH 1)
    Volume I, Characteristics of the Population.
    (Series PC(1)). 57 parts in 54 vols.
    First issued in four chapters for each area. Later, chapters for each area were bound into single books and published as parts of Vol. I. Also, the 57 CHAPTER A reports are available in a single bound edition designated Volume I, Part A: Number of Inhabitants.
        Chapter A: Number of Inhabitants.
    57 reports.
    Final population counts for states and counties and their urban and rural parts, and for standard metropolitan statistical areas, urbanized areas, all incorporated places, unincorporated places of 1,000 or more inhabitants, and minor civil divisions.
        Chapter B: General Population Characteristics.
    57 reports.

Statistics on sex, age, marital status, color or race, and relationship to head of household.

Chapter C: General Social and Economic Characteristics.
53 reports.

Nativity and parentage, state of birth, country of origin of
foreign stock, mother tongue, place of residence in 1955, year
moved into present house, school enrollment by level and type,
years of school completed, families and their composition,
fertility, veteran status, employment status, weeks worked in
1959, year last worked, occupation group, industry group,
class of worker, place of work, means of transportation to
work, and income of persons and families.

Chapter D: Detailed Characteristics.   53 reports.

Most of the subjects covered in Chapter C, above, cross-
classified by age, color, and other characteristics. Additional information on families; data on single years of age, detailed
occupation, and detailed industry.

Volume II, Subject Reports. (Series PC (2)). 35 reports
planned.

As indicated below, each report deals with a particular subject. Detailed information and cross-relationships are generally provided on a national and regional level. Some reports
give data for states or standard metropolitan statistical areas.

1A,   Nativity and Parentage. 167 p.

1B,   Persons of Spanish Surname. 219 p.

1C,   Nonwhite Population by Race. 274 p.

1D,   Puerto Ricans in the United States. 118 p.

1E,   Mother Tongue of the Foreign Born. 38 p.

2A,   State of Birth.   190 p.

2B,   Mobility for States and State Economic Areas.
       490 p.

2C,   Mobility for Metropolitan Areas.   365 p.

2D,   Lifetime and Recent Migration. 506 p.

2E,   Migration Between State Economic Areas. 388 p.

3A,   Women by Number of Children Ever Born. 343 p.

3B,   Childspacing. 206 p.

3C,   Women by Children Under Five Years Old. 160 p.

4A,   Families. 477 p.

4B,   Persons by Family Characteristics. 227 p.

4C,   Sources and Structure of Family Income. 255 p.

4D,   Age at First Marriage. 194 p.

4E,   Marital Status. 191 p.

5A,   School Enrollment. 150 p.

5B,   Educational Attainment. 204 p.

5C,   Socioeconomic Status. 282 p.

6A,   Employment Status and Work Experience. 248 p.

6B,   Journey to Work. 579 p.

6C,   Labor Reserve. 218 p.

7A,   Occupational Characteristics. 551 p.

7B,   Occupation by Earnings and Education. 318 p.

7C,   Occupation by Industry. 163 p.

7D,   Characteristics of Teachers. 74 p.

7E,   Characteristics of Professional Workers. 161 p.

7F,   Industrial Characteristics. 216 p.

8A,   Inmates of Institutions. 312 p.

8B,   Income of the Elderly Population. 219 p.

8C,   Veterans. 114 p.

Volume III, Selected Area Reports. (Series PC (3)).

5 reports.

1A,   State Economic Areas. 482 p.

1B,   Size of Place. 97 p.

1C,   Americans Overseas. 151 p.

1D,   Standard Metropolitan Statistical Areas. 767 p.

1E,   Type of Place. 481 p.

CENSUS of Population, 1960: Supplementary Reports. (Series PC
(S1)). Washington, D. C.: Bureau of the Census, 1961-   (DH 2)
     The first 16 reports give final figures on the population of
     particular kinds of areas (states, cities, wards, congression-
     al districts, SMSA's).   The others provide miscellaneous types
     of data, issued in advance of their publication in Vols. I and II,

selected tables from previously published reports, and special
use statistics of public interest.

A housing census was taken as part of the decennial
censuses of 1940, 1950, and 1960. The 1960 census included the
Survey of Components of Inventory Change and Residential Finance
which measured gains and losses in the housing inventory after
1950, and changes after December 1956 when the National Housing
Inventory was conducted.

CENSUS of Housing, 1960. Washington, D. C.: Government Printing Office, 1961-1963. 7 vols.   (DH 3)
> Volume I, State and Small Areas. (Series HC (1)).
> 55 reports. (also issued in 9 bound parts)
> One report for each state, the District of Columbia, Virgin
> Islands, Guam, Puerto Rico, and a United States summary.
> Information for states, urbanized areas, standard metro-
> politan statistical areas and places of 1,000 population and
> over. Data on tenure, color, vacancy status, population
> per occupied housing unit, number of persons per room,
> structural characteristics, and plumbing facilities, financial
> characteristics and other subjects.

> Volume II, Metropolitan Housing. (Series HC(2)). 202
> reports. (Also issued in 7 bound parts).
> Cross tabulations of housing and household characteristics
> with separate reports for the United States, nine geographic
> divisions, and each standard metropolitan statistical area with
> 100,000 inhabitants or more in the United States and Puerto
> Rico.

> Volume III, City Blocks. (Series HC(3)).   421 reports.
> Separate reports for cities with 50,000 population or more and
> smaller places which arranged for block statistics. Selected
> housing characteristics are presented by blocks.

Volume IV, Components of Inventory Change...
These data also update findings of the National Housing
Inventory conducted in December 1956.

Part 1A: 1950-1959 Components ... Standard
Metropolitan Statistical Area. (Series HC(4) Part
1A). 18 reports.
One report for each of the 17 metropolitan areas and the United
States. Data on new construction, conversions, mergers, and
demolitions.

Part 1B: Inventory Characteristics; (Series
HC(4) Part 1B). 18 reports.
One report for each of the 17 metropolitan areas and the
United States. Additional characteristics data, including
characteristics of present and previous residences of recent
movers.

Part 2: 1957 to 1959. United States and Selected Metropolitan Areas. (Series HC(4) Part 2). 10 reports.
One report for each of nine areas and for the United States
by regions. Give measurements and characteristics of the components of changes since 1956.

Volume V, Residential Finance.
Part 1, Homeowner Properties. xxix, 416 p.
Data for the United States, regions and selected metropolitan
areas include characteristics of mortgages, properties, and
homeowners.

Part 1, Supplement: Homeowner Properties,
Nonwhite Families. 5 p.
Only national summaries on the mortgage status and on selected characteristics of the property, the nonwhite owner and the
mortgage. Data relate to one-dwelling-unit nonfarm properties
which were owner occupied as of early 1960.

Part 2, Rental and Vacant Properties: United
States. xxix, 70 p.
Data similar to those in Part 1 will be presented on the financ-

ing and characteristics of rental and vacant properties for the United States.

Volume VI, Rural Housing: Economic Subregions.
xvii, 770 p.
Cross tabulations of housing and household characteristics for 121 economic subregions.

Volume VII, Housing of Senior Citizens. xxx, 297 p.
Characteristics of persons 60 years old and over and the housing units and households in which they live, for the United States, each state, the District of Columbia, and selected standard metropolitan statistical areas.

CENSUS of Housing, 1960: Special Reports for Local Housing Authorities. (Series HC(S1)). Washington, D. C.: Bureau of the Census, 1961-62. 140 reports. (DH 4)

One report for each participating locality, plus a summary on substandard occupied housing units. Requested by and planned in cooperation with the Public Housing Administration. Data presented on owner and renter occupied units defined as substandard by PHA. Emphasis on gross rent, family size, and income of renter families.

Major Censuses: Population and Housing -- Combined Reports

U. S. CENSUSES of Population and Housing, 1960: (DH 5)

CENSUS Tracts. (Series PHC(1)). Washington, D. C.: Government Printing Office, 1961-62. 180 reports.
One report for each of 180 tracted areas in the United States and Puerto Rico. Population subjects: age, race, marital status, country of origin of the foreign stock, relationship to head of household, school enrollment, etc. Housing subjects: tenure, color of head of household, vacancy status, condition and plumbing facilities, number of rooms and bathrooms, housing units in structure, heating equipment, etc.

Geographic Identification Code Scheme. (Series
PHC (2)). (See CA 13)
Census County Division Boundary Descriptions.
(Series PHC (3)). (See CA 14)

Major Censuses: Population and Housing -- Guides to 1960 Censuses

SUBJECT Guide to 1960 Census Data for the Negro Population. (Census of population, 1960; Supplementary reports, Series PC (S1) no. 46). Washington, D. C.: Bureau of the Census, 1964. 4 p. (DH 6)
> Indicates specific reports which contain data on the Negro population and the demographic and geographic (city, county, standard metropolitan statistical area, state) detail available.

U. S. Census of Population, 1960: Availability of Published and Unpublished Data. Washington, D. C.: Bureau of the Census, Rev. Oct. 1964. 36 p.   (DH 7)
> Describes the publication program and tabulates the detail available for each subject and each level of geographic area in printed, unpublished or computer tape form.

U. S. Census of Housing, 1960: Availability of Published and Unpublished Data. [Washington, D. C.: Bureau of the Census] Rev. Feb. 1966. 13 p.   (DH 8)
> Presents in outline form the items covered in the published reports and in the principal unpublished tabulations. Useful as a finding guide and index.

Population and Housing -- Current Reports: Population

A monthly survey conducted by the Bureau of the Census interviewers among a selected sample of the population yields current population and labor force data. The latter are listed with the publications of the Bureau of Labor Statistics which analyzes and reports the results.

Population findings on personal and family characteristics,

mobility, income, education, school enrollment, and other detail appear mostly on an annual basis. Population estimates are issued monthly; long-range forecasts occasionally. These data are published in a number of separate series. Those of immediate interest to market analysis are listed below.

CURRENT Population Reports: Washington, D. C.: Bureau of the Census.

Population Characteristics. (Series P-20). 10-12/yr.

(DH 10)

School enrollment, mobility, household and family characteristics.

Special Technical Studies. (Series P-23).   (DH 11)

Infrequent reports on methods, concepts, and miscellaneous data.

Population Estimates. (Series P-25). 20/yr.   (DH 12)

Estimates by geographic area and population characteristics. Also projections

Farm Population. (Census-ERS Series P-27). 2-3/yr.

(DH 13)

Prepared jointly with the Economic Research Service of the Department of Agriculture.

Special Censuses. (Series P-28). Irregular with quarterly and annual summaries.   (DH 14)

Taken at the request and expense of city or county involved, these reports show population changes in each locality since the last decennial census. Generally, the scope includes age, race and sex. No. 1447 (May 1967. 34 p.) summarizes all special censuses conducted since April 1, 1960 through 1966.

Consumer Income. (Series P-60). 1-3/yr.   (DH 15)

Consumer Buying Indicators. (Series P-65). Quarterly.

(DH 16)

Buying plans for automobiles, houses and major household appliances are tabulated by planning period, income and age groups.

Population and Housing -- Current Reports: Housing

Current housing statistics cover housing vacancies (rates, condition and characteristics) on a quarterly basis, television data annually, and other housing characteristics irregularly in the following separate series. Other important current statistics which update the housing data are produced regularly by the Bureau's Construction Statistics Division.

CURRENT Housing Reports: Washington, D. C.: Government Printing Office.

Housing Vacancies. (Series H-111). Quarterly.   (DH 17)
Vacancy rates and vacancies by housing characteristics for the country as a whole, geographic regions and inside and outside SMSA's.

Housing Characteristics. (Series H-121). Irregular

(DH 18)

In recent years this series has reported mainly on television sets for the United States, by regions, divisions and by inside vs outside SMSA's.

Construction Statistics

The construction data on housing starts, building permits, value of new construction put in place, regularly collected and published by the Bureau of the Census are planned to be augmented by the coverage of the construction industry as part of the regular Census of Business beginning with the one scheduled to cover the year 1967. Current construction statistics, issued in a series of separate releases, are being refined by the introduction of revised procedures and new survey data.

HOUSING Construction Statistics, 1889 to 1964. Washington, D. C.:
Government Printing Office, 1966. v, 805 p.   (DI 1)
   Historical compilation of 26 statistical time series issued in
   the Bureau's Construction Reports Series C20, C40 and
   C42 (listed below) and their predecessor publications. Data
   cover: housing starts; new units authorized, tabulated for
   regions, states, standard metropolitan statistical areas, cities
   of 100,000 or more, and individual permit-issuing places.

CONSTRUCTION Reports:

   Housing Starts. (Series C20). Washington, D. C.:
   Government Printing Office. Monthly.   (DI 2)
   Housing starts by geographic regions, by location in metropolitan and nonmetropolitan areas, by number of units in
   structure. Quarterly data on distribution of apartment houses
   by number of housing units, floors in structure and number of
   bedrooms in units.

   Housing Sales. (Series Census-HUD: C25). Washington, D. C.:
   Bureau of the Census. Monthly; Quarterly supplements;
   Annual Summary.   DI 3)
   Data on sales and unsold inventory of new, private nonfarm,
   one-family homes. Quarterlies provide additional data by
   regions and types of financing. Annual summary reports additional information on financing and characteristics of homes
   sold as well as data on metropolitan-nonmetropolitan location.

   Construction Activity: Value of New Construction
   Put in Place. (Series C30). Washington, D. C.: Government Printing Office. Monthly.   (DI 4)
   Estimates of private and public construction by type of construction (residential, nonresidential, public utility, etc.).

Housing Authorized by Building Permits and Public Contracts: Individual Permit-issuing Places.
(Series C40). Washington, D. C.: Government Printing Office.
Monthly; Annual summary.   (DI 5)
Units authorized in approximately 4,000 places, by place (county, city, étc.) arranged by state and SMSA or nonmetropolitan location. Annual summary provides data for 12,000 permit-issuing places.

Authorized Construction -- Washington, D. C., Area.
(Series C41). Washington, D. C.: Bureau of the Census.
Monthly.   (DI 6)
Housing units and valuation of building construction authorized by permit and by federal construction contract awards.

Housing Authorized by Building Permits and Public Contracts: States and Selected Standard Metropolitan Statistical Areas.
(Series C42). Washington, D. C.: Bureau of the Census.
Monthly; Annual summary.   (DI 7)
Valuation and number of units are shown for permit-issuing places by census divisions, states, and within 99 specified standard statistical metropolitan areas. Annual summary provides similar data covering 12,000 permit-issuing places for 62 standard metropolitan statistical areas.

Residential Alterations and Repairs. (Series C50). Washington, D. C.: Bureau of the Census. Annual.   (DI 8)
Annual and Quarterly expenditures by type of work, size of property, farm nonfarm status and geographic region.

Foreign Trade Statistics
    A wide selection of foreign trade statistics, collected from Shippers' Export Declarations and import entries filed with customs officials, is available in considerable detail. Basic data include dol-

lar value and net quantity of United States imports and exports by
commodity, country of origin and destination, and customs district.

Effective with the statistics for January 1967, some changes
were introduced. Several new reports replaced some previous ones
which were discontinued. One important change was the inclusion
in many reports and tabulations of separate information on movements
by vessel and air in addition to information for all methods of transportation combined. Significant changes in the coverage and presentation of the statistics are explained in the appropriate publications.

Detailed information on the new program is presented in the
following guide:

GUIDE to Foreign Trade Statistics, 1968. [Washington, D. C.]
Bureau of the Census, 1968. 120 p.   (DJ 1)
    Contains description of the foreign trade statistics program,
    samples of published tabulations, unpublished data available.

New reports and unpublished data are announced regularly in the
Bureau's catalog.

For the purposes of this handbook only publications of general
interest data have been included. Omitted are the reports on the
movement of gold and silver, bunker oil and coal, cotton manufactures, trade with Puerto Rico and United States possessions, and
the reports on air and waterborne trade.

After a long hiatus, the Bureau resumed, in 1965, the publication of
its basic historical annual:

FOREIGN Commerce and Navigation of the United States, 1946-1963.
Washington, D. C.: Government Printing Office [1965] 936 p. (DJ 2)
    Summary volume. Bridges the gap between the annuals pub-
    lished from 1821 through 1945 and the 1964 and subsequent annu-
    als which began publication in 1968. Among the statistics on ex-
    ports and imports are total figures, annual and monthly, in-

cluding seasonally adjusted monthly data; and country and
customs district data with comprehensive country and district
schedules for the 17-year period.   For the more recent
years, Standard International Trade Classification (3-digit)
commodity-by-country and country-by-commodity tables are
shown.

Recurring foreign trade reports fall basically into two
groups depending on whether they contain summary or detailed
data.   Three special reports have been included with the detailed
reports both in the tabular indexes and in the listing which follows.

EXPORT and Import Merchandise Trade.   (FT900).   Washington,
D. C.:   Bureau of the Census.   Monthly.   (DJ 3/DJ 4)
   Value of United States exports, general imports, and imports
   for consumption.   Combined reports issued previously as
   series FT900-E (United States Foreign Trade: Total Export
   Trade) and FT900-I (United States Foreign Trade: Total
   Import Trade).

HIGHLIGHTS of U. S. Export and Import Trade.   (FT900).
Washington, D. C.:   Government Printing Office.   Monthly Cumulative.   (DJ 5)
   Trade by commodity, country, U. S. customs district and
   method of transportation for total exports and imports and
   for vessel and air shipments.

Foreign Trade Statistics -- Detailed Export Reports
U. S. Exports: Commodity by Country.   (FT410).   Washington,
D. C.:   Government Printing Office.   Monthly cumulative.   (DJ 6)
   Dollar value by 1-, 2-, 3-, and 4-digit Schedule B commodi-
   ty groupings;   quantity and value for each individual 7-digit
   Schedule B commodity number, by country of destination.

TABULAR INDEX OF FOREIGN TRADE REPORTS: EXPORTS

Type of Data	Summary Reports*	Detailed and Special Reports*
Total	FT900-FT990	
Commodity		
Schedule B** detail		
Selected groupings	FT990	
Section	FT900	
1- through 4-digit		FT410 FT450 FT455
4-digit		FT450 FT455
7-digit		FT410
SIC-based code**		FT610
Value	FT900-FT990	FT410 FT450 FT455 FT610
Quantity	FT990	FT410 FT610
Country (or area)		
of destination	FT990	FT410 FT450 FT455 FT610
U. S. customs regions		
or districts	FT990	
Method of transportation	FT990	FT450 FT455
Shipping weight	FT990	FT450 FT455

* The numbers listed in this column are the series numbers of the individual reports. In the listing which accompanies this table the series number, enclosed in parentheses, appears after the title of each report.

** To facilitate statistical compilation various classification schedules are used for translating data into numeric codes. Referred to here are Schedule B, Statistical Classification of Domestic and Foreign Commodities Exported From the United States, and Sic, or the Standard Industrial Classification.

TABULAR INDEX OF FOREIGN TRADE REPORTS: IMPORTS

Type of Data	Summary Reports*	Detailed and Special Reports**
Total	FT900-FT990	
Commodity		
Schedule A** detail		
Selected groupings	FT990	
Section	FT990	
1- through 4-digit		FT135 FT150 FT155
4-digit		FT150 FT155
7-digit		FT135
SIC-based code**		FT210
TSUSA number**		FT246
Value	FT900-FT990	FT135 FT150 FT155 FT210 FT246
Quantity	FT990	FT135 FT210 FT246
Country (or area) or origin	FT990	FT135 FT150 FT155 FT210 FT246
U. S. customs regions or districts	FT990	
Method of Transportation	FT990	FT150 FT155
Shipping weight	FT990	FT150 FT155

* The numbers listed in this column are the series number of the individual reports. In the listing which accompanies this table the series number, enclosed in parentheses, appears after the title of each report.

** To facilitate statistical compilation various classification schedules are used for translating data into numeric codes. Referred to here are Schedule A, Statistical Classification of Commodities Imported into the United States; Sic, or the Standard Industrial Classification; TSUSA, or Tariff Schedules of the United States Annotated.

U. S. Exports: Schedule B Commodity Groupings: Geographic
Area, Country, and Method of Transportation. (FT 450). Washington, D. C.: Government Printing Office. Monthly cumulative. (DJ 7)
    Data for 1-, 2-, 3-, and 4-digit Schedule B commodity
    groupings; 4-digit Schedule B subgroup by world area and
    by country of destination showing dollar value for all methods
    of transportation and value and shipping weight for vessel and
    air.

UNITED States Exports, Geographic Area, Country, Schedule B
Commodity Groupings, and Method of Transportation. (FT455).
Washington, D. C.: Government Printing Office. Annual.   (DJ 8)
    Data in terms of 1-, 2-, 3-, and 4-digit Schedule B com-
    modity groupings by continent and country of destination;
    world area by 4-digit Schedule B groupings showing dollar
    value for all methods of transportation.

U. S. Exports of Domestic Merchandise: SIC-based Products and
Area. (FT610). Washington, D. C.: Government Printing Office.
Annual.   (DJ 9)
    Figures on net quantity and value of shipments of exports
    shown by Standard Industrial Classification based export
    product code, arranged by commodity and world area of
    destination. Additional tables show the conversion of
    Schedule B to a classification system based on the SIC.

See also D 3.

Foreign Trade Statistics -- Detailed Import Reports
    In some of the publications listed below, data are presented
for "imports for consumption" as well as for "general imports." The

Census Bureau defines these groups as follows:

> Imports for consumption consist of merchandise released from customs custody immediately upon arrival, merchandise entered into bonded manufacturing warehouses (other than smelting and refining warehouses), merchandise withdrawn from bonded storage warehouses for release into domestic consumption channels, and imported ores and crude metals which have been processed in bonded smelting warehouses. General imports represent total arrivals of imported goods (except for intransit shipments), i.e., merchandise released from customs custody immediately upon arrival plus merchandise entered into bonded storage warehouses, bonded manufacturing warehouses, and bonded smelting and refining warehouses immediately upon arrival.

U. S. Imports, General and Consumption, Schedule A Commodity and Country. (FT135). Washington, D. C.: Government Printing Office. Monthly cumulative.   (DJ 10)

Net quantity and dollar value for approximately 2,000 to 3,000 7-digit Schedule A commodity classifications by country of origin. Summary data show dollar value for 1-, 2-, 3-, and 4-digit Schedule A commodity groupings.

U. S. General Imports: Schedule A Commodity Groupings: Geographic Area, Country, and Method of Transportation. (FT150). Washington, D. C.: Government Printing Office. Monthly cumulative.   (DJ 11)

Data in terms of 1-, 2-, 3-, and 4-digit Schedule A commodity totals; 4-digit Schedule A subgroup by world area and by country of origin showing dollar value for all methods of transportation and value and shipping weight for vessel and air.

U. S. General Imports, Geographic Area, Country, Schedule A Commodity Groupings, and Method of Transportation. (FT155). Washington, D. C.: Government Printing Office. Monthly cumulative.   (DJ 12)

Data in terms of 1-, 2-, 3-, and 4-digit Schedule A commodity totals; world area by 4-digit Schedule A subgroup;

and continent and country of origin by Schedule A 1-, 2-, 3-,
and 4-digit commodity showing dollar value for all methods
of transportation and value and shipping weight for vessel and
air.

U. S. Imports for Consumption and General Imports, SIC-based
Product Classification, by Area. (FT210). Washington, D. C.:
Government Printing Office. Annual.   (DJ 13)

Import data originally compiled under the approximately
10,000 classes of the Tariff Schedules of the United States
Annotated (TSUSA) are rearranged and summarized into approximately 2,000 classes based on the Standard Industrial
Classification (SIC). Net quantity and value of general imports for consumption are shown for each commodity group
by area of origin.

U. S. Imports for Consumption and General Imports, TSUSA Commodity by Country. (FT246). Washington, D. C.: Government
Printing Office Annual.   (DJ 14)

Net quantity and value of imports by commodity, unit of
quantity, and country of origin. Also contains a table showing TSUSA commodity totals which differ from imports for
consumption totals by $10,000 or more.

See also D3.

Geographic Reports

The Geography Division is responsible for establishing the
boundaries of statistical areas and preparing maps for use by the
Bureau of the Census. Listed with manuals are the area delinea-
tion publications of interest. Enumerated below are the more general use report and map series.

GEOGRAPHIC Reports. (GE-10). Washington, D. C.: Govern-
ment Printing Office. Irregular.   (DK 1)

Reports oriented to geographic areas and presenting unpublished information already available at the Bureau, or compilations, in ,more useful form, of information scattered in published Bureau reports.

AREA Measurement Reports. (GE-20). Washington, D. C.:
Government Printing Office, 1964-   51 reports.   (DK 2)

One report for each state and a summary provide land, water, and total area in square miles for each county, minor civil division or census county division, and each place with 1,000 or more population in 1960.

UNITED States Maps. (GE-50). Washington, D. C.: Government
Printing Office. Irregular.   (DK 3)

Reference maps which present basic statistical data cartographically.

Notes

(1) Taeuber, Conrad. "Look It Up in the Census Reports."
Special Libraries, vol. 54, no. 1, January 1963, p. 35-39.

OTHER

FEDERAL SOURCES

Complete enumeration of the multitudinous publications issued by federal agencies is beyond the scope of this guide. Consequently, greater emphasis has been placed on periodic reports of current general-use data, less on occasional studies and special purpose statistics.

Since it is well known that every agency sums up its operations in annual reports only those are listed whose statistical content provides a useful summary or supplement to the periodic reports mentioned.

Similarly, only those special studies are included which provide historical or unique sources of general-purpose statistics. Statistical sources excluded here can be readily traced through the manuals previously mentioned and the research aids outlined in a subsequent chapter.

EXECUTIVE OFFICE OF THE PRESIDENT

In recent years there has been an increasing flow of publications from the Executive Office of the President and its constituent units. Although these reports are not entirely primary sources of quantitative data, their presentation and analysis merit analysis.

THE PRESIDENT

ECONOMIC Report of the President ... Together with the Annual Report of the Council of Economic Advisers. Washington, D. C.: Government Printing Office. Annual. (E 1)

Analysis of current developments and goals of the national economy supported by voluminous statistics on income, production, employment, and other indicator series.

MANPOWER Report of the President and a Report on Manpower
Requirements, Resources, Utilization, and Training by the United
States Department of Labor ... Washington, D. C.: Government
Printing Office. Annual.   (E 2)

> This report, submitted under the requirements of the Man-
> power Development and Training Act of 1962, is documented
> with detailed current and historic data on population, labor
> force, employment and unemployment, productivity, and oc-
> cupational trends.

Special reports, similarly documented by statistical and administrative agencies, are also issued from time to time as the oc-
casion arises.

COUNCIL OF ECONOMIC ADVISERS

Analysis of the national economy is one of the major functions of this body. Its interpretations appear in its ANNUAL RE-
PORT published with that of the President as cited above. In addition, the Council prepares a monthly compilation of major statistical series for publication by the Joint Economic Committee of the
U. S. Congress under the title ECONOMIC INDICATORS.

BUREAU OF THE BUDGET

The major activity of the Bureau of the Budget is the preparation of the federal budget which is reported in the publications
listed below. These are supplemented by occasional special studies, such as the 10-year projection of federal budget expenditures,
and staff reports on federal fiscal affairs. The Bureau's role in
coordinating and improving the federal statistical program is discussed in the preceding chapter and the resultant publications are
classed with their related bibliographical groups.

BUDGET of the United States Government. Washington, D. C.:
Government Printing Office. Annual.   (E 3)

Detailed official text of the President's budget message and budget for current and coming fiscal year.

THE BUDGET in Brief. Washington, D. C.: Government Printing
Office. Annual.   (E 4)
    Summary edition, including all basic data, presented in less technical style.

THE ... BUDGET Review. Washington, D. C.: Government
Printing Office. Annual.   (E 5)
    Official revised estimates of the budget issued after the adjournment of Congress.

COMMITTEES AND COMMISSIONS

Committees and commissions created by Congress or appointed by the President delve into many business aspects of commerce and industry. Their findings, reported to the President, reveal not only much basic and detailed information but also trends likely to develop with or without the benefit of governmental influence. Among such reports of current significance are the following.

U. S. National Commission on Food Marketing. Food From Farmer to Consumer. Washington, D. C.: Government Printing Office, 1966. 10 vols.

U. S. National Commission on Technology, Automation, and Economic Progress. Technology and the American Economy. Washington, D. C.: Government Printing Office, 1966. 7 vols.

THE CONGRESS

Congressional documents, hearings, and reports, compiled as guides for specific legislative action, often constitute a rich source of analytic information and occasionally of original data. Among the some 6,000 issued during a Congress there are a number which summarize current developments in particular industries, markets, or segments of the economy. These are often supplemented by comprehensive reports of committees or commissions established to study specific national problems and recommend appropriate measures to the President and Congress. Many include statistical documentation provided by federal agencies or independent authorities in a form not easily available elsewhere.

For example:

HOUSE. Committee on Interstate and Foreign Commerce. National Transportation Policy. Washington, D. C.: Government Printing Office, 1961. xx, 732 p.

World Newsprint Supply-Demand; Outlook Through 1968. Washington, D. C.: Government Printing Office, 1966. 31 p.

SENATE. Committee on Commerce. Helicopter Air Service Program; Hearings Before the Aviation Subcommittee ... Washington, D. C.: Government Printing Office, 1965. 494 p.

SENATE. Committee on Government Operations. Drug Literature; Report Prepared for the Study of "Interagency Coordination in Drug Research and Regulation" ... Washington, D. C.: Government Printing Office, 1963. 171 p.

SENATE. Committee on the Judiciary. Subcommittee on Antitrust and Monopoly. Administered Prices [of] Drugs. Washington, D. C.: Government Printing Office [1961] 374 p.

SENATE. Special Committee on Aging. Basic Facts on the Health and Economic Status of Older Americans. Washington, D. C.: Government Printing Office, 1961. 38 p.

JOINT ECONOMIC COMMITTEE
Because its functions entail the appraisal of economic programs and the analysis and interpretation of economic trends, the
reports, hearings, and study papers published by the Joint Economic Committee for itself and for its subcommittees (particularly its
Subcommittee on Economic Statistics and Subcommittee on Economic
Progress) deserve more consistent attention. Prices, family income, inventory fluctuations, private investment expenditures for
plant and equipment, labor force, and other aspects of economic
growth and stability are some of the subjects covered by its publications.

Widely used is the Committee's periodic report:

ECONOMIC Indicators. Washington, D. C.: Government Printing
Office. Monthly.   (E 6)
>   Prepared for the Committee by the Council of Economic Ad-
>   visers. Presents basic series on total output, income, and
>   spending; production and business activity; prices; employ-
>   ment, unemployment and wages; money, credit, and security
>   markets; and federal finance.
>   Supplement. Washington, D. C.: Government Printing
>   Office. Biennial.
>   Prepared by the Office of Statistical Standards, Bureau of the
>   Budget, and the Committee staff. Contains historical tables
>   of the various series published monthly, with explanatory text
>   on their compilation, uses and limitations.

Recent special studies worthy of note:

TECHNOLOGY in Education. Washington, D. C.: Government
Printing Office. 1966. 273 p.

U. S. Economic Growth to 1975: Potentials and Problems.
Washington, D. C.: Government Printing Office, 1966. 63 p.

Less publicized is the Committee's interest in assembling and assessing basic statistical data as illustrated here by some current reports:

GOVERNMENT Price Statistics. Washington, D. C.: Government Printing Office, 1966. 19 p.
  Reviews the reliability and scope of existing price indexes and the need for additional price indexes.

IMPROVED Statistics for Economic Growth. Washington, D. C.: Government Printing Office. 1966. 84 p.

PRODUCTIVITY, Prices and Incomes. Washington, D. C.: Government Printing Office, 1967. 213 p.
  Updates a 1957 report of the same title. Collection of statistics from various sources, with an indication of the characteristics and limitations of data in these fields.

All studies and reports issued free or for purchase are detailed in a complete list of publications:

COMMITTEE Publications and Policies Governing Their Distribution. Washington, D. C.: Joint Economic Committee. Annual. (E 7)
  Checklist of documents issued over approximately the last ten years arranged by publication date under each Congress.

DEPARTMENT OF AGRICULTURE

Because the Department of Agriculture is required by law to assemble and disseminate useful information on agricultural subjects in the most comprehensive sense, it produces an impressive amount and variety of data on all phases of agricultural economics, marketing, and distribution.

Many statistical studies are issued regularly, or occasionally, some with periodic supplements, on such subjects as food con-

sumption, dairy products, tobacco, wool and other agricultural
commodities.

Often overlooked are its research activities in the field of
human nutrition and home economics. Findings define not only the
farm market for a large variety of products but also the consumer,
industrial, and institutional markets for the nation's agricultural output, raw and processed.

Studies of sales potentials, consumer preferences, merchandising methods, buying practices, wholesaling, store layout and
other topics are specific and frequent and can be easily located
through the agency's catalog of publications. Detailed here are the
statistical programs which result in periodic reports of the general-
use type.

AGRICULTURAL Statistics.   Washington, D. C.: Government
Printing Office. Annual.   (EA 1)
    Compendium of the principal statistical series on agriculture
    and related subjects.   Historical data limited to the most re-
    cent 10 to 15 years.

AGRICULTURAL ECONOMICS

    This agency, comprised of the Statistical Reporting Service
and Economic Research Service, represents the main data collecting unit of the Department of Agriculture.

AGRICULTURAL Outlook Chartbook. Washington, D. C.: Government Printing Office.   Annual.   (EA 2)
    Published as a section of the November issue of THE FARM
    INDEX. Charts and maps accompanied by data and text on
    food supplies and consumption; farm production, costs,
    prices, income, expenditure; commodity highlights; family
    living. 1962 edition combined domestic and foreign economic
    data for the first time.

    Of major interest to marketers are the data collected and is-
sued by the Statistical Reporting Service: estimates and reports on

the production, supply, and prices of crops and livestock; farm employment; wage rates.

The broad program of the Economic Research Service produces quantities of statistics in the following areas:

Economic and statistical analyses on factors affecting agricultural prices and income; commodity outlook and situation; food demand, supply and consumption; farm population, manpower, levels of living.

Marketing, including research in market costs, structure and development; market potentials; distribution and merchandising of agricultural products. Emphasis is placed on products in abundant supply requiring additional outlets.

Economic and statistical research on farm efficiency and productivity, including optimum utilization of manpower, land, buildings, equipment; agricultural real estate and finance; adjustment to changing market patterns and technological developments.

Statistical reports issued by both these units are numerous and varied.

Statistical Reporting Service

STATISTICAL Summary. Washington, D. C.: Agricultural Economics. Monthly.   (EA 3)

In addition to summarizing crop and livestock production estimates this report is also the first to publish data on cash receipts by states, farm marketings index, farm-retail price spreads and farmer's share of the consumer's dollar, and farm output indexes.

AGRICULTURAL Situation. Washington, D. C.: Government Printing Office. Monthly.   (EA 4)

Contains brief reviews of current marketing and economic

developments affecting farmers.

AGRICULTURAL Prices. Washington, D. C.: Agricultural Economics. Monthly.   (EA 5)
    Prices received and paid by farmers compared to parity prices;
state and regional analyses for selected farm products.

FARM Labor. Washington, D. C.: Agricultural Economics. Monthly.   (EA 6)
    Data on farm employment, wage rates, and related subjects.

COLD Storage Report. Washington, D. C.: Agricultural Economics.
Monthly.   (EA 7)
    Information collected from warehouses and other storage facili-
ties gives holdings by commodity, space and occupancy, and
other data.

CROP Production. Washington, D. C.: Agricultural Economics.
Monthly.   (EA 8)
    Content varies with season. Data on plantings, stocks, prices
yields; production statistics by states.

    A large number of crop and livestock reports are issued for
the country as a whole and generally include estimates by states.
Segments, with emphasis on local conditions, are reissued through
the 43 offices of the state agricultural statisticians. Production,
utilization, stocks and other data are published as they become
available, with little or no economic analysis. Commodities covered
fall into the following groups: field and seed crops; fruits and nuts;
vegetables; milk and dairy products; livestock and livestock products;
poultry and eggs; miscellaneous (cut flowers, nursery products, cotton). A detailed publication schedule and description of contents is
available from the agency upon request.

Economic Research Service

THE Farm Index. Washington, D. C.: Government Printing Office.

Monthly.   (EA 9)

> Begun in October 1962, this nontechnical magazine reports on ERS research and information developed in cooperation with state agricultural experiment stations. Editorial content covers farming, marketing, the foreign market, and the consumer. Current agricultural outlook, leading economic developments, and annotated list of recent ERS publications are regular features.

AGRICULTURAL Economics Research. Washington, D. C. : Government Printing Office. Quarterly.   (EA 10)

> Contains technical articles on methods, results and findings of research in agricultural economics, statistics and marketing.

AGRICULTURAL Finance Review. Washington, D. C. : Agricultural Economics. Annual with supplement.   (EA 11)

> Basic source of financial data pertaining to agriculture: capital used; credit; financing of specialized activities; agricultural risk and insurance; bankruptcies; real estate values and transfers; taxation; interrelations of agriculture and public finance. Appendix contains detailed data by states and regions.

AGRICULTURAL Outlook Digest. Washington. D. C. : Agricultural Economics. 11/yr.   (EA 12)

> A four-page newsletter summarizing, for the most part, the content of the Demand and Price Situation and of the commodity situation reports.

The economic analysis lacking in the crop and livestock reports is provided in the outlook and situation reports. Those listed below contain review and trend data, special analyses, and an annual appraisal of the outlook for the coming year. Some publish important statistics for the first time.

DEMAND and Price Situation. Washington, D. C. : Agricultural

Economics. 4/yr.   (EA 13)

   Reviews domestic and foreign demand for farm products, including output, supply, employment, income, commodity
   prices and related factors.

FARM Income Situation. Washington, D. C.: Agricultural Economics.
4/yr.   (EA 14)

   Estimates of gross and net farm income, production expenses,
   and cash receipts appear first in this report.

MARKETING and Transportation Situation. Washington, D. C.: Agricultural Economics. 4/yr.   (EA 15)

   Carries special articles, and retail cost return received by
   farmers and the spread between the two for individual food
   products, a group of cotton clothing articles and housefurnish-
   ings, and cigarettes. This report is also the first to publish
   price spreads or marketing charges, farmer's share of the consumers' food dollar, and the national farm food marketing bill.

NATIONAL Food Situation. Washington, D. C.: Agricultural Economics
4/yr.   (EA 16)

   Per capita food consumption data are first published in this report. Other statistics include production of major food commodities, indexes of supply, retail food prices.

FARM Cost Situation. Washington, D. C.: Agricultural Economics.
Annual.   (EA 17)

   Reviews farm labor, power and machinery, feeds, seeds, fertilizer, building materials, pesticides, land values and rentals,
   interest, taxes and insurance, and related data, on costs on
   farms of various types.

AGRICULTURAL Finance Outlook. Washington, D. C.: Agricultural
Economics. Annual.   (EA 18)

   Reports on farm income situation and outlook, financial conditions, real estate, debts, assets, and the regional situation
   and outlook.

   The following commodity situation reports carry special studies and analyze the supply, demand, price and outlook for the products
indicated. Tables give data on current acreage, yield, production,
stocks, consumption and prices.

COTTON Situation, Washington, D. C.: Agricultural Economics.
6/yr.   (EA 19)

DAIRY Situation. Washington, D. C.: Agricultural Economics.
5/yr.   (EA 20)

FATS and Oils Situation. Washington, D. C.: Agricultural Economics. 5/yr.   (EA 21)

FEED Situation. Washington, D. C. Agricultural Economics. 5/yr.
                                                         (EA 22)

FRUIT Situation. Washington, D. C.: Agricultural Economics.
4/yr.   (EA 23)

LIVESTOCK and Meat Situation. Washington, D. C.: Agricultural
Economics. 6/yr.   (EA 24)

POULTRY and Egg Situation. Washington, D. C.: Agricultural
Economics. 5/yr.   (EA 25)

RICE Situation. Washington, D. C.: Agricultural Economics.
Annual.   (EA 26)

TOBACCO Situation.   Washington, D. C.: Agricultural Economics. 4/yr.   (EA 27)

VEGETABLE Situation. Washington, D. C.: Agricultural Economics.
4/yr.   (EA 28)

WHEAT Situation. Washington, D. C.: Agricultural Economics.
4/yr.   (EA 29)

WOOL Situation. Washington, D. C.: Agricultural Economics.
4/yr.   (EA 30)

        The population, manpower and level-of-living reports include
the following:

FARM Population Estimates. Washington, D. C.: Agricultural
Economics. Annual.   (EA 31)
        Provide data on distribution and components of annual change
        (births, deaths, and migration) for the United States and geo-
        graphic regions and divisions. Some estimates for intercensal
        years are by states.

CENSUS-ERS Series. Washington, D. C.: Agricultural Economics.

2-3/yr.   (EA 32)

Prepared cooperatively with the Bureau of the Census. Gives
annual estimates of farm population by age, sex, labor force
status, and, at times, by other characteristics.

HIRED Farm Working Force. Washington, D. C.: Government
Printing Office. Annual.   (EA 33)

Reports for agricultural workers, 14 years old and over, time
worked and wages earned by race, sex, age, duration of employment, migratory status, residence, and chief activities of
the worker.

FARM Operator Level-of-Living. Indexes for Counties of the United
States 1950, 1959, and 1964. Washington, D. C.: Economic Researc
Service, 1967. 73 p. tables, maps. (Statistical Bulletin No. 406)

(EA 34)

Published every five years. Indexes are constructed from
data provided in the agriculture censuses for the United States,
regions, divisions, states, state economic areas and metropolitan areas as well as for counties.

Three periodic reports on farm production costs and returns:

FARM Costs and Returns. Washington, D. C.: Economic Research
Service. Annual.   (EA 35)

Continuing nationwide study. Summarizes results of farm operations for about 42 important types of commercial farms and
ranches, by type and size, in major producing areas.

CHANGES in Farm Production and Efficiency. Washington, D. C.:
Economic Research Service. Annual with four supplements. (EA 36)

Latest information for appraising production trends, changes
in farm inputs and practices, uses of cropland, animal units
of breeding livestock, improvement in labor productivity, an
the progress of farm mechanization.

THE Balance Sheet of Agriculture. Washington, D. C.: Economic
Research Service. Annual.   (EA 37)
> Treats agriculture as a single enterprise. Brings together the
> individual series of farm assets and the claims to these assets.

> Farm real estate reports cover taxes, debt, mortgages and
> developments in the farm land market.

CONSUMER AND MARKETING SERVICE

Among the activities of the Consumer and Marketing Service
are the commodity standardization, inspection, grading and classing
program, and the Market News program whereby information is
collected and disseminated on the supplies, demand, prices, movements, locations, quality and condition of farm commodities in
specific markets and marketing areas. Special studies are issued
in line with these and other activities of the Service.

AGRICULTURAL Marketing. Washington, D. C.: Government
Printing Office. Monthly.   (EA 38)
> Reviews the current marketing programs, regulation activi-
> ties, consumer food programs and protection activities.

MARKET News Reports. Washington, D. C.: Consumer and Marketing Service. Frequencies vary.   (EA 39)
> The Consumer and Marketing Service, in cooperation with
> many of the state agriculture departments and through a na-
> tionwide network of field offices, gathers and distributes
> market news reports on supply, demand, prices, and move-
> ment of agricultural products. These are issued on all major
> farm commodities and are published with varying frequencies
> depending on the nature of the commodity and on the season.

OTHER UNITS

Other agencies in the Department of Agriculture also maintain statistical programs of interest to market research.

The Agricultural Stabilization and Conservation Service, is responsible for production and adjustment activities, including acreage allotments and farm marketing quotas.

THE Pesticide Review. Washington, D. C.: Agricultural Stabilization and Conservation Service. Annual.   (EA 40)

The Agricultural Research Service conducts research relating to the production, utilization and marketing of agricultural products. It is responsible for nutrition, consumer and industrial-use research; farm research; foreign research; and, effective July 1, 1964, for the marketing research program which is directed toward more efficient assembling, handling, packing, packaging, transporting, storing, processing, wholesaling, and retailing of agricultural products.

AGRICULTURAL Research. Washington, D. C.: Government Printing Office. Monthly.   (EA 41)
> Presents results of Department of Agriculture research projects.

The Cooperative State Research Service coordinates the agricultural experiment stations' research programs, including those in agricultural marketing and rural life, both among the states and between the states and the Department of Agriculture.   (EA 42)

The Farmer Cooperative Service conducts research and service activities on organizational, management, merchandising, costs, efficiency and other problems. Its publications report the results of such studies as well as quantitative data on farmers' cooperatives.
(EA 43)

The Forest Service studies the economics of forest resources and utilization, as well ast timber and forest products marketing.
(EA 44)

The Commodity Exchange Authority supervises the trading of some 15 commodities on 17 contract markets. For public information it publishes a number of commodity futures reports giving volume of trading, prices and related statistics. (EA 45)

The Rural Electrification Administration publishes statistics on REA borrowers, electricity consumers and telephone subscribers.
(EA 46)

DEPARTMENT OF COMMERCE

By statute, the Department of Commerce is responsible for the development of the foreign and domestic commerce, the industries and the transportation facilities of the United States. Through its bureaus and subordinate agencies it is by far the largest single purveyor of marketing data.

COMMERCE Business Daily. Washington, D. C.: Government Printing Office. Daily (Monday-Friday). (EB 1)

Synopsis of federal proposed procurement, sales and contract awards. Of value to firms interested in bidding on government purchases and contracts, surplus property for sale, or in seeking subcontract opportunities from prime contractors. Lists current information received daily from military and civilian procurement offices.

BUSINESS AND DEFENSE SERVICES ADMINISTRATION

Of interest to market research are BDSA's activities in promoting the nation's industry and commerce. It provides information needed by business and government to stimulate the national economy. Its studies of national and regional economic problems, of broad and specific aspects of business and industry, of long-range industrial growth are often marked by an emphasis on world trade and global markets.

Programs of the Business and Defense Services Administration are executed by 26 business and industry divisions grouped into seven offices: Marketing and Services; Chemicals and Consumer Products; Industrial Equipment; Metals and Minerals; Scientific and Technical Equipment; Construction and Materials Industries; Textiles.

The Office of Marketing and Services, within the Administration, develops and distributes basic information on production development, market potentials, and domestic distribution of goods and services.

Its Commodity-Industry Offices compile and publish historical and trend data on production, consumption, prices, sales, distribution, employment, foreign trade and other aspects of numerous products and industries.

Timeliness, variety and scope, rather than periodicity, characterize the major portion of the agency's information output. Several statistical programs, however, provide data on a continuing basis:

U. S. Industrial Outlook. Washington, D. C.: Government Printing Office. Annual.   (EB 2)
>   In text and tables gives background data, review of past year
>   and projections for current year for over 100 key industries.

INDUSTRY Reports. Washington, D. C.: Government Printing Office.   (EB 3)
>   These reports offer analyses of supply, demand and outlook
>   with statistics on production, consumption, inventories, ex-
>   ports, imports, etc.
>>   Chemicals. Quarterly.
>>   Containers and Packaging. Quarterly.
>>   Copper. Quarterly.
>>   Printing and Publishing. Quarterly.
>>   Pulp, Paper and Board. Quarterly.

CURRENT Industrial Reports ... (Series BDSAF).
>   These are issued jointly with the Bureau of the Census and are
>   treated with the Bureau's publications.

CONSTRUCTION Review. Washington, D. C.: Government Printing

Office. Monthly.   (EB 4)

Contains analytical articles as well as almost all current construction data (new nonfarm housing, building permits, contract awards, cost indexes, building materials stocks, shipments, prices) from government and some private sources.
CONSTRUCTION Statistics, 1915-1964; A Supplement to
Construction Review. Washington, D. C.: Government
Printing Office, Jan. 1966. 90 p.

Other industry data are issued annually (confectionery sales
and distribution, lumber exports and imports) or irregularly (Aluminum Fact Book, industrial diamond stones consumption, trade
in jewel bearings). The agency also prepares a number of OVER-
SEAS Business Reports (see EB 31) useful to exporters, importers, investors and manufacturers. These cover data on international trade and economic conditions, worldwide and by individual countries, or present market characteristics for specific products in
specific countries.

In addition BDSA has published a variety of statistical and
market analysis tools: indexed bibliographies of statistical data for
a number of industries; guides to available market data illustrated
with case histories; and statistical compendia, based on data compiled by other agencies, such as the following.

FACTS for Marketers. Washington, D. C.: Government Printing
Office, 1966. 9 reports (one for each geographic region).   (EB 5)

Selected data from federal sources for the 100 largest SMSA's.
Included are population and housing characteristics, employment, income, industry sales by retail, wholesale and selected
service trades, consumer expenditures, where available.

INDUSTRY Profiles, 1958-1966. Washington, D. C.: Government
Printing Office, 1968. 154 p.   (EB 6)

A picture of economic developments in each of 417 manufacturing industries (shown at 4-digit SIC level), it contains year-by-
year breakdowns of comparable statistics: 16 basic data series

relating to employment, payroll, man-hours, value of shipments, value added by manufacture, capital expenditures and
selected ratios.

EXPORT/Import Summaries. Springfield, Va.: Clearinghouse for
Federal Scientific and Technical Information. Monthly cumulative.

(EB 7)

Statistics are drawn from the more detailed reports of the
Bureau of the Census. Data by country of origin and destination reported for over 1,000 groups of individual items. Each
product group assembles related items in meaningful product
totals. Reports are published in two series:

Export Subsections:

E-1,   Chemical and Consumer Goods including Sporting
       Goods, Toys and Games

E-2,   Foods and Beverages; Rubber, Leather and Prod-
       ucts Thereof

E-3,   Transportation Equipment, Metalworking Machinery
       and Other General and Special Industry Machinery
       and Equipment

E-4,   Metals and Minerals

E-5,   Electronic, Scientific, Photographic and Business
       Equipment

E-6,   Building Materials, Containers, Lumber, Paper
       and Printed Matter

E-7,   Textiles

Import Subsections:

I-1,   Chemicals and Consumer Goods including Sporting
       Goods, Toys, Games and Sheet Glass

I-2,   Foods and Beverages

I-3,   Rubber, Leather and Products Thereof

I-4,   Transportation Equipment, Metalworking Machinery
       and other General and Special Industry Machinery
       and Equipment

I-5,   Metals and Minerals

I-6,   Electronic, Scientific, Photographic and Business
       Equipment

I-7,   Building Materials, Containers, Lumber, Paper
        and Printed Matter

Similar data for textile imports are available from EDSA's
Office of Textiles.

Detailed guides showing the individual items reported in each
of the 14 subsections are available free from the Department
of Commerce.

OFFICE OF BUSINESS ECONOMICS

This agency provides basic economic measures and current
analyses of the national economy as well as statistics on the nation's
foreign investments and transactions.   Besides its national income
and product work it analyzes the business outlook and factors affecting regional economic development, and formulates economic
and statistical indicators.   Its work is concentrated in six principal
operating units: National Income Division, Regional Economics
Division, Business Structure Division, and the Balance of Payments
Division.

A major new OBE program is the Interindustry Relations
Study which involves the periodic preparation of a set of input-output
tables as part of an integrated system of national accounts.   Various
aspects of the 1958 study were published in the Survey of Current Business (November 1964, p. 10+; May 1965, p. 13+;
September 1964, p. 33+; October 1965, p. 7+; April 1966, p. 14+).
The data are usually presented in an input-output table in which each
industry is represented by a row and a column; each final market by
a column; and value added by one or more rows.   The row for an
industry shows the distribution of its output to itself and to other industries and final markets.   The column shows its consumption of
goods and services of the various industries and its value added.   Not
only does this analysis provide a tool for probing economic changes
but also makes it possible for a company to compare its marketing
position with that of the industry as a whole and to note possible areas
of additional market potential.

OBE's major publication is the monthly Survey of Current

Business which is augmented by a number of supplements issued at
irregular intervals. Cited here are a number of those of general
interest.

BUSINESS Statistics. (see B 5)

NATIONAL Income and Product Accounts of the United
States, 1929-1965: Statistical Tables. (A supplement
to the Survey of Current Business). Washington,
D. C.: Government Printing Office [1966] xiii, 165 p.
                                                                (EB 20)
Updated in the July issue of the Survey of Current
Business.

STATE Personal Income, 1948-1965. In: Survey of Current
Business, Aug. 1966, p. 11+.   (EB 21)
Data on total and per capita personal income for each state by
type of income and industrial sources. This basic revision
supercedes all previously published estimates. Updated annually in the August issue of the Survey of Current Business.

GROWTH Patterns in Employment by County, 1940-1950 and 1950-
1960. Washington, D. C.: Government Printing Office, 1966. 8
vols. (by regions)   (EB 22)
Employment changes and their analytical components for each
of 32 industries by regions, states and counties are compared
to the national average.

BALANCE of Payments Statistical Supplement, rev. ed. (A supplement to the Survey of Current Business). Washington, D. C.:
Government Printing Office [1963] xi, 260 p.   (EB 23)
Data cover transactions with principal areas, merchandise
trade, international transportation, international travel, miscellaneous services, private remittances, U. S. government
transactions, private U. S. investments abroad, foreign investments in the United States, gold transactions, international in-

vestment position.   Provides historical (through 1960-1961) statistics to be used in conjunction with current data and analysis published quarterly (March, June, September, December issues) in the Survey of Current Business.   Related to this supplement are the two publications cited below.

UNITED States Business Investments in Foreign Countries. Washington D. C.: Government Printing Office, 1960. 147 p.   (EB 24)

A report on the foreign expansion of American industry abroad from 1929 to 1959. Shows investment pattern by major industry and area. A companion volume to this report is listed below.

FOREIGN Business Investments in the United States: A Supplement to the Survey of Current Business. Washington, D. C.: Government Printing Office, 1962. v, 58 p. charts, tables.   (EB 25)

First comprehensive study in some twenty years of foreign controlling interests in United States business firms in terms of their output, expenditures, tax payments, assets employed, and use of United States as well as of foreign financing.   1959 data have been carried back to 1950 and forward through 1961.   A companion volume to the 1960 study listed above.

The Office of Business Economics also issues a number of monthly and quarterly BUSINESS NEWS REPORTS. These provide text and tables on such indicators as cash dividend payments; national income and corporate profits, personal income; new plant and equipment expenditures. Data in these press releases are later incorporated in the Survey of Current Business.

BUREAU OF INTERNATIONAL COMMERCE

This agency is the successor to the Bureau of Foreign Commerce. It is the principal source of information on foreign markets and of commercial intelligence useful to the American firm trading abroad.

INTERNATIONAL Commerce. Washington, D. C.: Government
Printing Office. Weekly.   (EB 30)

> Official periodical of the Bureau covering trends in overseas
> commerce, trade opportunities and other aspects of foreign
> trade and international marketing. Quarterly cumulative index.

OVERSEAS Business Reports. Washington, D. C.: Government
Printing Office. About 200 reports/yr.   (EB 31)

> Irregular series numbered consecutively. Individual reports
> devoted to basic market and investment information on foreign
> countries; foreign trade regulations; how to establish a
> business abroad; foreign market indicators; foreign trade
> statistics; overseas market and industry surveys. Some re-
> ports originate with the Business Defense and Services Admini-
> stration. New reports are listed, as published, in the Depart-
> ment of Commerce Business Service Checklist and sum-
> marized semiannually in the Bureau's Checklist [of] Inter-
> national Business Publications.

MARKET Share Reports. Springfield, Va.; Clearinghouse for
Federal Scientific and Technical Information. Annual.   (EB 32)

> Issued in two series, commodity and country, currently covering
> data for 1962-66. The Commodity Series tabulates the dollar
> value of 1,127 manufactured commodities exported to the 90
> major importing countries by the United States and 13 other
> major exporting countries. The United States percentage share
> has been computed to show this country's competitive perform-
> ance. Summary totals are shown for four broad groups of
> manufactures. The 1,127 commodity categories consist of
> 380 subgroups (4-digit products) and 747 items (5-digit prod-
> ucts) as listed in the United Nations' Standard International
> Trade Classification.
>
> The Country Series consists of 69 country reports presenting
> dollar values for shipments of 1,127 manufactured commodities
> into a single foreign market. For each product the values of
> shipments are shown separately not only for the United States

but for eight other principal supplier countries. The United
States percentage share for each commodity has also been com-
puted for this series. In addition to individual products, summary totals are shown for the four broad groups of manufactures, as in the commodity series.

The application of new computer and reproduction techniques
has increased the availability of voluminous data collected by the
Bureau at home and abroad. These are offered in a form more closely resembling services:

FOREIGN Market Reports Service. Springfield, Va.: Clearinghouse
for Federal Scientific and Technical Information.   (EB 33)

These reports, prepared by the 280 Foreign Service posts in
about 130 countries, present, by country, economic conditions
and commodity information. The economic-type reports provide dispatches on broad economic trends and on specific commercial, industrial and financial developments. The commodity-
oriented reports deal with new developments in industry, production levels, demand analysis, changing trade patterns or
consumer preferences, import regulations, tariff changes and
similar subjects.

INSTANT Trade Lists. Washington, D. C.: Bureau of International
Commerce.   (EB 34)

A computer bank, based on the Bureau's WORLD TRADE
DIRECTORY REPORTS, which permits a selective printout of
importers, exporters,dealers, manufacturers of specific products by 5-digit SIC codes. Information covers firm name and
address, relative size, products handled, territory, size of
sales force. This is a refinement of the regularly published
country and commodity trade lists.

AMERICAN International Traders Index. Washington, D. C.: Bureau of International Commerce.   (EB 35)

A computerized file of the international business interests of individual United States companies. Voluntary registration statements submitted by firms permit the matching of foreign business opportunities for exports, licensing and investment.

The Bureau's publications and services are described in its semiannual Checklist [of] International Business Publications, a catalog of all foreign trade sources. New publications are announced in its International Commerce. The Foreign Market Report Accessions List, issued monthly, announces the Foreign Service reports received during the preceding four weeks. Selected BIC publications are also listed in the weekly Business Service Checklist (see QB 13).

OTHER UNITS

Other agencies within the Department of Commerce are sources of more specialized data.

The Economic Development Administration, among its other programs, provides assistance to state and local agencies concerned with the expansion of the economic resources and facilities in their areas. Technical assistance studies, based on specific area industries, resources and needs are prepared under contract to the Department of Commerce. These are available on interlibrary loan from the Department's library through the facilities of local lending libraries.

INDUSTRIAL Location as a Factor in Regional Economic Development. Washington, D. C.: Government Printing Office, 1967. 125 p.   (EB 40)
     Reviews plant location process, information on location trends and techniques.

TOURISM and Recreation. Washington, D. C.: Government Printing Office. 1967. 308 p.   (EB 41)
     Assembles much of the research already done on outdoor recreation and domestic travel as an aid to planning and measur-

ing their impact on the regional economy.

The Maritime Administration collects data on world merchant fleets, ship utilization, cargoes carried in domestic and foreign trade, data on ports and port administration.

Weather Bureau publications provide data useful to commerce, industry and agriculture.

WEEKLY Weather and Crop Bulletin. Washington,D. C.: Government Printing Office. Weekly.   (EB 42)

AVERAGE Monthly Weather Resume and Outlook. Washington, D. C.: Government Printing Office. Semimonthly.   (EB 43)

CLIMATOLOGICAL Data. Washington, D. C.: Government Printing Office. Monthly; Annual.   (EB 44)
  Temperature, precipitation and other weather information published in 47 sections (state, possession or group of states) and national summary.

CLIMATES of the States. Washington, D. C.: Government Printing Office.   (EB 45)
  Summaries of weather characteristics issued in a series of special reports, one for each state.

SELECTIVE Guide to Published Climatic Data Sources, Prepared by U. S. Weather Bureau. (Key to Meteorological Records Documentation, no. 4.11). Washington, D. C.: Government Printing Office, 1963. xv, 84 p.   (EB 46)
  A useful guide, illustrated with brief examples of basic tables and indexed by time-period breakdowns (hourly, daily, weekly, etc.) and climatological categories (temperature, precipitation, humidity, etc.).

DECENNIAL Census of United States Climate, 1960. Washington,

D. C.: Government Printing Office [1961-   ]   (EB 47)
Information submitted by over 11,000 localities, many of them
with records covering the 30-year period 1931-1960, issued in
several bulletin series.

The United States Travel Service is active in the study of the
economic aspects of tourism and patterns of international travel. It
reports primarily on foreigners' travel to the United States.

The need for product innovation and the pressure of technological advances focus on the functions and services of the Patent
Office. This agency records the assignment of patents and trademarks, maintains a search file of American and foreign patents for
public use and supplies copies of patents. The specifications and
drawings of patents are published on the day they are granted and
copies may be purchased by the public from the Patent Office only.
The patent must be identified by its number or full name of inventor
and approximate date of issue.

OFFICIAL Gazette. Washington, D. C.: Government Printing Office. Weekly.   (EB 48)
Contains a brief description of each patent issued; illustrations
of each trademark published for opposition; patents for sale,
license or expiring. Its annual indexes, issued in two volumes (Patents; Trademarks), list patentees, patent numbers,
trademark registrants, registration numbers, disclaimers
filed.

The major purpose of the National Bureau of Standards is the
application of science to advance technology in industry and commerce.
In cooperation with industry groups, it formulates and promulgates
Product Standards, previously referred to as Commodity Standards
and Simplified Practice Recommendations.

LIST of Commercial Standards and Simplified Practice Recommendations. Washington, D. C.: National Bureau of Standards. Irregular.

A classified listing with instructions for ordering those currently available.

DIRECTORY of United States Standardization Activities. Washington,
D. C.: Government Printing Office, 1967. 280 p.   (EB 50)
Lists 486 American organizations that consider standardization
to be a major or important part of their work. Their activities
in the fields, products, and services in which they specialize
are described. Government agencies are grouped separately
from nongovernmental organizations.

Through its Clearinghouse for Federal Scientific and Technical Information, the National Bureau of Standards distributes reports and technical information based on government-sponsored research.

DEPARTMENT OF HEALTH, EDUCATION, AND WELFARE

Although most of the primary data emanate from the subordinate agencies of the Department, the following publication is a
most useful summary.

HEALTH, Education and Welfare Indicators. Washington, D. C.:
Government Printing Office. Monthly; Annual supplement. (EC 1)
Articles and current statistics on health, education, social
security, population and vital statistics, welfare and related
subjects. Its annual supplement, HEALTH, EDUCATION AND
WELFARE TRENDS, presents national and selected state data
(including some state rankings) from many government agencies
and private organizations. All tables are fully documented.

PUBLIC HEALTH SERVICE

The Public Health Service supports one of the major general-
purpose statistical programs of the federal government principally
through its National Center for Health Statistics. In cooperation

with the states, it collects vital statistics (births, deaths, marriages, divorces), tabulates and analyzes such data. It publishes detailed data on specific diseases. In addition, through its Bureau of State Services, PHS supports studies in the areas of community and environmental health which bear on air pollution control, water and waste supply and treatment, community sanitation. Its biennial inventories of municipal waste and water facilities were recently transferred to the Federal Water Pollution Control Administration.

VITAL Statistics of the United States. Washington, D. C.: Government Printing Office. Annual.   (EC 2)
    Official final data on natality, mortality, marriages, and
    divorces. Geographic detail includes cities, counties, standard metropolitan statistical areas.

MONTHLY Vital Statistics Report. Washington, D. C.: Public Health Service. Monthly; Annual summary.   (EC 3)
    Data on births, deaths and infant mortality, marriages and
    marriage licenses, and divorces. Selected data by states and
    certain cities.

MORBIDITY and Mortality. Atlanta: National Communicable Disease Center. Weekly.   (EC 4)
    Cases of specified notifiable diseases by states; deaths
    registered in each of over 100 major cities.
    Annual Supplement; Reported Incidence of Notifiable Diseases
    in the United States. Atlanta: National Communicable Disease
    Center. Annual.
    Data by years for past ten years; for current year, totals for
    states by age groups, months, and other detail.

VITAL and Health Statistics. (Public Health Service Publication, no. 1000). Washington, D. C.: Public Health Service, 1963- Irregular.
                                                 (EC 5)
    Material previously published in Vital Statistics -- Special
    Reports and Health Statistics from the U. S.

NATIONAL Health Survey, as well as new kinds of reports,
are included in this series grouped as follows:

Series 1:   Programs and Collection Procedures.

Series 2:   Data Evaluation and Methods Research.

Series 3:   Analytical Studies
            Interpretive reports on vital and health statistics
            treated quantitatively in other series.

Series 4:   Documents and Committee Reports.

Series 10: Data From the Health Interview Survey.
            Statistics on illness, accidental injuries, disabili-
            ty, use of hospital, medical, dental, and other
            services, and other health-related topics.

Series 11: Data From the Health Examination Survey.
            Data from direct examination, testing, and
            measurement of national samples provide estimates
            of prevalence of specific diseases and the physical,
            physiological and psychological characteristics of
            the population.

Series 12   Data From the Health Records Survey.
   & 13:   Health characteristics of persons in institutions,
            and hospital, medical, nursing, and personal care
            received.

Series 20: Data on Mortality.
            Various statistics on mortality other than as in-
            cluded in annual or monthly reports.   Special
            analyses by cause of death, age, and other demo-
            graphic variables; also geographic and time series
            analyses.

Series 21: Data on Natality, Marriage, and Divorce.
            Statistics other than as included in annual or month-
            ly reports.   Special analyses by demographic vari-
            ables.

Series 22: Data From the National Natality and Mortality
            Surveys.
            Characteristics of births and deaths, based on
            sample surveys.   Topics include mortality by socio-

economic class, medical experience in the last
year of life, and characteristics of pregnancy.

HEALTH Resources Statistics ... Washington, D. C.: Government
Printing Office.   (EC 6)
   The first, 1965 edition, presents health manpower data for
   some 140 health occupations. Subsequent editions are planned
   to be more comprehensive, including statistics on manpower,
   facilities, and other resources in the health field.

OFFICE OF EDUCATION

   The Office of Education is most useful as a source of statistical studies in practically all educational fields and for all educational levels.   Its periodic reports present statistics on libraries;
the staff, finances, receipts, expenditures of educational institutions;
enrollments and graduates for specific study fields and institutions;
construction, rehabilitation and equipment of physical facilities.

DIGEST of Educational Statistics. (OE-10024). Washington, D. C.:
Government Printing Office. Annual.   (EC 10)
   Current and historical data on schools, enrollment, graduates,
   and other phases of the American educational system compiled
   from a variety of official sources, published and unpublished.
   Well documented and indexed.

PROJECTIONS of Educational Statistics. Washington, D. C.:
Government Printing Office. Annual.   (EC 11)
   Companion volume to the DIGEST OF EDUCATIONAL STATIS-
   TICS.   Contains forecasts, for about 10 years ahead, of a
   great variety of educational statistics such as enrollments ,
   graduates, teachers, expenditures.

FALL Enrollment, Teachers, and Schoolhousing. Washington, D.
C.: Government Printing Office. Annual.   (EC 12)
   Title varies.   Data by states for the public school system on

enrollment, teachers, school capacity. Similar data for the 15 largest cities.

OPENING (Fall) Enrollment in Higher Education. Washington, D. C.: Government Printing Office. Annual. (EC 13)
Enrollment (total and first-time degree-credit students) by sex and individual institution.

EARNED Degrees Conferred by Higher Educational Institutions. Washington, D. C.: Government Printing Office. Annual. (EC 14)
Degrees by level, field and sex of recipient, and by institution.

SOCIAL SECURITY ADMINISTRATION

In administering its social insurance, public assistance, and related activities, this agency collects and analyzes data on the economic and social conditions of the population subject to its programs.

SOCIAL Security Bulletin. Washington, D. C.: Government Printing Office. Monthly: Annual statistical supplement. (EC 20)
Reports current data on benefits recipients, payments, collections, and other programs, as well as results of pertinent research and analyses.

WORKERS Under Social Security. Washington, D. C.: Government Printing Office. Irregular. (New edition in preparation) (EC 21)
Data on wage and employment experience of covered workers. Previous title: Handbook of Old Age and Survivors Insurance Statistics.

THE Aged Population of the United States: The 1963 Social Security Survey of the Aged. (Office of Research and Statistics, Research Report no. 19). Washington, D. C.: Government Printing Office, 1967. 431 p. (EC 22)

Nationwide survey of persons aged 62 and over, undertaken in
1963, reports on income, work experience, assets, medical
costs, health insurance coverage and hospital utilization in
1962. Follow-up study and second national survey are planned.

DEPARTMENT OF HOUSING AND URBAN DEVELOPMENT

The department was established in 1965 to centralize the
housing, residential financing, urban growth and development programs of the federal government. Its activities also encompass the
support of urban transportation improvements, water and sewer
construction, community beautification programs.

STATISTICAL Yearbook. Washington, D. C.: Government Printing
Office. Annual.   (ED 1)

Information on the activities and operations of the Department
and its programs. Data from government and other sources
on housing production and costs, home financing, urban renewal, community facilities projects.

HOUSING and Urban Development Trends. Washington, D. C.: Department of Housing and Urban Development. Monthly; Annual summary.

(ED 2)

Construction costs, housing production, home financing and
data on operations of departmental programs.

CONSTRUCTION Reports: Housing Sales. (Series Census-HUD: C25).
(see DI 3)

FEDERAL HOUSING ADMINISTRATION

Under its loan and mortgage insurance programs FHA collects a considerable amount of data on the characteristics of housing units which, although limited in scope, can serve to fill a number of statistical gaps.

ANNUAL Statistical Summary. Washington, D. C.: Federal Housing Administration. Annual.   (ED 3)

FHA mortgage and insurance activity for homes, projects and property improvement. In addition to property value, price and mortgage data, includes information on number of stories, rooms, bedrooms, garages, carports, heating and utilities, as well as on mortgagor's age, income and total fixed obligations.

FHA Homes. Washington, D. C.: Federal Housing Administration. Annual.   (ED 4)

Data, similar to that in the ANNUAL STATISTICAL SUMMARY, for states and selected counties and metropolitan areas on characteristics of FHA operations under Section 203.

FHA Trends. Washington, D. C.: Federal Housing Administration. Quarterly with supplements.   (ED 5)

Issued with two supplements: AREA TRENDS, for selected counties and metropolitan areas; STATE TRENDS. All three update the statistics published annually in the ANNUAL STATISTICAL SUMMARY and FHA HOMES;

RENEWAL ASSISTANCE ADMINISTRATION

This agency is responsible for slum clearance, urban renewal, and urban parks and beautification programs.

URBAN Renewal Project Characteristics. Washington, D. C.: Renewal Assistance Administration. Semiannual.   (ED 6)

Statistical data on the physical and financial characteristics of urban renewal projects under federal loan-grant contracts.

DEPARTMENT OF THE INTERIOR

General-purpose statistics as well as much special interest data originate in the various agencies of the Department of the Interior.

BUREAU OF MINES

The Bureau of Mines conducts economic and statistical
studies of domestic and foreign production, distribution, consumption and stocks of minerals, mineral fuels and products.   Industry
and product reports are published individually and in periodic series.
Special reports and additional information on minerals are sometimes
available from other offices in the Department (see EE 20-EE 22).

MINERALS Yearbook.   Washington, D. C. : Government Printing
Office.   Annual.   (EE 1)
> This basic statistical handbook is issued in four volumes:
> Metals and Minerals (Except Fuels); Mineral
> Fuels; Area Reports: Domestic: Area Reports:
> International. Data, some of them by counties, on pro-
> duction, shipments, value, prices, reserves, consumption,
> foreign trade, mining technology, employment and injuries.
> Separate chapters on each mineral, fuel, state and territory.

MINERAL Industry Surveys.   Pittsburgh, Pa. : Bureau of Mines.
Weekly, monthly, quarterly, annual depending on the report. (EE 2)
> Periodic reports dealing with various mineral commodities and
> with mine accidents and facilities.   Update the statistics in
> Minerals Yearbook.

MINERAL Facts and Problems.   Washington, D. C. : Government
Printing Office.   Quinquennial.   (EE 3)
> Consists of 89 chapters each of which is devoted to a non-
> technical discussion of a mineral commodity.   Topics covered
> for each include geology, prospecting, mining and processing,
> uses and substitutes, reserves, production, consumption,
> world trade, employment and transportation, research and
> outlook.   Each chapter also available separately.

THE Interindustry Structure of the U. S. Mining Industries, 1958.
Washington, D. C. : Government Printing Office, 1967. 190 p.
                                                                   (EE 4)
Report on a technical economic research study to determine

the input-output relationships of the domestic mining industries. This basic data source also provides a framework for aggregate economic impact analysis with respect to the mining industries.

FISH AND WILDLIFE SERVICE

Since it is concerned with the conservation and recreational use of fish and wildlife, the Service, through its Bureau of Sport Fisheries and Wildlife, collects data on fishing and hunting and publishes annual statistics on license holders. In recent years it has also undertaken national surveys of the sport aspects of the resources which it administers. Detailed findings of such studies have been published in comprehensive reports about every five years.

Production, processing, storage and marketing of fish and fishery products are researched and documented by the Service through its Bureau of Commercial Fisheries. In addition to the periodic data detailed here the Bureau, in cooperation with the Bureau of the Census, conducted in 1963 the first census of the commercial fishing industry to be taken since 1908.

COMMERCIAL Fisheries Review. Washington, D. C.: Government Printing Office. Monthly. (EE 10)

Developments and news of fishery industries - production, marketing, statistics, government actions.

FISHERY Statistics of the United States. Washington, D. C.: Government Printing Office. Annual. (EE 11)

Detailed data on the domestic fishing industry: volume and value of raw and processed products; exports and imports; industry equipment and employment. These and related statistics presented for the United States and by regional fisheries.

CURRENT Fishery Statistics. Washington, D. C.: Bureau of Commercial Fisheries. Monthly, quarterly, annual depending on release series. (EE 12)

Current data issued in a series of bulletins which may be categorized as follows:

State landings bulletins include volume and value by species.

Fisheries bulletins, for the United States and each of nine regions, report annual catch and operating activity.

Processed products bulletins (seven) cover production and cold storage of various types of processed fish and by-products.

In addition, the Bureau maintains market news offices in important fish producing and distributing centers. These issue daily, monthly and annual reports on landings, shipments, prices, imports, production and related information for areas within their jurisdiction.

FOOD Fish Situation and Outlook. Washington, D. C.: Bureau of Commercial Fisheries. Quarterly. (EE 13)

SHELLFISH Situation and Outlook. Washington, D. C. Bureau of Commercial Fisheries. Quarterly; Annual. (EE 14)

OTHER UNITS

Useful data are also available from other units in the Department of the Interior.

The Office of Minerals and Solid Fuels is responsible for an adequate mobilization base and emergency management of the solid fuels, metals and minerals industries. In line with these responsibilities the Office initiates specialized studies; develops, assembles and evaluates data concerning materials, equipment, manpower, transportation and other industry requirements; compiles information on production, capacity, employment at these facilities. (EE 20)

The Office of Oil and Gas is a liaison and communications channel between the petroleum and gas industries and the federal government with respect to the strategic and economic factors affecting these industries at home and abroad. In this respect it develops, evaluates and coordinates oil and gas information neces-

sary to the implementation of national policies and programs affecting these commodities.   (EE 21)

The Office of Coal Research has the responsibility of developing, through research, new and more efficient methods of mining,
preparing and utilizing coal. It does this primarily by contracting
for research in the economic as well as the scientific and technical
fields.   (EE 22)

The Office of Saline Water provides research and development
of means for production of usable water from saline sources. Although much of its work is technological, the Office does initiate
studies of industry and municipality requirements and of the economics and costs of water conversion.   (EE 23)

A major function of the Federal Water Pollution Control Administration is the development of special programs for the control
of water pollution. The biennial inventories of municipal waste and
water facilities, previously conducted by the Public Health Service
were transferred to this office in the course of the reorganization
which followed the enactment of the Water Quality Act of 1965.
                                                              (EE 24)

The Geological Survey evaluates water resources and public
water supplies and has published information used in identifying hard
and soft water areas. The following reports present about the same
information for each city: Population supplied, ownership, source,
treatment, storage capacities for both raw and treated water, and
chemical analyses of supplies.

THE INDUSTRIAL Utility of Public Water Supplies in the United States,
1952 ...by E. W. Lohr and S. K. Love. (Geological Survey Water-
Supply Paper 1299, 1300). Washington, D. C.: Government Printing Office, 1954. 2 vols.   (EE 25)
    Gives water characteristics data for 1,315 places in states
    east (Part 1) and west (Part 2) of the Mississippi.

PUBLIC Water Supplies of the 100 Largest Cities in the United
States, 1962, by C. N. Durfor and Edith Becker. (Geological Water
Supply Paper 1812). Washington, D. C.: Government Printing Of-
fice, 1964. 364 p.   (EE 26)

    For the 100 largest cities, updates the findings published in its
Geological Survey Water-Supply Paper 1299, 1300 (above).*

CHEMICAL Characteristics of Public Water Supplies of Alaska,
Hawaii and Puerto Rico, 1954,by E. W. Lohr. (Geological Survey
Water- Supply Paper 1460-A). Washington, D. C.: Government
Printing Office, 1957. 39 p.   (EE 27)

    Information for 13 places in Alaska, 12 in Hawaii, and 12 in
Puerto Rico.

    The preparation and publication of a national atlas is a new
project undertaken in accordance with the recommendation from the
National Academy of Sciences-National Research Council:

THE National Atlas. Washington, D. C.: Geological Survey. (In
preparation)   (EE 28)

    Planned to be a volume of some 475 pages consisting mostly
of thematic maps covering the country's salient physical characteristics, climate, water resources, soils and vegetation,
history, economic status (agriculture, industry, resources,
transportation and finance), social conditions (population distribution and structure, educational achievement, recreation,
income, labor force), world affairs. Detailed index. Many
of the maps will be sold separately. Revision is planned on
a continuing basis.

    The National Park Service collects data on accommodations
and visitors to areas under its jurisdiction.   (EE 29)

    The Bureau of Reclamation reports on the status of irrigable
lands and irrigation projects.   (EE 30)

The Bureau of Outdoor Recreation is responsible for promoting the coordination and development of effective outdoor recreation programs. Although it publishes no periodic reports of general-use statistics, its special studies carry useful data.   (EE 31)
An example:

OUTDOOR Recreation Trends. Washington, D. C. : Government
Printing Office, 1967. 24 p. illus.
> Participation in summer outdoor recreation activities for 1960
> and 1965 are compared with projected participation for 1980
> and 2000.

DEPARTMENT OF LABOR

BUREAU OF LABOR STATISTICS

The Bureau is the principal federal factfinding agency in the field of labor economics, prices, cost of living and related areas. Major BLS series are widely used in economic and market analysis. The Bureau also publishes numerous reports on productivity, wages and related benefits, work injuries and stoppages, and allied subjects. Employment, prices, cost of living and similar data reflecting local conditions are distributed by its regional offices.

HANDBOOK of Labor Statistics. Washington, D. C. : Government
Printing Office. Annual.   (EF 1)
> Statistical compendium on all phases of labor economics. Its
> tables start at the earliest time from which continuous con-
> sistent series are available. Many series report for states and
> areas as well as for the nation as a whole.

Basic information appears in its official organ:

MONTHLY Labor Review. Washington, D. C. : Government Printing Office. Monthly.   (EF 2)
> Includes articles on methodology, summaries of all major BLS
> studies and a comprehensive statistical section containing labor

force, employment, price and other series.

The Bureau's statistical activity of general business and marketing interest falls into three broad areas each with a series of periodic publications reporting current data.

Prices and Cost of Living

PRICES: A Chartbook, 1953-62. (Bulletin no. 1351). Washington, D. C. : Government Printing Office, 1962. v, 207 p. charts, tables.

(EF 3)

Price trends, based primarily on BLS consumer and wholesale price indexes, are arranged to reveal relationships among price index series and between prices and other economic measures. Currently updated by periodic supplements.

PRICES in [month] Washington, D. C. : Bureau of Labor Statistics. Monthly.   (EF 4)

Text and tables giving preliminary data on wholesale and consumer price indexes.

Prices and Cost of Living: Consumer Prices

CONSUMER Price Index. Washington, D. C. : Department of Labor. Monthly.   (EF 5)

Presents, for the United States and selected cities and standard metropolitan statistical areas, average changes in prices of goods and services usually bought by city wage earners and clerical workers, both families and individuals living alone.

ESTIMATED Retail Food Prices by Cities. Washington, D. C. : Department of Labor. Monthly; Annual.   (EF 6)

Monthly average prices and price indexes of individual foods for the United States and for each of 12 large metropolitan areas.

RETAIL Prices and Indexes of Fuels and Electricity. Washington,

D. C.: Department of Labor. Monthly.   (EF 7)

    Indexes and average retail prices for the United States and for each of 22 metropolitan areas.

CONSUMER Price Indexes for Selected Items and Groups. Washington, D. C.: Bureau of Labor Statistics. Quarterly.   (EF 8)

    Presents quarterly retail price indexes for individual commodities and services (except foods and fuels) and for selected minor classes of related items which are included in the Consumer Price Index.

CITY Worker's Family Budget for a Moderate Living Standard, Autumn 1966. (Bulletin 1570-1) Washington, D. C.: Government Printing Office, 1967. 40 p.   (EF 8.1)

    Annual estimates for a family of four in four regions and 39 metropolitan areas. Covers food, housing, transportation, clothing, personal care, medical care and other items. Supplemented by "Revised Equivalence Scale" for estimating costs for families differing from the specific family for which the budget was constructed.

Prices and Cost of Living: Primary Market Prices

DAILY Spot Market Price Indexes and Prices. Washington, D. C.: Bureau of Labor Statistics. Daily; Weekly summary.   (EF 9)

    These daily indexes measure price trends and are particularly sensitive to factors affecting spot markets.

WHOLESALE Prices and Price Indexes. Washington, D. C.: Department of Labor. Monthly; Annual.   (EF 10)

    Average prices and indexes for individual commodities, commodity groups, subgroups, product classes. Historical data for these series are available in Bulletins issued at regular intervals of varying frequency.

Employment and Labor Force

EMPLOYMENT and Earnings Statistics for the United States ... (Bulletin 1312.) Washington, D. C.: Government Printing Office. Annual.
(EF 11)

> Presents national historical data on employment, hours, earnings and labor turnover by industry detailed by 4-digit SIC code. Data are given by years beginning with 1909.

EMPLOYMENT and Earnings Statistics for States and Areas ... (Bulletin no. 1370). Washington, D. C.: Government Printing Office. Annual.
(EF 12)

> Industry data, detailed by 2- and 3-digit Standard Industrial Classification code, show annual average employment, hours and earnings for production or nonsupervisory workers for all states, 179 standard metropolitan statistical areas and regional comparisons. Data are for years beginning with 1939. Updated by monthly statistics in the report listed below. (EF 13).

EMPLOYMENT and Earnings and Monthly Report on the Labor Force. Washington, D. C.: Government Printing Office. Monthly including annual supplement.
(EF 13)

> Detailed statistics on employment, unemployment, labor force and turnover, hours and earnings, payroll and manhour indexes. Gives data for over 350 industries and for industry groups by states and metropolitan areas.

LABOR Turnover. Washington, D. C.: Department of Labor. Monthly.
(EF 14)

> Preliminary release on factory labor turnover rates, by major industry group.

SPECIAL Labor Force Reports. Washington, D. C.: Department of Labor. Irregular.
(EF 15)

> Series of detailed studies on the labor force, its work experience, marital and family characteristics, and other aspects. First published in the Monthly Labor Review; most of the reprints

contain additional tables.

INCOME, Education and Unemployment in Neighborhoods. Washington, D. C.: Bureau of Labor Statistics, 1963. 37 reports. (EF 16)
Although not a continuing series, these reports present information in a form not easily available otherwise. Originally prepared in connection with the work of the President's Committee on Youth Employment, they represent a cooperative effort on the part of the Bureau of Labor Statistics and the Bureau of the Census. Special tabulations, based on data from the 1960 population and housing censuses, were compiled for 36 cities, including all those with a population of 500,000 or more in 1960 plus a few smaller cities. Data are provided by census tract on the ethnic composition of the population, the male civilian labor force and unemployment rate, median family income, educational attainment and school enrollment, migration to metropolitan area of current residence.

OCCUPATIONAL Employment Statistics; Sources and Data. (Report no. 305). Washington, D. C.: Bureau of Labor Statistics, June 1966. 87 p.   (EF 17)
Brings together statistics, documented for source, on employment in individual occupations nationwide, in selected industries and local areas.

Consumer Expenditures

Studies of consumer expenditures are conducted from time to time, usually in conjunction with a revision of the Consumer Price Index. The 1960-61 survey was issued in two series by the Bureau of Labor Statistics and the Agricultural Research Service of the Department of Agriculture:

SURVEY of Consumer Expenditures, 1960-1961. (USDA report CES; BLS report 237 - ...). Washington, D. C.: Bureau of Labor Statistics, 1964-1966. 15 CES reports; 15 BLS reports; 30 BLS-CES

Detailed tables present income, savings and expenditures for a
long list of household goods and services by income class;
family size; age, education and occupation of family head, location in and out of cities and standard metropolitan statistical
areas, and other socioeconomic characteristics. Conducted in
cooperation with the Department of Agriculture, this survey
added farm and rural nonfarm data to urban data providing, for
the first time since 1941, a nationwide study of spending patterns.

The reports for farm areas were issued by the Department of
Agriculture under the CES series number; those for urban
areas were issued by BLS under the BLS series number. The
reports for rural nonfarm and urban-rural totals are joint
publications and carry both CES and BLS series numbers. Each
population group is represented by separate reports for each of
four regions and a United States total. They range in detail as
tabulated below:

Reports Presenting Summary Tables Classified by
Single Characteristics of Families

Population Group	Report Number
Farm:	
Northeast	CES 1
North Central	CES 2
South	CES 3
West	CES 4
U. S.	CES 5
Rural Nonfarm:	
Northeast	CES 6; BLS 237-84 and supplement 1
North Central	CES 7; BLS 237-85 and supplement 1
South	CES 8; BLS 237-86 and supplement 1
West	CES 9; BLS 237-87 and supplement 1

U. S.	CES 10; BLS 237-88 and supplement 1

Urban:

Northeast	BLS 237-34 and supplement 1
North Central	BLS 237-35 and supplement 1
South	BLS 237-36 and supplement 1
West	BLS 237-37 and supplement 1
U. S.	BLS 237-38 and supplement 1

Total Urban and Rural:

Northeast	CES 11; BLS 237-89 and supplement 1
North Central	CES 12; BLS 237-90 and supplement 1
South	CES 13; BLS 237-91 and supplement 1
West	CES 14; BLS 237-92 and supplement 1
U. S.	CES 15; BLS 237-93 and supplement 1

Reports Presenting Summary Tables Classified By

Pairs of Characteristics of Families

Population Group	Report Number
Farm:	
Northeast	CES 16
North Central	CES 17
South	CES 18
West	CES 19
U. S.	CES 20
Rural nonfarm:	
Northeast	CES 21; BLS 237-84, supplement 2
North Central	CES 22; BLS 237-85, supplement 2
South	CES 23; BLS 237-86, supplement 2
West	CES 24; BLS 237-87, supplement 2
U. S.	CES 25; BLS 237-88, supplement 2
Urban:	
Northeast	BLS 237-34, supplement 2
North Central	BLS 237-35, supplement 2
South	BLS 237-36, supplement 2

West	BLS 237-37, supplement 2
U. S.	BLS 237-38, supplement 2.

Total urban & rural:

Northeast	CES 26; BLS 237-89, supplement 2
North Central	CES 27; BLS 237-90, supplement 2
South	CES 28; BLS 237-91, supplement 2
West	CES 29; BLS 237-92, supplement 2
U. S.	CES 30; BLS 237-93, supplement 2

Reports Presenting Detail of Expenditures
and Income

Population Group	Report Number
Farm:	
Northeast	CES 31
North Central	CES 32
South	CES 33
West	CES 34
U. S.	CES 35
Rural nonfarm:	
Northeast	CES 36; BLS 237-84, supplement 3
North Central	CES 37; BLS 237-85, supplement 3
South	CES 38; BLS 237-86, supplement 3
West	CES 39; BLS 237-87, supplement 3
U. S.	CES 40; BLS 237-88, supplement 3
Urban:	
Northeast	BLS 237-34, supplement 3
North Central	BLS 237-35, supplement 3
South	BLS 237-36, supplement 3
West	BLS 237-37, supplement 3
U. S.	BLS 237-38, supplement 3
Total urban & rural:	
Northeast	CES 41; BLS 237-89, supplement 3
North Central	CES 42: BLS 237-90, supplement 3
South	CES 43: BLS 237-91, supplement 3
West	CES 44; BLS 237-92, supplement 3
U. S.	CES 45; BLS 237-93, supplement

MARKETING Uses of Consumer Expenditure Survey Data. (BLS report, no. 238-15). Washington, D. C.: Bureau of Labor Statistics, 1967. 7 p.   (EF 18a)

> Discussion illustrated with examples of studies which have applied CES data.

Analytical reports based on this survey: (EF 19)

CLOTHING for Urban Families: Expenditures per Member by Sex and Age, 1960-61. (Bulletin 1556). Washington, D. C. : Government Printing Office, 1967. 149 p.

CLOTHING the Urban American Family, How Much for Whom? (BLS report 238-16). Washington, D. C.: Bureau of Labor Statistics, 1968. 6 p.

Special Reports

Some BLS reports are of particular interest to industry planners:

TECHNOLOGICAL Trends in Major American Industries. (Bulletin 1474). Washington, D. C.: Government Printing Office, 1966. 269 p.   (EF 20)

> Appraises developments in equipment, products, and materials in the next decade with special attention to 40 separate industries. Bibliography.

[CONSTRUCTION Labor and Material Requirements Studies] Washington, D. C.: Government Printing Office. Irregular.   (EF 21)

> Series of studies summarized in the Monthly Labor Review and published in full as BLS bulletins. For selected types of construction (e. g. sewer works, highways, college housing, hospitals) covers labor required per unit of dollar volume of construction on site and in the manufacture and distribution of building materials; types and quantities of materials used.

In recent years, a vast new program was centered at the Bureau of Labor Statistics: Interagency Growth Study Project. This project was started by the Department of Labor in cooperation with other government and private agencies, in an effort to utilize the interindustry relationship tables for developing projections of the economy in industry detail under alternative assumptions regarding rates and patterns of growth.   The program works within guidelines provided by an interagency coordinating committee chaired by the representative from the Council of Economic Advisers. Other committee members come from the Departments of Labor and Commerce and from the Bureau of the Budget.   Elements of the projections are developed by a number of government and private organizations including the Department of Agriculture, Bureau of Mines, Harvard Economic Research Project and the National Planning Association. The central project staff is located at the BLS which has the major responsibility for integrating the results of the various studies. The following publication represents one of the first reports on a major phase of the work of this project.   (EF 22)

PROJECTIONS 1970: Interindustry Relationships, Potential Demand, Employment. (Bulletin 1536). Washington, D. C.: Government Printing Office, 1966. 155 p.   (EF 23)

> Using the 1958 input-output study for manpower analysis, this report presents estimates of industry employment-output relationship and converts the interindustry output requirements per dollar of final demand into employment requirements based on the level of productivity in 1962.

1970 Input-Output Coefficients. (BLS report 326). Washington, D. C. Bureau of Labor Statistics, Sept. 1967. 11 p.   (EF 23a)

> Presents the input-output relationships which underlie the 1970 interindustry employment estimates.   Includes a table which shows how much each industry would buy from every other industry in order to produce a dollar's worth of output.   Relationships are stated in 1958 prices at producers' value.

MAJOR BLS Programs -- A Summary of Their Characteristics ...
Washington, D. C.: Bureau of Labor Statistics. Annual. (EF 24)
Brief guide to data available in terms of source, detail,
coverage, reference period, publication schedule, special
characteristics and uses. State and area index to nine statistical categories.

GUIDE to Employment Statistics of BLS: Employment, Labor Turnover, Hours and Earnings. Washington, D. C.: Bureau of Labor
Statistics, 1961. i, 134 p. (EF 25)
This volume presents tables showing the earliest date for
which national historical data are available and gives industry
definitions according to the 1957 Standard Industrial Classification. Revised edition in process.

GUIDE to Area Employment Statistics. (see FB 9)

GUIDE to State Employment Statistics ... (see FA 13)

OFFICE OF MANPOWER POLICY, EVALUATION AND RESEARCH

This office initiates and coordinates basic research and statistical programs related to manpower development and utilization.
Although it prepares the materials for the President's and Labor
Secretary's annual manpower reports (see E 2), its publications are
not of a periodic nature. However, of particular interest are those
which touch upon the long-range effects on industry of automation,
technology and the manpower supply. Such, for example, were the
bulletins: Technology and Manpower in Design and Drafting,
1965-75 (1966); Technology and Manpower in the Health
Service Industry, 1965-75 (1967); Technology and Manpower
in the Telephone Industry, 1965-75 (1966); Automation,
Skill and Manpower Predictions (1966).

BUREAU OF EMPLOYMENT SECURITY

To implement its employment services program the BES collects and analyzes operational and economic data which are of value in assessing labor markets, employment anu unemployment trends in various industries and areas.

HISTORICAL Statistics of Employment Security Activities, 1938-1966. Washington, D. C.: Bureau of Employment Security, 1968. 144 p.   (EF 35)

> Data on federal-state employment security system activities presented from year of initiation. Supplementary volumes planned for publication every five years.

AREA Trends to Employment and Unemployment. Washington, D. C. Bureau of Employment Security. Monthly.   (EF 36)

> Summary of employment, unemployment, manpower conditions and outlook in 150 labor market areas classified into six labor supply groups.

EMPLOYMENT And Wages. Washington, D. C.: Department of Labor. Quarterly.   (EF 37)

> Wages and employment of workers, covered by state unemployment insurance laws, tabulated for major industries and subgroups with state and regional breakdowns. First issue of each year reports these data by size of firm for major industry divisions in each state and 2-, 3-, and 4-digit manufacturing detail by size of reporting unit for the nation as a whole.

WOMEN'S BUREAU

Data collected by this agency concern the social and economi climate of the working woman, her employment and characteristics.

HANDBOOK on Women Workers. Washington, D. C.: Government Printing Office. Triennial.   (EF 40)

> Text and tables on women's employment occupations, age, marital status, earnings and income, education and related information.

DEPARTMENT OF TRANSPORTATION

Under the Department of Transportation Act of October 15, 1966 which became effective April 1, 1967, this department was established to develop national transportation policies and programs by identifying transportation problems, coordinating public and private projects, and stimulating technological advances. The bulk of its departmental structure was drawn from existing agencies.

FEDERAL AVIATION ADMINISTRATION

This agency is concerned with the development of air commerce and civil aeronautics. It publishes data on registered civil aircraft and their utilization, the characteristics and uses of airports, air carrier operations in relation to airway facilities, and the movement of passengers, cargo and mail. Data are issued in a series of special studies and annual reports. Recently added was the first census of air taxi operators. Its three principal periodic reports:

FAA Statistical Handbook. Washington, D. C.: Government Printing Office. Annual. (EG 1)

FAA Air Traffic Activity. Washington, D. C.: Government Printing Office. Annual (calendar and fiscal year). (EG 2)

AVIATION Forecasts, F. Y. 1965-75. Washington, D. C.: Government Printing Office. Annual. (EG 3)
   Includes aircraft production, carrier and general aviation
   fleets, passenger traffic.

FEDERAL HIGHWAY ADMINISTRATION

This agency was formed to coordinate highways with other modes of transportation. Its programs cover the responsibilities of the Bureau of Public Roads (transferred from the Department of Commerce) and of the United States Coast Guard (transferred from the Department of the Treasury), the functions of the Army Corps

of Engineers relating to tolls, and the motor carrier safety functions
provided by the Interstate Commerce Act.

HIGHWAY Statistics. Washington, D. C.: Government Printing Office. Annual.   (EG 4)
> Basic statistics on highway mileage, finance and taxation;
> motor vehicle registrations; fuel consumption; driver licens-
> ing. Statistical tabulations predating this volume by over a
> year are available upon request from the agency. Summary
> editions, published from time to time, recapitulate data from
> earlier annuals. Current summary is the 1965 edition.

PUBLIC Roads. Washington, D. C.: Government Printing Office.
Bimonthly.   (EG 5)
> Reports on the results of highway research and on traffic
> characteristics.

UNITED STATES COAST GUARD

In addition to the merchant marine data listed below, this
service compiles statistics on recreational vessels, and boating accidents.

MERCHANT Marine Statistics. Washington, D. C.: Government
Printing Office. Annual.   (EG 6)
> Statistics on all U. S. merchant marine documented vessels
> (including yachts) and those removed from documentation dur-
> ing the preceding year.

MERCHANT Vessels of the United States. Washington, D. C.:
Government Printing Office. Annual; monthly supplements. (EG 7)
> List of all documented U. S. vessels belonging to the com-
> mercial merchant marine, including yachts of five net tons and
> over. Gives name of vessel, owner, number, rig, tonnage,
> home port, place and date of build.

DEPARTMENT OF THE TREASURY

In its role of national fiscal agent the Treasury Department collects and disseminates a large amount of statistical data as a by-product of its administrative and regulatory activities.   Its studies and reports reflect not only the financial condition of the federal government but also the fiscal health and activity of the country's business, industrial, and consumer communities.

FISCAL SERVICE

The Bureau of Accounts of the Fiscal Service plans, compiles and publishes a number of periodic and special reports on the financial operations of the federal government.

DAILY Statement of the United States Treasury. Washington, D. C.: Government Printing Office. Daily and month-end.   (EH 1)

MONTHLY Statement of Receipts and Expenditures of the U. S. Government. Distributed with the above.   (EH 2)
> Official vehicle for current statements of federal budget surplus or deficit.

COMBINED Statement of Receipts, Expenditures and Balances of the United States Government. Washington, D. C.: Government Printing Office. Annual.   (EH 3)

TREASURY Bulletin.   Washington, D. C.: Government Printing Office. Monthly.   (EH 4)
> Current and comparative statistics on federal finance and monetary data.

INTERNAL REVENUE SERVICE

Statistics on businesses and individuals, as well as miscellaneous data on certain industries and products, are compiled by the Internal Revenue Service as a by-product of its revenue collecting activity. Particularly revealing of product movement from manufacturer to consumer are the tax collection data.

ANNUAL Report ... Washington, D. C. : Government Printing
Office. Annual.   (EH 5)
    Considerable detail on tax collections by source, type of tax,
and geographic area.

FEDERAL Tax Collections. Washington, D. C. : Internal Revenue
Service. Monthly; Annual.   (EH 6)
    Individual and corporate income, distilled spirits, beer, wine
and tobacco products tax collections shown by internal revenue
regions, districts, states and other areas.

ALCOHOL and Tobacco Summary Statistics. (Publication 67). Wash-
ington, D. C. : Government Printing Office. Annual.   (EH 7)
    Production, withdrawal, stocks and related statistics on
distilled spirits, alcohol, beer, wine and tobacco products.
This report is supplemented by a series of STATISTICAL RE-
LEASE publications, most of them monthly, issued by its
Alcohol and Tobacco Tax Division.

STATISTICS of Income. Washington, D. C. : Government Printing
Office. Annual.   (EH 8)
    Three reports in this series merit special attention. Each is
preceded by a less detailed preliminary.
    Individual Tax Returns. (Publication 79).
    Data on income (including adjusted gross income) and its
sources. Selected statistics reported by states and for the
100 largest standard metropolitan areas.
    Corporation Income Tax Returns. (Publication 16).
    Income, deductions, assets, liabilities, tax credit and
dividends paid. Returns are classified by major and minor
industry and trade groupings, size of total assets, business
receipts or net income.
    U. S. Business Tax Returns. (Publication no. 438).
    Based on returns filed by sole proprietorships, partnerships,

and corporations, report includes: number of establishments,
receipts, profits, financial ratios, and other balance sheet
data, with classification by industry, states, size of profits,
receipts, assets.

STATISTICS of Income: Supplemental Report ... Washington, D. C.:
Government Printing Office. Irregular.   (EH 9)

Recently inaugurated, these reports present special analyses
of income tax data. Examples of those published to date:
STATE and Metropolitan Area Data for Individual Income Tax
Returns, 1959, 1960, and 1961.   1964.
FOREIGN Tax Credit Claimed on Corporation Income Tax
Returns ... Annual.
Useful for information on American holdings of foreign cor-
porations.
FARMERS' Cooperatives, 1963.   1966.
Detailed balance sheet data which, for exempt cooperatives,
is presented by type of product marketed and by state.
PERSONAL Wealth, 1962.   1967.

SOURCE Book of Statistics of Income. Washington, D. C.: Internal
Revenue Service.   (EH 10)

Unpublished annual tables showing balance sheet and income
statement data from corporation returns for each of about
270 major and minor industry groups. Detail is greater than
that carried in the published reports. Reproductions are available from the Director of the Statistics Division of the IRS.

OTHER UNITS

Some examples of other data published by the Department
of the Treasury are gold and silver production statistics (Bureau of
the Mint); conditions of national banks (Comptroller of the Currency).   (EH 11)

BOARD OF GOVERNORS OF THE FEDERAL RESERVE SYSTEM

The Board's principal duties consist of influencing monetary policy and credit conditions, and supervising the Federal Reserve Banks and member banks. For setting policy the Board has developed a number of statistical series useful in analyzing current business conditions and forecasting economic trends. Its supervisory activity produces voluminous data on money and banking.

The principal series used in economic and market analysis appear in the publications listed below.

FEDERAL Reserve Bulletin. Washington, D. C.: Board of Governors of the Federal Reserve System. Monthly. (EI 1)

> Principal source for current data on money and banking, credit, FRB indexes of industrial production, and other business statistics. Special articles on financial and economic developments; descriptions of new series.

BUSINESS Indexes. Washington, D. C.: Board of Governors of the Federal Reserve System. Monthly. (EI 2)

> Indexes of industrial production, output of consumer durables, and selected series compiled by other agencies.

Banking and Finance

BANKING and Monetary Statistics. Washington, D. C.: Board of Governors of the Federal Reserve System, 1943. 979 p. (EI 3)

> Compendium of historical data (primarily 1914-1941) with explanatory text. Its SUPPLEMENT, in the process of publication, is being issued in a series of numbered sections.

DISTRIBUTION of Bank Deposits By Counties and Standard Metropolitan Areas. Washington, D. C.: Board of Governors of the Federal Reserve System. Biennial. (EI 4)

> Demand and time deposits of individuals, partnerships, and corporations in all banks in the United States.

Numerous periodic reports and releases supply such current data as all-bank assets and liabilities; Reserve Banks' condition;

member bank income, loans, deposits, reserves, assets and liabilities, etc.   (EI 5)

Consumer Credit and Finances

SURVEY of Financial Characteristics of Consumers. Washington, D. C.: Board of Governors of the Federal Reserve System, August 1966. 166 p.   (EI 6)

> Data on the size and composition of wealth as of December 31, 1962. The analyses deal with the determinants of size of wealth, the components of wealth and debt and their diffusion throughout the population, the changes in composition of wealth as it increases, and the variation in patterns of ownership among consumer units of differing characteristics.

SURVEY of Changes in Family Finances. (In preparation)   (EI 7)

> Detailed analysis and evaluation of data obtained from a reinterview survey of the consumer units who had cooperated in the earlier survey listed above.

A number of releases report credit statistics many of which also appear in the Federal Reserve Bulletin:

CONSUMER Credit ... Washington, D. C.: Board of Governors of the Federal Reserve System.   Monthly.   (EI 8)

CONSUMER Credit at Consumer Finance Companies. Washington, D. C.: Board of Governors of the Federal Reserve System. Monthly.   (EI 9)

CONSUMER Instalment Credit at Commercial Banks. Washington, D. C.: Board of Governors of the Federal Reserve System. Monthly.   (EI 10)

SALES Finance Companies. Washington, D. C.: Board of Governors of the Federal Reserve System. Monthly.   (EI 11)

Federal Reserve Banks

From time to time the 12 Federal Reserve Banks publish
economic and market data for states and areas within their district.
For example:

FEDERAL Reserve Bank of Chicago. Economic Fact Book, rev. ed.
Chicago: Federal Reserve Bank of Chicago, 1966. 49 p.
    Revision of 1964 edition. Data are for states and selected
    cities within the Seventh Federal Reserve District and cover:
    banking, construction, agriculture, population, employment,
    income.

FEDERAL Reserve Bank of Philadelphia.   Mainsprings of Growth.
Philadelphia: Federal Reserve Bank of Philadelphia: 1967. 109 p.
    Studies on the economy of the Philadelphia metropolitan area,
    present and future. Covers the growth prospects for the area's
    research and development industry, employment, income,
    finance, trade, and other aspects.

Each Bank also publishes a bulletin which contains articles
on business developments of general interest as well as reviews of
regional conditions and local statistics.   These publications are
available upon request from the individual Banks.

MONTHLY Review. Atlanta: Federal Reserve Bank of Atlanta.
Monthly.

NEW England Business Review. Boston: Federal Reserve Bank
of Boston. Monthly.

BUSINESS Conditions. Chicago: Federal Reserve Bank of Chicago.
Monthly.

ECONOMIC Review. Cleveland. Federal Reserve Bank of Cleveland. Monthly.

BUSINESS Review. Dallas: Federal Reserve Bank of Dallas.
Monthly with statistical supplement.

MONTHLY Review.   Kansas City, Mo. : Federal Reserve Bank of
Kansas City. Every 2 months.

NINTH District Conditions. Minneapolis: Federal Reserve Bank of Minneapolis. Monthly.

MONTHLY Review. New York: Federal Reserve Bank of New
York. Monthly.

BUSINESS Review. Philadelphia: Federal Reserve Bank of Philadelphia. Monthly.

MONTHLY Review. Richmond: Federal Reserve Bank of Richmond. Monthly.

REVIEW. St. Louis: Federal Reserve Bank of St. Louis. Monthly.

MONTHLY Review. San Francisco: Federal Reserve Bank of San
Francisco. Monthly.

The following index provides ready access to the information
in all 12 bulletins.

FEDERAL Reserve Bank of Philadelphia. Federal Reserve Bank
Reviews, Selected Subjects ... Philadelphia: Library,
Federal Reserve Bank of Philadelphia. Biennial.   (EI 12)

Cumulated index to all 12 Federal Reserve Bank bulletins.
Interedition additions are maintained on cards by the library
of the bank.

FEDERAL TRADE COMMISSION

Prevention of unfair competition and deceptive practices in
commerce is the major function of the Federal Trade Commission.

Some fact-finding results from the inquiries and hearings
conducted into the methods of marketing of specific products. Recent
investigations probed the advertising and merchandising of tires, the
marketing practices of the gasoline industry, vertical integration in
the cement industry. Summaries of these investigations are sometimes published for general distribution either as Senate or House
documents or as Commission publications.

Occasional economic studies of individual industries are
made from the monopoly aspect. These are rich in detail and often
treat of marketing practices in the broadest sense. Thus, for
example, the Commission's research into the food industry was

made available in a series of staff reports: Concentration and
Integration in Retailing (Jan. 1960); The Frozen Fruit, Juice,
and Vegetable Industry (Dec. 1962); The Canned Fruit, Juice,
and Vegetable Industry (June 1965).

    Periodic statistical publications report financial statement
data:

QUARTERLY Financial Report of Manufacturing Corporations. (see
EI 41)
    Issued jointly with the Securities and Exchange Commission.

RATES of Return for Identical Companies in Selected Manufacturing
Industries. Washington, D. C.: Federal Trade Commission. Annual.
                                                        (EI 20)

Related to the above is the following special report:

REPORT on Profit Rates of Manufacturing Corporations, 1947-
1962. Washington, D. C.: Federal Trade Commission, 1963. 70 p.
                                                        (EI 21)
    Special report showing profits per dollar sales and rates of
    profit on equity for 63 industry and size groups of manufactur-
    ing corporations in each calendar quarter 1947-62.

UNITED STATES TARIFF COMMISSION

    Industry information is also available from the United States
Tariff Commission which investigates and reports on the effect of
imports on domestic enterprise. Its special studies have covered
such products as ceramic mosaic tile, straight pins, sheet glass,
flatware, and watch movements. The Commission also issues
periodic reports on the production and sales of synthetic organic
chemicals, and synthetic plastics and resin materials.   (EI 30)
    In 1966 USTC initiated the publication of a new series of
SUMMARIES OF TRADE AND TARIFF INFORMATION. The complete project will include about 1,800 summaries covering all

tariff items.   Publication of the 62 volumes projected for the series
is scheduled under a three-year program.   Individual volumes are released as they are prepared.   Each summary is to provide an ac-
curate description of the item with indications of its uses, methods
of production, number of producers, world supplies, and appraisals
of its importance in trade and in our economy.   Each also includes
substantive analytical material on the factors affecting trends in
consumption, production, and trade, and those bearing on the competitive position and economic health of domestic industries.   The
current edition of volumes, too limited for general distribution, is
being made available for consultation in the field offices of the Department of Commerce and in selected public and university libraries
in the larger cities.   Following the completion of the volumes projected for each tariff schedule, it is expected that the separate volumes will be obtainable from the Government Printing Office.   (EI 31)

SECURITIES AND EXCHANGE COMMISSION

The Commission's principal responsibility is the protection of
investors in their securities transactions.   Its major sources of information are the registration and other statements filed with it by a
variety of businesses, national security exchanges, public utility
holding companies and investment trusts.

STATISTICAL Bulletin.   Washington, D. C.: Government Printing
Office.   Monthly.   (EI 40)
  Data on new securities, securities sales, stock prices and
  transactions and other phases of securities exchange; volume
  and composition of individuals' savings; plant and equipment
  expenditures, actual and anticipated; current assets and liabilities of United States corporations.

QUARTERLY Financial Report of Manufacturing Corporations.
Washington, D. C.: Government Printing Office. Quarterly.   (EI 41)
  Published jointly with the Federal Trade Commission. Contains financial and operating data, including ratios of profits
  to sales, and related statistics classified by asset size and

major industry groups.

SMALL BUSINESS ADMINISTRATION

Although the primary purpose of SBA is direct advice and assistance to the small businessman, the agency has developed a number of publications bearing on marketing as well as on management (Management Aids), production methods (Technical Aids), and on buying from or selling to the federal government.

U. S. Government Purchasing, Specifications and Sales Directory. Washington, D. C. : Government Printing Office. Irregular.   (EI 50)
> Directory of federal military and civilian purchasing agencies and guide to sources of specifications for products used.

MANAGEMENT Research Summaries [series] Washington, D. C. : Small Business Administration. Irregular.   (EI 51)
> Highlights of studies made under research grants. Many provide data on local industries or markets for local products.

SMALL Marketers Aids [series] Washington, D. C. : Small Business Administration. Irregular.   (EI 52)
> Informative and advisory brochures on subjects of interest to retail, wholesale, and service enterprises.

POST OFFICE DEPARTMENT

Recently marketing research has directed its attention to the usefulness of the Zip Code system in establishing marketing units related to demographic, economic and environmental factors.   The department's Zip Code maps and distribution of 1960 population by Sectional Centers are available from its Office of Special Projects.

NATIONAL SCIENCE FOUNDATION

In the light of the increased application and impact of scientific and technological developments on industry, the costs and findings of research, as reported by the National Science Foundation, are of interest.

BASIC Research, Applied Research, and Development in Industry.
Washington, D. C.: Government Printing Office. Annual.   (EI 60)
    Statistical presentation of research and development costs by
    type of research, size of firm, industry, geographic distribu-
    tion, and method of funding.

CURRENT Projects on Economic and Social Implications of Science
and Technology. Washington, D. C.: Government Printing Office.
Annual.   (EI 61)
    Summaries of university-based research in progress. Among
    the 14 subject categories: impacts on selected industries;
    economic development; innovation including inventions and new
    processes; patents and trademarks.

OTHER AGENCIES

A number of government agencies maintain statistical programs whose total output is of interest only in studies of specific
industries and products. A few such are characterized here. Greater detail on these and others can be located through the guides and
research aids cited in the preceding and subsequent chapters of this
work.

For industrial marketers and those interested in selling to
the government the General Services Administration issues a guide:
INDEX of Federal Specifications and Standards. Washington, D. C.: Government Printing Office. Annual with cumulative
supplements.   (EJ 1)

A similar publication, directed to those wishing to sell to
the military market, is issued by the Department of Defense:
DEPARTMENT of Defense Index of Specifications and
Standards. Washington, D. C.: Government Printing Office.
looseleaf.   (EJ 2)

Other publications of this department cover administrative and operating statistics, medical and manpower data, and contract awards. More recently initiated are its continuing studies of the economic impact of defense spending on industries and geographic areas:

SELECTED Economic Indicators. Washington, D. C.: Department
of Defense. Monthly.   (EJ 3)

> Superseded by the Census Bureau's DEFENSE INDICATORS
> (Washington, D. C.: Government Printing Office. Monthly).
> Employment impact data collected from defense contractors under
> its Economic Information System and supplemented by statistics
> from other sources are planned for release in periodic statistical
> summaries.

The Corps of Engineers of the Department of the Army is concerned, in addition to its other duties, with the operation and maintenance of port facilities. An outgrowth of this responsibility is the compilation of waterborne commerce statistics. In the latter part of 1965 this activity was consolidated at a new installation, Waterborne Commerce Statistics Center, in New Orleans.

WATERBORNE Commerce of the United States. New Orleans:
U. S. Army Engineer District. Annual.   (EJ 4)

> Published in five parts with supplements: Part 1, Atlantic
> Coast; Part 2, Gulf Coast, Mississippi River System and
> Antilles Areas; Part 3, Great Lakes; Part 4, Pacific Coast,
> Alaska, and Hawaii; Part 5, National Summaries. Gives
> detailed statistics on freight traffic by commodities and
> characteristics of vessels using United States ports and water-
> ways.

In the field of travel, two agencies publish statistical data. The Passport Office of the Department of State tabulates and analyzes statistics on passports issued and renewed:

SUMMARY of Passport Statistics. Washington, D. C.: Passport
Office. Quarterly.   (EJ 5)

Data show travellers' age, occupation, citizenship, state and metropolitan area of residence; means of transportation; countries to be visited.

FORECAST of Citizen Departures to Europe. Washington, D. C.: Passport Office. Monthly.   (EJ 6)

Gives two-month forecast on basis of historical data.

The Immigration and Naturalization Service of the Department of Justice reports on intercountry migration as well as on passenger travel.

ANNUAL Report. Washington, D. C.: Immigration and Naturalization Service. Annual.   (EJ 7)

Includes series on immigrants admitted by sex, age, marital status, occupation, country of birth, destination in the United States; and arrivals from and departures to foreign countries by country of embarkation and debarkation and by port of arrival and departure.

REPORT of Passenger Travel Between the United States and Foreign Countries. Washington, D. C.: Immigration and Naturalization Service. Monthly, semiannual and annual.   (EJ 8)

For aliens and citizens arriving and departing gives means of transportation, flag of carrier, country of embarkation or debarkation, and United States ports of arrival and departure.

In transportation, air carrier financial and operating statistics are published by the Civil Aeronautics Board which regulates the accounting practices of the industry. It also compiles the passenger origin and destination studies which are issued by the Air Transportation Association of America.   (EJ 9)

The Interstate Commerce Commission regulates common and contract motor and water carriers, freight forwarders, interstate railroads, pipelines (except water and gas) and sleeping-car com-

panies. It publishes comprehensive statistics on the finances,
equipment, traffic, and operations of these industries as well as on
freight shipments by commodity group or class.   (EJ 10)

Public and private electric utilities, pipelines and producers
engaged in interstate gas commerce are regulated by the Federal
Power Commission which publishes statistics on their finances,
rates, operations and equipment. Particularly detailed data are
available on electric power supply and requirements, production,
plant capacity, sales and customers.   (EJ 11)

Communications carriers are subject to Federal Communications Commission control. Detailed financial and operating data
on telephone, telegraph, cable, radio and television broadcasting
industries are available from the commission's reports.   (EJ 12)

Data on insured banks and on all banks in the United States,
including the structure of the banking system, assets and liabilities,
and related statistics are compiled by the Federal Deposit Insurance
Corporation.   (EJ 13)

The Federal Home Loan Bank Board, on the other hand,
publishes statistics on savings and loan associations, on savings
banks and insurance companies engaged in home financing, as well
as on nonfarm mortgage activity.   (EJ 14)

REGIONAL
AND LOCAL SOURCES
Official and Quasi-Official

Historically, the amount and nature of the statistical supply available from states and localities has varied from area to area. Even within the same area, diversitv in data collection, reporting and analysis and an overlap in agencies' statistical projects is to be expected.

GOVERNMENTS

In recent years, the growth of state and local government programs has generated a trend toward an improved data base for official decision-making. Consequently, attention is being directed toward a better statistical output, standardization in coverage and quality, coordination of statistical activities and on means of exchanging information on all matters of statistical interest.

Some effort has been put into the coordination of federal, state, and local statistics both by government and private groups. Federal agencies have increased their supply of guides to area data. Notable, too, is the Census Bureau's newsletter (see FB 1) recently inaugurated to provide a communications medium on all matters of area statistics. Similar publications are appearing on state and local levels.

In general, however, data available from state and local governments, like that from the federal government, are strongly characterized by the administrative, regulatory and planning functions of the respective agencies.

Permits, fees, licenses, registrations, taxes immediately suggest the existence of quantitative facts on the local level in published or unpublished form. Vital statistics and certain industry data are collected locally in cooperation with or for transmittal to federal agencies.

Officials charged with the activities of planning departments, development commissions, departments of commerce, and their equivalents are also in a position to supply information and advice out of their knowledge and experience.

STATE

Each state issues a number of periodic publications of value in local market and economic analysis. Unpublished data are often available upon application to the proper authorities. Such information may be loosely grouped into several types common to most of the states.

Directories of manufacturers, products, new plant locations have been issued consistently by many states -- some with basic industrial data added. These are treated in greater detail in a subsequent chapter.

A number of states publish statistical compendia of varying frequencies but on a regular basis. These abstracts are a good source of current and historical facts. Moreover, they constitute useful guides to the research data collected regularly. A list of current editions is included in the Appendix.

Periodicals containing reviews of state economic activity are issued by some states -- a few by state agencies, others by university bureaus of business research.

Among the many periodic statistical reports, those on labor and agriculture stand out in terms of quantity and detail. Most states have issued series on employment and unemployment, hours and wages, cost of living, labor supply and turnover, on a continuing basis for a number of years. Similarly, state agriculture departments collect and disseminate production statistics; demand, supply and price information; movement and storage data on agricultural products of importance to their economies. State agricultural experiment stations, many of which are located at colleges and universities, supplement and augment this output with studies on the

markets for and on the marketing of specific agricultural commodities.

Tax collections by source reflect income, sales of certain
products, number and location of licensed retail and service establishments and other economic activity subject to state assessment.
These and similar data on such subjects as housing, vital statistics,
vehicle registrations, banks, utilities, transport, manufacturing
industries are either published or made available for consultation
by the agency concerned.

Area market studies (consumer and industrial), market
analyses, industrial censuses, resources and growth reports,
prompted by state economic and industrial planning activity, are
issued from time to time.

Under the impact of the national highway modernization program over 200 cities are reported to be involved in intensive land
use and transportation studies (1).   Research data, current and
projected, developed for these include population and employment
distribution, family income, retail sales, travel habits.   The highway department of each state would be the source for all such information, published and unpublished.

Guides to state sources of information appear in the last
section of this chapter.

LOCAL

Like states many local governments collect statistics in the
course of their regulatory and administrative activities but seldom
publish them for wide distribution.

Although a certain amount of unpublished data is available
from local agencies, the basic statistical supply for these areas
emanates primarily from federal and state governments, chambers
of commerce and other sources.

Where close state-local economic relationships exist, such
as in population, income, local business activity, state interests
usually activate research and development and state publications
provide city, county and regional breakdowns.

Guides to sources of local information appear in the last

section of this chapter.

CHAMBERS OF COMMERCE

The Chamber of Commerce of the United States was organized as a privately supported national organization by President Taft and his Secretary of Commerce to provide a business viewpoint on matters of federal policy of concern to the business community.

A large study staff produces for its membership numerous bulletins and studies on economic, business and governmental developments affecting American enterprise on national and international levels. It also issues a monthly magazine, Nation's Business, and informational reports of interest to business management.

State and local chambers of commerce, because of their aggressive and competitive interest in promoting and developing the commercial, industrial and other economic activity of their areas, provide a number of useful publications.

The two most prevalent types closely parallel and complement those issued by state and local governments and university bureaus of business research. Industrial directories often carry descriptive information on the state and its resources. Some include similar detail for their municipalities. Further discussion of this source appears in the chapter on directories. Monthly bulletins, reviewing general business conditions and statistical data affecting the local economic climate, are issued by a number of state and city chambers. Also available is information on building projects and plant expansions, and occasional projections of population, housing and employment.

City chambers of commerce also compile and distribute occasional area studies dealing with their markets as a whole or with particular factors of current local interest.

Both state and local organizations can assist in supplying unpublished information and pertinent advice relating to their areas. The larger organizations maintain collections of directories, trade journals, government publications and other reference materials for servicing the business interests of their community.

OTHER

Although not distinguished by quantities of published data,
several other local groups constitute sources of information.

One notable development has been the establishment of a
coordinating statistical agency by the local chapter of a professional
association. (see FB 6)

Regional plan organizations, supported by citizen and business interests in a number of localities, maintain research programs
and develop data for long-range area projects.

A current example:

THE REGIONS' Growth. (Bulletin 105) New York: Regional Plan Association, Inc. , 1967.   143 p.

>One of several reports. Projects population, jobs, house-
>holds and income for the New York metropolitan region to the
>year 2000 and relates its growth to the urbanization of the
>eastern seaboard.

Another regional source are interstate agencies active in
pollution control, land and water resources development and transportation planning.

Commerce and industry associations, local merchant and
similar groups, organized on a city or on smaller district levels,
exist in large metropolitan areas. Concerned with the business activity in their immediate community, they constitute a relatively
obscure but often unique source of information and assistance.

The self-supporting, quasi-governmental port authorities are
a source of information not only for the facilities under their jurisdiction but also for the geographical areas where they are concerned
with the maintenance and development of their activities.

A recent example:

THE Next Twenty Years. New York: The Port of New York
Authority, 1966.

>Forecasts to 1985 area conditions, including population and
>employment growth, in the New York-New Jersey-Connecticut

metropolitan region.

GUIDES TO SOURCES

Regional, state and local data sources are scattered throughout all levels of government and business. Local newspapers, university bureaus of business research, field units of federal agencies and other suppliers of area statistics are treated in subsequent chapters. Nor to be overlooked is the Appendix list of state statistical abstracts.

Gathered here, however, are a number of comprehensive guides either generally or topically oriented toward area data. Not only the presence but also the scope of the list indicates a notable recent development: the initiative of government agencies and professional associations in coordinating these elusive sources and in closing the information gap on their resources.

Regional

DIRECTORY of Interstate Agencies. Chicago: The Council of State Governments. Biennial (?)   (F 1)

> Purpose, activities, publications, executive personnel, including research directors, given for interstate agencies established by compact.

INDEX to Reports by Geographic Areas. In U. S. Bureau of the Census. Bureau of the Census Catalog. (See OD 6)

U. S. Bureau of the Census. Census Bureau Programs and Publications: Area and Subject Guide ... Washington, D. C.: Government Printing Office, 1968. 152 p.   (F 2)

> Tabular presentation of major statistical publications and periodic reports annotated for types of areas and subjects covered. Geographic area index.

FEDERAL Reserve Bank of Philadelphia. Federal Reserve Bank

Reviews, Selected Subjects ... (See EI 12)

State: Omnibus Guides

THE BOOK of the States. Chicago: The Council of State Governments.
Biennial with two supplements.   (FA 1)
  Authoritative guide to the structure and functions of state
  governments. Its "Summer Supplement" contains a detailed
  list of administrative officials classified by function and is
  thereby an excellent key to state statistical data sources.

STATE Manual Procurement Guide, by Donald O. Hotaling. Special
Libraries, vol. 54, no. 4, April 1963, p. 206-9.   (FA 2)
  Detailed descriptions of state legislative manuals, the best
  source on state agencies and their functions.

SOURCES of State Information and State Industrial Directories. Washington, D. C.: Chamber of Commerce of the United States. Irregular.   (FA 3)
  Directory of public and private agencies which provide information about their states. Also lists manufacturers' directories issued by state and private agencies and codes these
  for type of data and indexes included.

WORLD Wide Chamber of Commerce Directory. Loveland, Colo.:
Johnson Publishing Co., Inc. Annual.   (FA 4)
  Domestic and foreign chambers of commerce arranged geographically. Gives names of acting executives, addresses and
  telephone numbers.

FEDERAL Reserve Bank of Philadelphia. Federal Reserve Bank
Reviews, Selected Subjects ... (see EI 12)

U. S. Bureau of the Census. Census Bureau Programs and
Publications: Area and Subject Guide ... (see F 2)

---DIRECTORY of Federal Statistics for States, 1967. Washington, D. C. : Government Printing Office, 1968. 372 p.   (FA 5)
   A companion volume to FB 5.

INDEX to Reports by Geographic Areas. In U. S. Bureau of the
Census.   Bureau of the Census Catalog.   (see OD 6)

State: Single-State Guides

Colorado
CRAMPON, L. J. and Label, Maurice. Business Information
Sources in Colorado State Government. Boulder, Colo.:
University of Colorado Bureau of Business Research, 1963. xi,
109 p.   (FA 6)
   Prepared under a grant from the Small Business Administration. Agencies, with descriptions of their functions and annotated lists of publications issued in 1961 and earlier reports still in effect, are grouped in six categories: Agriculture; Business, commerce, and professions; Economic
   resources; Mining and extractive industries; Government;
   Population characteristics and social conditions. Agency and
   subject indexes.

Mississippi
KENNEY, Brigitte L. An Informational Manual to Assist
Chambers of Commerce with Research. Jackson, Miss.:
Mississippi Economic Council, 1965. 40 p.   (FA 7)
   Classified, annotated bibliography of basic business sources.
   Included here for its coverage of Mississippi state sources.
   Author, title, subject indexes.

New York
NEW YORK (State) Office of Statistical Coordination. Statistical
Series of New York State. Albany: New York State Division
of the Budget, Office of Statistical Coordination, Nov. 1966. 99 p.
                                                             (FA 8)
   Provides: descriptions of state agencies, their recurring

publications and statistical data produced; tabular presentation
of the scope, detail, geographic unit covered, year of origin,
frequency, compiling agency and published or unpublished
source of all major statistical series of interest outside of
the originating agency; alphabetical list of recurring statistical publications; subject index.

---New York State Statistical Reporter.   Albany: New York
State Division of the Budget, Office of Statistical Coordination. Every
2 months.   (FA 9)

Reports on completed, current and prospective studies and on
related materials.

Pennsylvania

PENNSYLVANIA.   Bureau of Statistics. Index of State Sources of
Statistical Data.   Harrisburg: Pennsylvania Bureau of Statistics. Irregular.   (FA 10)

Latest edition is 1961. New edition planned.

Washington

AMERICAN Marketing Association Puget Sound Chapter.   Directory
of Marketing Information Sources for the State of Washington.
Olympia: State of Washington Department of Commerce and
Economic Development,   July 1966. v, 65 p.   (Revision
in process)   (FA 11)

Classifies 460 publications and references from national and
local sources under 21 broad topics.   Also describes facilities
of local business libraries and information centers.

State: Topical Guides

U. S. Business and Defense Services Administration.   Measuring
Markets;   A Guide to the Use of Federal and State Data.
Washington, D. C.:   Government Printing Office, 1966. v,
94 p. illus.   (FA 12)

Concise explanation of federal data and its application to the
market analysis of consumer and industrial goods.   Illustrated

with eight case histories. Main feature is a tabulation of
federal publications on population, income, employment and
sales showing for each: type of data, geographic coverage,
frequency of data and of publication, name of issuing agency.
Similar information is given for state sources of population,
employment, sales and tax collection statistics.

U. S. Bureau of Labor Statistics. Major BLS Programs. (see
EF 24)

---Guide to State Employment Statistics: Employment, Hours
and Earnings. Washington, D. C.: Bureau of Labor Statistics, 1960.
ii, 71 p.   (FA 13)
     The tables in this guide list for each state the 1957 SIC in-
     dustry titles and codes for which employment, hours, and
     earnings statistics are available from the cooperating state
     agencies.

U. S. Bureau of the Census. Inventory of State and Local
Agencies Preparing Population Estimates; Survey of
1965. (Current population reports: Population estimates, P-25, no.
328). Washington, D. C. Bureau of the Census, March 8, 1966. 23
p.   (FA 14)
     Revised at irregular intervals. Sources and types of current
     population estimates and forecasts available are listed by
     regional, state, county and city agency. Besides name and
     address of agency, reports on the method or type of data,
     source and frequency of data.

---State Reports on State and Local Government Finances.
(Census of Governments, 1962, vol. 6, no. 3). Washington, D. C.:
Government Printing Office, 1964. 55 p.   (FA 15)
     Provides a summary descriptive listing, by states, of peri-
     odic state government publications that contain statistics on
     state and local government finances.

U. S. Bureau of the Census. Small-Area Data Activities.
Washington, D. C.: Bureau of the Census . Irregular.   (FB 1)
    Newsletter intended to keep both users and producers of small-
    area data informed on the needs, programs, publications of
    interest to them.   Articles are directed toward state and
    local officials, planning personnel, and leaders in the civic,
    educational, and business sectors.

U. S. Congress. Joint Economic Committee.   A Directory of
Urban Research Centers ...   Washington, D. C.: Government
Printing Office, 1967. x, 77 p.   (FB 2)
    Includes university-sponsored centers and nonprofit research
    institutes with studies ranging from broad aspects of urban
    planning to special projects on land-use, water resources,
    waste disposal, transportation design.   Descriptions cover
    current and past projects, publications, names of profession-
    al staff and their specialties.   State index.

U. S. Business and Defense Services Administration. Measuring
Metropolitan Markets;   A Guide to the Use of U. S.
Government Data.   Washington, D. C.: Government Printing
Office, 1963. v, 48 p. maps, tables.   (FB 3)
    Using Rochester, N. Y. , as an example, describes and
    illustrates the application in market analysis of the data
    published by federal agencies relating to standard metro-
    politan statistical areas.

THE MUNICIPAL Year Book. Chicago: International City Managers-
Association.   Annual.   (FB 4)
    Text and tables summarize trends and statistics compiled by
    the Bureau of the Census, association and local officials.
    Data are presented for cities grouped by population size.
    Sources of the data are cited at the end of each chapter In-
    cludes a directory of city managers, officials in cities over

10,000 , and mayors and city clerks in cities of 5,000 to
10,000 population.

WORLD Wide Chamber of Commerce Directory. (see FA 4)

FEDERAL Reserve Bank of Philadelphia. Federal Reserve
Bank Reviews, Selected Subjects ... (see EI 12)

U. S. Bureau of the Census. Directory of Federal Statistics for Local Areas; A Guide to Sources, 1966. Washington, D. C.: Government Printing Office, 1966. 162 p.   (FB 5)
  Finding guide to published statistics for units below the state
  level.   Covers latest data available, including one-time programs, provided they are at least as recent as 1960. Subject
  and tabular detail arranged topically for population and its
  characteristics; health and vital statistics; climate and
  physical environment; construction and housing; labor and
  employment; prices; banking and finance; commerce and
  trade; manufacturing; transportation and communication;
  agriculture and fisheries; mining and mineral products;
  governments; law enforcement; civil defense. Subject index.

---CENSUS Bureau Programs and Publications: Area and Subject
   Guide ... (see F 2)
   INDEX to Reports by Geographic Areas. In U. S. Bureau of the
   Census. Bureau of the Census Catalog. (see OD 6)

Local: Single-Area Guides

New York City
NEW YORK (City) Inter-Agency Research Council. Research Re-
porter. New York: Inter-Agency Research Council. Semiannual.
                                                              (FB 6)
  A communication organ containing an annotated listing of re-
  search projects initiated or completed by agencies of the
  City of New York. Notable, too, is the work of the Inter-

Agency Research Council which is composed of representatives from municipal agencies engaged in research activities or requiring the results of such activities as part of their work programs. Among the aims of the Council are: to serve as a clearing house for the exchange of information, ideas and proposed projects; to reduce, through interchange of information, duplication of effort in research activities; to inform members of the Council of new research techniques, applications, and developments; to foster joint research efforts by city agencies with other levels of government, academic institutions, foundations, and private industry.

NEW YORK Regional Statistical Center.   (FB 7)

In January 1966, the New York Area Chapter of the American Statistical Association established the New York Regional Statistical Center encompassing the 22-county area in the states of New York, New Jersey and Connecticut. In an effort to encourage the development of more adequate statistics within this region, the Center planned to initiate an inventory of statistical generating sources and data resources within the region; to publish a regional statistical bulletin, papers on regional data problems, reports on new and revised data; to identify statistical gaps for cooperative effort and to obtain technical and financial support for these activities. An antecedent project resulted in the publication listed below.

A GUIDE to Sources of Social and Economic Statistics for the New York Metropolitan Area, prel. ed. , October 1963. New York: Columbia University Bureau of Applied Social Research [1963] 36 p.
(FB 8)

Compiled with the cooperation of the New York Area Chapter of the American Statistical Association. Names and addresses of organizations and individuals producing or familiar with the availability of local data are listed for the three cities, 22 counties, and three states followed by multi-area sources and census tract personnel familiar with U. S. census data.

U. S. Bureau of Labor Statistics. Major BLS Programs ...
(see EF 24)

---Guide to Area Employment Statistics: Employment, Hours and
Earnings, Area Definitions. Washington, D. C.: Bureau of Labor
Statistics, 1960. iii, 227 p.   (FB 9)
    For each metropolitan area lists, by new and old SIC code,
    those nonagricultural industries for which employment, hours
    and earnings data are available from state agencies.

U. S. Bureau of the Census. Inventory of State and Local
Agencies Preparing Population Estimates ... (see FA 14)

U. S. Business and Defense Services Administration. Personal
Income, a Key to Small-Area Market Analysis.   Washington, D. C.: Government Printing Office, 1961. iv, 60 p.   (FB 10)
    Comprehensive survey of federal, local noncommercial and
    commercial sources of personal income data existing and
    planned at time of publication.   Arranged by state with
    emphasis on county breakdowns.   Includes samples and dis-
    cusses uses for such data.

Notes

1. "A Vast New Storehouse of Transportation and Marketing Data,"
   by Henry K. Evans. Journal of Marketing.   Jan. 1966,
   p. 33-40.

UNIVERSITY
PROGRAMS

One of the significant trends in business is the adoption of academic contributions by management and research. With the advent of the computer further breakthroughs in economics, communications and the allied social sciences hold promise of furnishing new techniques and sophisticated data tools. Substantial bases for such advances have been and will continue to be laid within the framework of university programs.

Moreover, as in other areas, institutions of higher learning are assuming an increasingly prominent and diversified role in the field of marketing. Faculty and students in recent years have undertaken both basic and applied research projects of interest to the business community. Staff members continue to contribute widely as consultants to industry and government. Pure research, on the institutional and individual professional level, continues to produce new methods and refinements of value to economic and market analysis.

PRIVATE GRANT PROJECTS

Notable, too, is the growing amount of research conducted under private grant by universities and their affiliated units. Organizations such as the Institute of Life Insurance, Carnegie Corp., Ford Foundation have financed probes of family decision-making, factors which influence consumer economic behavior, buying habits of housewives and industrial companies. A National Aeronautics and Space Administration grant sponsored the Wharton School's input-output analysis of Greater Philadelphia's economy. This is a detailed study which shows the buying and selling relationships of some 490 industrial sectors.

Thus, applied research, similarly spurred by contracts from

government, trade associations, foundations and business firms, has also been increasing in volume and variety. Such projects are usually undertaken by university research centers in addition to their own staff studies and continuing programs. Consequently, it is well to bear in mind that reports produced under contract are often available only from the sponsoring body. Some are commercially published; others are restricted to intramural use. Publications resulting from a university's own project or continuing program are usually distributed by the institution itself.

CONTINUING PROGRAMS AND PUBLICATIONS

Although much university research stems from individual effort, continuing projects reflect cooperative work on a departmental or institutional level.

Such, for example, have been the operating results studies issued regularly.

DEPARTMENTAL Merchandising Results in Small Department Stores. Ann Arbor, Mich.: University of Michigan Graduate School of Business Administration. Biennial.

OPERATING Results of Food Chains. Ithaca, N. Y.: Cornell University, New York State College of Agriculture. Annual.

OPERATING Results of Self-Service Discount Department Stores. Ithaca, N. Y.: Cornell University. Annual.

Among the continuing research projects of interest to business the following can be cited:

The Wharton School capacity utilization data, a series on the utilization rate of industrial capacity.

Harvard Economic Research Project input-output studies with emphasis on the structure of the economy.

University of Michigan econometric model of the United States economy
used to forecast the economic outlook.

INSTITUTES

Another source of information is the research centers and institutes supported by universities and colleges. As the advances of
science and technology exert an increasing influence on the products
of industry, the work and resources of these units become of greater
importance in research. Although most numerous in agriculture,
engineering, physics and similar fields, there are some concerned
directly with mass communications and marketing. Well known, for
example, for its annual survey of consumer finances is the Institute
of Social Research at the University of Michigan.

THESES AND DISSERTATIONS

Graduate theses and dissertations in business, economics and
marketing and in the allied sciences offer a growing volume of information. Yet, they are often neglected because their content and
availability are probably the least publicized of any source among
practitioners.

BUREAUS OF BUSINESS RESEARCH

More familiar are the activities of university bureaus of business research. For researchers, faced with specific geographic or
product marketing problems, they provide a variety of applicable
facts. Quantitatively, the largest body of information concerns local
and regional business and economic conditions and presents analyses
of previously published and original data.

Graduate business schools and other university units, too,
issue a number of useful publications on economics and marketing
topics of more universal scope.

Available data from both these sources, therefore, fall into
two general categories: regional and "national."

Regional data are issued in periodicals, statistical compendia,
industrial directories, area studies and industry reports.

Although the preponderance of "national" studies are critical analyses or evaluative treatments of various industries and phases of business, a certain amount of primary data not available elsewhere is presented either on a continuing basis or in single reports.

Periodical publications of business schools, research bureaus and other university divisions consist of journals, bulletins, newsletters. These carry summaries of the region's business and economic conditions, timely articles on economic developments, analyses of principal industries -- all documented with local statistics. From time to time faculty and research bureau studies are reported in this press.

The following college and university periodicals reflect state and regional interests. Others, more management or single-industry oriented, have been omitted since they more closely resemble business periodicals and are treated as such in periodical indexes and directories.

Alabama
ALABAMA Business. University, Ala.: University of Alabama Bureau of Business Research. Monthly.   (G 1)

ALABAMA Retail Trade. University, Ala.: University of Alabama Bureau of Business Research. Monthly.   (G 2)

Arizona
ARIZONA Business Bulletin. Tempe, Ariz.: Arizona State University Bureau of Business Research and Services. 10/yr.   (G 3)

ARIZONA Review. Tucson, Ariz.: University of Arizona Division of Economic and Business Research. Monthly.   (G 4)

PLANNING Urban Arizona. Tucson, Ariz.: University of Arizona Division of Economic and Business Research. Bimonthly.   (G 5)

Arkansas
ARKANSAS Business Bulletin. Fayetteville, Ark.: University of

Arkansas Bureau of Business and Economic Research. Quarterly.

(G 6)

ARKANSAS Economist. Little Rock, Ark.: University of Arkansas
Industrial Research and Extension Center. Irregular.   (G 7)

California

BUSINESS Inquiry. San Diego, Calif.: San Diego State College Bureau of Business and Economic Research. Semiannual.   (G 8)

FRESNO Facts and Trends. Fresno, Calif.: Fresno State College
Bureau of Business Research and Service. Monthly.   (G 9)

Colorado

COLORADO Business Review. Boulder, Colo.: University of
Colorado Bureau of Business Research Division, Graduate School
of Business Administration. Monthly.   (G 10)

Florida

BUILDING-Permit Activity in Florida. Gainesville, Fla.: University
of Florida Bureau of Economic and Business Research. Monthly.

(G 11)

BUSINESS and Economic Dimensions. Gainesville, Fla.: University
of Florida Bureau of Economic and Business Research. Monthly.

(G 12)

ECONOMIC Leaflets. Gainesville, Fla.: University of Florida Bureau of Economic and Business Research. Monthly.   (G 13)

Georgia

ATLANTA Economic Review. Atlanta, Ga.: Georgia State College
School of Business Administration, Bureau of Business and Economic
Research. Monthly.   (G 14)

GEORGIA Business. Athens, Ga.: University of Georgia Bureau of

Business and Economic Research. Monthly.   (G 15)

Illinois

ILLINOIS Business Review. Urbana, Ill.: University of Illinois Bureau of Economic and Business Research. Monthly.   (G 16)

QUARTERLY Review of Economics and Business. Urbana, Ill.: University of Illinois Bureau of Economicaand Business Research. Quarterly.   (G 17)

BUSINESS Perspectives. Carbondale, Ill.: Southern Illinois University Business Research Bureau. Monthly.   (G 18)

Indiana

INDIANA Business Review. Bloomington, Ind.: Indiana University Bureau of Business Research. Monthly.   (G 19)

Iowa

IOWA Business Digest. Iowa City, Iowa: University of Iowa Bureau of Business and Economic Research. 11/yr.   (G 20)

Kansas

KANSAS Business Review. Lawrence, Kans.: University of Kansas Center for Regional Studies. Monthly.   (G 21)

Kentucky

RESEARCH Briefs. Lexington, Ky.: University of Kentucky Bureau of Business Research. Irregular.   (G 22)

Louisiana

CONSUMER Price Index. Baton Rouge, La.: Louisiana State University Division of Research. Quarterly.   (G 23)

LOUISIANA Business Review. Baton Rouge, La.: Louisiana State University Division of Research. Monthly.   (G 24)

Massachusetts

BUSINESS Topics. Boston, Mass.: Northeastern University Bureau
of Business and Economic Research. Bimonthly.   (G 25)

BENTLEY Economics and Business Review. Boston, Mass.: Bentley College Bureau of Business and Economic Research. Quarterly.
(G 26)

Michigan

MICHIGAN Business Review. Ann Arbor, Mich.: University of
Michigan Bureau of Business Research. 5/yr.   (G 27)

MSU Business Topics. East Lansing, Mich.: Michigan State University Bureau of Business and Economic Research. Quarterly.
(G 28)

MICHIGAN Economic Record. East Lansing, Mich.: Michigan State
University Bureau of Business and Economic Research. Monthly.
(G 29)

Mississippi

MISSISSIPPI Business Review. State College, Miss.: Mississippi
State University Bureau of Business and Economic Research. Monthly.   (G 30)

MISSISSIPPI Business. University, Miss.: University of Mississippi
Bureau of Business and Economic Research. Bimonthly.   (G 31)

Missouri

BUSINESS and Government Review. Columbia, Mo.: University of
Missouri School of Business and Public Administration Research
Center. Bimonthly.   (G 32)

Montana

MONTANA Business Quarterly. Missoula, Mont.: University of
Montana School of Business Administration, Bureau of Business and

Economic Research. Quarterly.   (G 33)

Nebraska

BUSINESS in Nebraska. Lincoln, Neb.: University of Nebraska
Bureau of Business Research. Monthly.   (G 34)

Nevada

NEVADA Business Review. Reno, Nev.: University of Nevada Bureau of Business and Economic Research. Monthly.   (G 35)

New Jersey

NEW JERSEY Economic Indicators. New Brunswick, N. J.: Rutgers
The State University Graduate School, Bureau of Economic Research.
Monthly.   (G 36)

New Mexico

ALBUQUERQUE Food Price Bulletin. Albuquerque, N. M.: University of New Mexico Bureau of Business Research. Quarterly.
                                                                    (G 37)

NEW MEXICO Business. Albuquerque, N. M.: University of New
Mexico Bureau of Business Research. Monthly.   (G 38)

Ohio

BULLETIN of Business Research. Columbus, Ohio: Ohio State
University Bureau of Business Research. Monthly.   (G 39)

MIAMI Business Review. Oxford, Ohio: Miami University School
of Business Administration, Bureau of Business Research. 5/yr.
                                                                    (G 40)

Oklahoma

OKLAHOMA Business Bulletin. Norman, Okla.: University of
Oklahoma Bureau of Business Research. Monthly.   (G 41)

GASOLINE Marketed in Oklahoma. Norman, Okla.: University of

OKLAHOMA Bureau of Business Research.   Monthly.   (G 42)

OKLAHOMA Industrialization. Norman, Okla.: University of Oklahoma Bureau of Business Research. Quarterly.   (G 43)

Oregon
OREGON Business Review. Eugene, Ore.: University of Oregon Bureau of Business and Economic Research. Monthly.   (G 44)

Pennsylvania
ECONOMIC and Business Bulletin. Philadelphia, Pa.: Temple University Bureau of Economic and Business Research. Quarterly.

(G 45)

PENNSYLVANIA Business Survey. University Park, Pa.: Pennsylvania State University Center for Research of the College of Business Administration.   Monthly.   (G 46)

PITTSBURGH Business Review. Pittsburgh, Pa.: University of Pittsburgh Bureau of Business Research. Monthly.   (G 47)

SUMMARY of Business Conditions in the Pittsburgh District. Pittsburgh, Pa.: University of Pittsburgh Bureau of Business Research. Weekly.   (G 48)

South Carolina
BUSINESS and Economic Review. Columbia, S. C.: University of South Carolina Bureau of Business and Economic Research. Monthly.

(G 49)

SOUTH CAROLINA Indicators. Columbia, S. C.: University of South Carolina Bureau of Business and Economic Research. Monthly(G 50)

South Dakota
SOUTH DAKOTA Business Review. Vermillion, S. D.: State University of South Dakota Business Research Bureau. Quarterly. (G 51)

Tennessee

TENNESSEE Survey of Business. Knoxville, Tenn.: University of
Tennessee College of Business Administration, Bureau of Business
and Economic Research. Monthly.   (G 52)

MEMPHIS State Business Review. Memphis, Tenn.: Memphis State
University Bureau of Business and Economic Research. Bimonthly.

(G 53)

Texas

BUILDING Construction in Texas. Austin, Tex.: University of Texas
Bureau of Business Research. Monthly.   (G 54)

THE Business Review. Houston, Tex.: University of Houston Center
for Research in Business and Economics. Quarterly.   (G 55)

INDEX of Credit Reporting.   Austin, Tex.: University of Texas
Bureau of Business Research.   Monthly.   (G 56)

TEXAS Business Review. Austin,Tex.: University of Texas Bureau
of Business Research. Monthly.   (G 57)

TEXAS Retail Trade. Austin, Tex.: University of Texas Bureau of
Business Research. Monthly.   (G 58)

TEXAS Industrial Expansion. Austin, Tex.: University of Texas
Bureau of Business Research. Monthly.   (G 59)

Utah

UTAH Construction Report. Salt Lake City, Utah: University of
Utah Bureau of Economic and Business Research. Monthly.   (G 60)

UTAH Economic and Business Review. Salt Lake City, Utah: University of Utah Bureau of Economic and Business Research. Monthly.   (G 61)

Washington

UNIVERSITY of Washington Business Review. Seattle, Wash.: University of Washington Graduate School of Business Administration.
Bimonthly.   (G 62)

Wyoming

WYOMING Trade Winds. Laramie, Wyo.: University of Wyoming
College of Commerce and Industry, Division of Business and Economic Research. Quarterly.   (G 63)

Statistical compendia for the home state are issued by a number of university research bureaus. Although varying in frequency and scope they are, however, useful sources of population, industry, service, trade, financial and other economic data for the state, its counties and metropolitan areas. A list of current editions appears in the Appendix.

Industrial directories, compiled by bureaus of business research, represent a unique marketing tool. and as such, are treated in greater detail in a subsequent chapter on directories.

Area studies cover economic analyses and projections of state resources and potentials; studies of personal income, retail sales, price trends; marketing analyses of consumer goods sold within the state or of the state's commodities produced for distribution elsewhere.

Industry reports highlight the status and development of those industries important to the area's economic growth. Information ranges from agricultural outlook reports to statistical analyses of local business and surveys of such factors as tourist trade.

Many topics relating to various aspects of the national economy, business management and marketing are treated in university periodicals and studies.

Some magazines, like the HARVARD BUSINESS REVIEW, Indiana University's BUSINESS HORIZONS, and Chicago University's JOURNAL OF BUSINESS, offer a mixture of academic and executive thinking on matters of concern to marketing managements; others are more specialized in their approach.

GUIDES TO PROJECTS AND PUBLICATIONS

Guides to University Research

RESEARCH Centers Directory. 2d ed. Detroit: Gale Research
Co. Triennial.   (GA 1)

> University-related and independent nonprofit research units
> are classified according to 16 broad categories. Descriptive
> information includes the activities of the research body, its
> special programs, serial publications, library facilities,
> directors' names. Indexes: sponsoring institutions, centers
> alphabetically, personal names, centers by subject. Supple-
> mented by the following publication.
> NEW Research Centers. .Detroit: Gale Research Co.
> Quarterly interedition service cumulatively indexed.

U. S. Congress. Joint Economic Committee. A Directory of
Urban Research Centers ... (see FB 2)

U. S. Small Business Administration. A Survey of University
Business and Economic Research Projects, 1959-1963; Prepared
by ... Bureau of Business Research, The University of Texas ...
Washington, D. C.: Government Printing Office, 1963, xiii. 690 p.
                                                                 (GA 2)

> Annotated listing of 3,623 faculty and doctoral research pro-
> jects reported by 284 colleges and universities as completed
> or in progress. Arranged in 27 chapters by major subject
> field. Author and subject indexes. Preceded by a 1957-61
> edition published in 1961.

U. S. National Science Foundation. Current Projects on Economic
and Social Implications of Science and Technology. (see EI 61)

Guides to Theses and Dissertations: Comprehensive

DISSERTATION Abstracts. Ann Arbor, Mich.: University Microfilms Library Services, Xerox Corp. Monthly.   (GB 1)

600-word authors' summaries of doctoral dissertations submitted by graduate students to the publisher for publication.
Arrangement is by broad subject and institution. Author and
specific subject index in each issue. Complete text available
from publisher in microfilm or Xerographic form.

AMERICAN Doctoral Dissertations. Ann Arbor, Mich.: University
Microfilms Library Services, Xerox Corp. Annual.   (GB 2)
Index to all doctoral dissertations accepted by American and
Canadian institutions of higher learning, whether published by
University Microfilms or not.

DATRIX. Ann Arbor, Mich.: University Microfilms Library Services, Xerox Corp.   (GB 3)
Computer search service inaugurated in July 1967. Input consists of the majority of all doctoral dissertations written in
over 160 American and Canadian universities since 1938 and
updated monthly. Terms selected by the inquirer from supplied key word lists provide a topical bibliography, including
title, author, university, degree, publication date, reference
to abstract in Dissertation Abstracts and order information for microfilm or hard copy.

Guides to Theses and Dissertations: Topical - Marketing

New York University. Graduate School of Business Administration.
Bibliography of Graduate Theses in the Field of
MARKETING Written at U. S. Colleges and Universities,
1950-1957. New York: New York University [1957] 92 p.   (GB 4)
Compiled for the President's Conference on Technical and
Distribution Research for the Benefit of Small Business. Listings were supplied in answer to a questionnaire by about half
of the higher institutions offering organized courses in business administration. Entries are grouped by author and title
under the name of institution and coded for main topic.
Presentation of citations is uneven ranging from complete

bibliographic information and annotations to brief titles without dates.

An approximately biennial compilation of doctoral dissertations and masters' theses previously published in the JOURNAL OF
MARKETING has been suspended.   (GB 5)

Guides to Theses and Dissertations: Topical   - Other

DOCTORAL Dissertations Accepted. Journal of Business. Chicago:
University of Chicago Press. Annual feature in January issue.

(GB 6)

Two-to-three page listing arranged by broad subject. Each
title is identified by author and university where completed.

LIST of Doctoral Dissertations in Political Economy in American
Universities and Colleges. American Economic Review. Evanston, Ill.: Northwestern University. Annual feature of September
issue.   (GB 7)

Doctoral degrees conferred, with abstracts of many of the dissertations, are listed by broad subject. Information given:
author, title, institution and year of completion.

JOURNALISM Abstracts. Chapel Hill, N. C.: University of North
Carolina School of Journalism. Annual.   (GB 8)

Published under the auspices of the Association for Education
in Journalism. Abstracts of theses in journalism, and mass
communications supplied by the degree candidates are arranged alphabetically by name of writer in two sections:
1) PhD dissertations; 2) MA and MS theses. Many cover
print and air media, audience analyses, advertising. Author
and subject indexes.

Guides to Business Bureaus

RESEARCH Centers Directory. (see GA 1)

ASSOCIATED University Bureaus of Business and Economic Research.
Membership Directory. Columbia, S. C.: University of South
Carolina Bureau of Business Research.   Annual.   (GC 1)

> Arranged by state. Gives: address and telephone number,
> director and personnel, periodicals published.

---Bibliography of ... Publications of University Bureaus of
Business and Economic Research. Eugene, Ore.: University of
Oregon Bureau of Business and Economic Research. Annual. (GC 2)

> Supplements its: INDEX OF PUBLICATIONS ... 1950-1956.
> Arranged in three sections: publications by institutions; sub-
> ject index; author index.

RESEARCH
INSTITUTIONS

Nonprofit research organizations, whose main purpose is to explore and disseminate basic knowledge, function in many subject and industry areas.

In marketing such institutions are comparatively new.

The Advertising Research Foundation is supported by advertising media, advertising agencies and advertisers. Its primary purpose is the promotion of scientific practices and the study and enhancement of advertising and marketing effectiveness through objective research. Specifically, it guides the development and application of new and existing techniques in the conduct of research projects. Although not directly engaged in market research problems, its Journal of Advertising Research touches on marketing data and its activities are of concern to all marketers interested in the productive use of advertising. (H 1)

Similarly, the Marketing Communications Research Center (formerly the Industrial Advertising Research Institute), created under the sponsorship of the Association of Industrial Advertisers, works toward increasing the effectiveness of industrial advertising and marketing. Its expanded activities are planned "to develop complete marketing communications function." Research studies issued have covered many phases of industrial advertising and marketing: characteristics of effective industrial catalogs, direct mail, exhibits; advertising budgets, inquiries, readership; motives in industrial buying; a series of reports on employment by job categories in various industries as defined by Standard Industrial Classification codes. (H 2)

The Marketing Science Institute was established in 1962 through the joint efforts of 29 of the nation's major companies. Its announced objective is "to develop a more definitive science of marketing and stimulate the application of science in marketing." Its research program covers a number of areas: significant changes in marketing institutions and functions since the end of World War II; identification of marketing management problems susceptible to scientific solution; international marketing developments; the development of marketing theory; the study and advancement of marketing education; the development of methods and techniques for testing theoretical structures in marketing. Books and reports resulting from this program have covered such topics as industrial buying, advertising measurement, personal selling, private brand practices, meaning and sources of marketing theory, marketing education in the United States.   (H 3)

Similar organizations exist in allied fields. Cited here are a number of institutions whose continuing programs in business and economics are of general interest to marketers.

The National Bureau of Economic Research, Inc. engages in objective and impartial determination and interpretation of important economic facts. It is well known for its pioneer work in the study of business cycles and for its research programs in economic growth; national income, consumption and capital formation; financial institutions and processes; industrial commodity prices; international economic relations, including price competitiveness; the accuracy and techniques of short term economic forecasts.   (H 4)

Two of its recent publications received wide notice:

INDICATORS of Business Expansions and Contractions, by Geoffrey H. Moore and Julius Shiskin. (National Bureau of Economic Research Occasional paper 103). New York: Columbia University Press, 1967. 127 p.   (H 4a)

Presents the Bureau's revised list of key business cycle

indicators.   These measures of business activity, reported
regularly in Business Conditions Digest (see B 8),
are widely used in predicting economic recessions and re-
coveries.   Included for the first time is a new scoring system
for evaluating the predictive worth of each measure.

SOURCE Book of Statistics Relating to Construction, by Robert E.
Lipsey and Doris Preston. New York: Columbia University Press,
1966.   307 p.   (H 4b)
   A compilation of the principal monthly, quarterly and annual
   time series on expenditures, contracts, permits, starts and
   construction materials. Coverage is from earliest available
   year through 1963.

   The National Industrial Conference Board conducts research
in economics, business management and human relations in industry.
Its reports cover business trends, sales and marketing, corporate
finance, organization planning and other areas of management operation, environment and responsibility.   As additional services to its
membership the Board organizes conferences and seminars on
economic and management problems and provides special assistance
through its information service and research staff.   (H 5)

   A large proportion of its work is published in a number of
continuing publications and in a number of special reports.   Some of
particular interest are:

CONFERENCE Board Record.   Monthly.   (H 5a)
   Reports the Board's own research as well as analyses of developments in industry, trade, commerce and government.

EXPERIENCES In Marketing Management. Irregular.   (H 5b)
   Executive views and experiences, presented at the Board's
   conferences and seminars, on a variety of questions and solutions arising in marketing management.

STUDIES In Business Economics. Irregular.   (H 5c)
    Comprehensive reports on economic factors affecting sales
    and profits cover consumer economics, business conditions,
    antitrust data and case material, fiscal and monetary research,
    international operations. Included in this series is an annual
    business outlook report and economic analyses of mergers and
    acquisitions.

STUDIES In Business Policy. Irregular.   (H 5d)
    Analyses of current practices, techniques and trends in busi-
    ness management. Reports have covered such topics as new
    product introduction by industrial marketers, sales analysis
    and forecasting, selecting distributors, measuring advertising
    results, cost reduction programs.

STUDIES In Personnel Policy. Irregular.   (H 5e)
    Reports on corporate organization planning, management de-
    velopment, compensation and benefits, communication, motiva-
    tion and employment, collective bargaining.

TECHNICAL Papers. Irregular.   (H 5f)
    Special reports on business economics. Of particular inter-
    est are no. 13 "Diffusion Indexes" and no. 17 "Discretionary
    Income" both of which are supplemented quarterly in the Con-
    ference Board Record.

ECONOMIC Almanac ... (see B 9)

CHARTBOOK of Weekly Business Indicators. Annual.   (H 5g)
    Graphic presentation of 23 leading business indicators. Week-
    ly figures are published in the Board's Weekly Desk Sheet.

CHARTBOOK of Current Business Trends. Annual.   (H 5h)
    Graphic presentation of important statistics on all aspects of
    the national economy. Updated by the monthly release,
    Selected Business Indicators.

MERGERS and Acquisitions.   Monthly.   (H 5i)
     Lists acquiring companies with their industry or product and
     total assets.

     In addition, the Board issues special reports and analyses.
Recent examples are its Expenditure Patterns of the
American Family (1965) and Market Profiles of Consum-
er Products (1967) which were based on the new Bureau of Labor
Statistics survey of consumer expenditures.   (H 5j)

     The American Management Association is a nonprofit educa-
tional organization concerned with the improvement of management
skills and techniques. Its program includes courses, conferences,
seminars, a research and information service. Its publications are
varied: books authored and edited by staff members as well as by
outside specialists; periodicals devoted to general management
topics, personnel relations, supervisory management; reports and
studies, drawn from conference activities or based on original research, on developments, policies and practices in such areas as
executive skills and compensation; organization; planning; administration; marketing; packaging; manpower planning, training, and
development; production management; etc.   (H 6)

     Stanford Research Institute focuses its activity on the solu-
tion of particular problems for industry, government and foundations, as well as on projects of a basic nature. Included within its
scope are research programs in the physical and life sciences,
economics and management sciences, and engineering. Its projects
cover specific industries, size and growth rate of markets, production and distribution, regional economies. Special emphasis is
placed on those areas which involve the application or impact of
developing technology. Clients are serviced through an information
center, consultation staff, seminars, annual conferences and a number of publications and services.   (H 7)

SRI Journal.   Quarterly.   (H 7a)

Devoted to economic and technical developments reflecting the Institute's work.

LONG Range Planning Service. Irregular.   (H 7b)
Series of reports based on a research program which evaluates the impact of technological and economic changes on companies' long range opportunities. Special attention is given to the effect of developments in scientific research, engineering and marketing on long term growth of products and services.

CHEMICAL Economics Handbook. Looseleaf.   (H 7c)
Provides comprehensive reports on chemicals and data sheets which, in graphic form, present basic statistics on economic indicators, major industries, chemical and allied industries, organic and inorganic chemicals, chemical product groups. Renewed over a period of two years by bimonthly scheduled replacement pages and supplemented by the bimonthly Manual of Current Indicators which contains monthly, quarterly and preliminary annual data indicating short term and newly developing trends. The Chemical Economics Newsletter, issued with the Handbook installments, highlights current research.

DIRECTORY of Chemical Producers. Looseleaf, updated quarterly.
                                                          (H 7d)
PRODUCTS section shows for each chemical its producing companies, plant locations, capacities, processes.
COMPANIES section shows for each producer, his subsidiaries and divisions, plants, and products made at each location.
REGIONS section is a listing of plants in a state-city arrangement with identification as to owning company and products made.
NEW Plants and Expansions volume lists plants which are planned, under construction, or just going on stream. Arrangement also permits access to this information by product,

by company and geographically.

The National Planning Association draws upon leaders in
labor, agriculture, business and the professions in assessing problems and mapping out goals in every field of national endeavor. It
is one of a group of private and government agencies cooperating
on the Interindustry Growth Project. Among its publications are
the monthly magazine Looking Ahead, a series of Planning
Pamphlets, case studies, staff and special committee reports on
economic growth, agriculture, various industries, and foreign conditions affecting American enterprise. Long established in the field
of economic projections, the Association also issues two subscription services to provide guidance to business management, labor and
government. The National Economic Projection Series includes detailed analyses of national output, government expenditures,
business investment, international trade, population, employment
and household incomes. The Regional Economic Projection
Series provides similar data for states and metropolitan areas.

(H 8)

The Institute for Interindustry Data, Inc. was established in
1967 as a nonprofit organization "to promote research and scientific
activities in input-output analysis and other econometric techniques
along sound and professional lines; to facilitate cooperation among
private industry, governmental bodies, educational institutions, research organizations, in connection with input-output projects; to
establish standards of data quality, classification and collection; to
facilitate the access to and the common use of input-output data that
are in the public domain; to disseminate, through publications and
meetings, information concerning input-output analysis and such other
econometric techniques as may be useful in conjunction with it."

Its program includes: setting up a data pool of all input-output data that is in the public domain, together with information on
proprietary or confidential studies; regularly scheduled seminars on
input-output applications; establishing contact with all government
agencies and private organizations engaged in input-output programs;

the provision, through the medium of its Newsletter, of a clearinghouse for all news on input-output studies and publications. (H 9)

Resources for the Future, Inc., established and financed by
the Ford Foundation, is a nonprofit corporation for research and
education in the development and use of natural resources. Part of
its work is carried out by its resident staff, part supported by grants
to universities and other nonprofit organizations. Among its works
are studies of trends and requirements, together with long range
projections, for water and land use; mineral, forest and other resources; outdoor recreation. A recent grant was made to Washington University to support its information services on urban economics.
(H 10)

The Twentieth Century Fund, like Resources for the Future,
is a nonprofit educational organization. Its research and publications are directed toward the examination of economic and social
problems. Its classic economic survey, "America's Needs and
Resources," has been followed by similar volumes on Canada and
Europe. Other studies have analyzed work and leisure in our industrial society, the rise and implications of urbanization, the
economic problems of the performing arts.   (H 11)

PROFESSIONAL
AND
TRADE ASSOCIATIONS

PROFESSIONAL SOCIETIES

Professional associations exist in many fields of business, science and technology to promote and promulgate scientific and fundamental advances in their respective disciplines. Through their meetings and publications researchers can keep abreast of current developments and find solutions to problems which can come only from an interchange of ideas.

MARKETING: GENERAL

The American Marketing Association is the leading professional organization in its field. Its some 15,000 members are drawn from both business and educational spheres. Its major publications are the Journal of Marketing and the Journal of Marketing Research. It also issues monographs and bibliographies; fosters research; promulgates standards for professional and ethical conduct; sponsors seminars, conferences and student marketing clubs. These activities are carried out both at the national and local chapter levels. (I 1)

The National Association of Market Developers includes in its membership individuals who are engaged in or interested in advertising and selling to the Negro market. (I 2)

The Sales and Marketing Executives- International, with affiliated clubs in 29 countries, provides its members with a marketing information center; a monthly journal, Sales Marketing Today; educational, research, publication, conference, and seminar

192

programs. Although dedicated primarily to the advancement of selling and sales management, a large part of its activity encompasses
marketing management, techniques and methods.   (I 3)

The National Accounts Marketing Association was established
in 1964 by a group of national account managers, a new type of
sales specialist. Its purpose is to provide, through meetings and
discussions, a forum for an exchange of ideas and techniques involved in national account selling.   (I 4)

The Marketing Research Trade Association membership represents field research and executive personnel concerned with interviewing and similar aspects of survey work.   (I 5)

The Special Libraries Association is an international organization of professional librarians and information experts concerned
with the organization, management and utilization of information resources in specialized subject areas for a specialized clientele.
Organized originally to serve the professional needs of librarians
employed by business and industry, the membership now includes a
sizeable representation from government agencies and other public
and private nonprofit institutions. Among its 25 subject interest
divisions and sections are Advertising and Marketing, Business and
Finance, Chemistry, Insurance, Publishing. It sponsors conferences
and seminars both on the science of information control and on the
art of information retrieval. Publications include a monthly journal,
bibliographies, manuals, as well as many subject-interest bulletins
and reference handbooks.   (I 6)

MARKETING: INDUSTRY ORIENTED

With the growing acceptance of the marketing concept there
has been a noticeable increase in the number of professional societies concerned with the marketing function in individual industries.
In some cases associations previously devoted to advertising interests have expanded their programs to include the total marketing
concept. Among these industry oriented marketing groups are:

The Chemical Marketing Research Association draws its
members from individuals engaged in marketing and related research
in the chemical and allied industries.   (I 7)

The National Agricultural Advertising and Marketing Association is supported by a membership drawn from advertising agencies,
media and advertisers. Its function is to provide for an exchange of
ideas, to promote standards and to encourage the study of agricultural marketing.   (I 8)

The Automotive Market Research Council announced its in-
corporation in 1966. Founded by market research executives of
leading original equipment and replacement parts manufacturers, its
membership was planned to include about 35 companies. Among its
objectives is the development of the professional abilities of market
research personnel and the improvement of market data and forecasts for its industry.   (I 9)

The Bank Public Relations and Marketing Association, formerly the Financial Public Relations Association, has expanded its program and projects to encompass those of marketing interest. (I 10)

The Savings Institutions Marketing Society of America was
formed in 1965 by a group of representatives from savings and loan
associations to advance a marketing and public relations program
for its segment of the industry.   (I 11)

ALLIED DISCIPLINES

Contributions of professional societies in allied fields bear
significant import for market research and marketing. Special
interest organizations such as the National Association of Accountants, National Association of Purchasing Agents, the American
Chemical Society (and particularly its Division of Chemical Marketing and Economics) maintain research, publication and conference
programs. All are potential sources of general and specific marketing information.

The following list includes those associations upon whose work marketing has drawn most frequently in the past.

American Economic Association members are drawn from a variety of professions.   The association fosters economic discussion; conducts research in current and past conditions; issues the American Economic Review, monographs, and other publications. (IA 1)

American Statistical Association members are active in promoting the theory, methodology and application of statistics in all branches of knowledge. Through special committees, the association acts as an advisor on statistical matters to the government and to industry. In addition to the quarterly Journal (see NA 6) it publishes American Statistician (5/yr.) and Technometrics (quarterly).   (IA 2)

The National Association of Business Economists is a society of practicing business economists.   Its program includes meetings, seminars and the journal, Business Economics (3/yr.).
                                                                      (IA 3)

The American Association for Public Opinion Research directs its interest to opinion and communications research, much of it as it applies to marketing and its related activities.   Its official journal is The Public Opinion Quarterly.   (IA 4)

The American Psychological Association is a professional society of psychologists and educators.   Its Consumer Psychology Division numbers industry, advertising agency and media people, as well as consultants and other occupational groups, among its members.   Among the dozen periodicals which it publishes is the bimonthly Journal of Applied Psychology which covers research of interest to marketing.   (IA 5)

American Sociological Association members are professional

sociologists and social scientists. Its bimonthly American Sociological Review (see NA 8) reports on research findings and
methodology of value to market and opinion researchers.   (IA 6)

The Operations Research Society of America is composed of
professionals active in operations research. The Society's official
journal, the bimonthly Operations Research, is a major news
medium for current developments in this field.   (IA 7)

TRADE ASSOCIATIONS

Business competitors operating in the same industry establish
and maintain trade associations 'to research common problems and
to assist the membership with information and advice for the achievement of common goals.

Some trade information is not available for general distribution. Other data, however, are collected and issued for public consumption in association journals, releases, convention proceedings,
statistical reports.

In the allied fields of media and advertising, trade associations have concentrated their efforts in promoting their primary interests.   They research the results of and the methods for more effective advertising and marketing and have broadened these programs
to include data quality, standardization and comparability suitable
to the needs created by computer technology. Occasional market
data publications are supplemented by working collections of market
information acquired and maintained to service client, member and
intramural activities. Some media associations act as clearing
houses for market research conducted and published by their memberships. Organizations servicing the newspaper (Bureau of Advertising) and consumer magazine (Magazine Advertising Bureau)
industries have published guides to member research reports and
services. Other media oriented sources include the Associated
Business Press, Inc. , The Transit Advertising Association, Inc. ,
the Institute of Outdoor Advertising , Radio Advertising Bureau and
Television Advertising Bureau.

Such organizations as the American Association of Advertising Agencies, Association of Industrial Advertisers, and the Association of National Advertisers, most immediately concerned as they are with the advertising function, are seldom represented by marketing publications. These organizations do, however, cover a wide range of topics vital to marketing management in their projects and conference programs.

The informational output of other industry and trade associations is rich and varied. Of particular value to research are several types of statistical compilations which often provide original data unavailable elsewhere.

"Facts and Figures"

These statistical factbooks are by far the largest and most useful category because of their continuity (usually annual) and comprehensive scope.

Historical and current data for each industry and its markets, from raw material utilization to end consumption of product, are culled from official government sources, special surveys, and original compilations submitted by the associations' memberships. Text and tables are, in the main, well documented and clearly dated.

Statistical Releases

Forecasts and current data on production, shipments, stocks, sales, etc., are often issued on a more frequent basis in the form of statistical releases.

Sometimes these supplement a basic factbook; in other instances they constitute the only source of data published by the association.

Many are not available for general distribution. Others are issued for publication in the trade press and are obtainable on a mailing list basis.

Operating Cost Studies

A number of retail and wholesale dealer associations issue annual studies of sales, profits, and operating expenses in their business lines. Detail usually includes inventory turnover, margin data, departmental sales, with groupings by geographic area and annual sales volume.

Special Reports and Analyses

Less prevalent, although issued by some associations on a continuing basis, are consumer surveys and industry reviews and forecasts.

Occasional publications, such as economic outlook studies, marketing maps, and similar materials, are particularly useful since they often represent the culmination of a broad research program necessitated by the previous lack of and need for such information.

Administrative Publications

Newsletters, membership rosters, conference programs and attendance lists are a good source of specialists in the field. Annual reports often include product and industry statistics, reviews and forecasts. Current industry developments are assessed at national conventions the proceedings of which are usually made available for general distribution.

Official association journals do not differ materially from commercially published periodicals and are treated as such in a subsequent chapter.

DIRECTORIES

Conventional bibliographic aids list association publications with the exception of statistical releases. The latter can be located only by direct inquiry to the respective organizations.

The following directory is an excellent guide to all professional and trade associations and to their major publications.

ENCYCLOPEDIA of Associations. Detroit: Gale Research Co. 3 vols. Irregular.   (IB 1)

Vol. 1, National Organizations of the United

States; vol. 2, Geographic-Executive Index; vol. 3,
New Associations. Most comprehensive and detailed
directory in print. Lists all types of commercial associations, including technical and professional societies, commodity exchanges and numerous special interest groups. In
volume 1 entries are arranged in sections, by type of organization, and indexed alphabetically and by key word. Descriptive information includes key personnel, founding date, size,
continuing publications and annual meeting schedule. Volume
2 is a state and city listing of all organizations (name and
address) in volume 1 and an alphabetical name index of chief
executives. Volume 3, an updating, inter-edition service issued every two months, resembles volume 1 in content and
format. Cumulative index.

SERVICES AND
FIELD RESEARCH

The term "service" has been defined as an agency which supplies information, especially current data, in easily accessible form, not readily available otherwise. It is also applied to such information supplied regularly and/or on request in printed, multilithed, loose-leaf or other format.

The types of agency so categorized range widely. The sole output of some consists of publications conveying specialized and/or advisory information. Others are consultant and contract firms which engage exclusively in special assignment work on a fee basis. Between the two lie a number of companies, and even nonprofit institutions, which complement their basic programs with special order work based on individual needs, and vice versa.

Published services, regardless of considerable variation in format and content, are characterized by timeliness and immediate applicability in daily business activity and planning. As a rule, they are the product of continuing research and reporting programs geared to the specific needs of a specialized clientele. Because of this definition, mailing list services, commercially published newsletters and directories, abstract journals, indexes and other publications are often classed with services. Here, however, they are treated in the respective chapters devoted to such sources.

SERVICES FOR MARKETING AND MARKET RESEARCH

In market research a number of firms offer continuous reporting programs on retail distribution, product acceptance, brand awareness, data banks and compendia, as well as special assignment facilities for custom investigations of various marketing factors. Cited here are a number of basic services available to con-

sumer and industrial marketers. Advisory and marketing assistance offered, usually free of charge, by national and local media
are treated in the following chapter.

CONSUMER MARKETING SERVICES

A. C. Nielsen Co. has long furnished basic syndicated services to manufacturers and advertising agencies.   (J 1)

NIELSEN Retail Indexes provide continuous market reports of
food, drug and other products sold through retail outlets.
Sales, inventories, stocks, purchases and advertising-mer-
chandising activity are inventoried in a sample of chain and
independent stores and the data expanded to represent national totals. Reports give breakdowns by client and competitive
brands, sizes, territories or sales areas, county-size, store
types and sizes.

NIELSEN New Product Service is based on special warehouse tabulations of all food and household items handled by
supermarkets. Data covering product groups show brand,
size, case pack, unit volume, retail price and distribution,
and provide a guide to new product areas of growing potential.
Similar in detail, the semiannual Expanded Coverage Reports
present a record of all product groups moving through supermarkets and thereby reflect the expansion and contraction of
product lines.

NIELSEN Major Market Service provides, for any product
sold through food stores, bimonthly reports on store distribution, inventories, purchases, stock, product prices and merchandising activity for any or all of the 23 major metropolitan
areas.

Audits & Surveys Co. , Inc. also provides a number of syndicated services.   (J 2)

NATIONAL Sample Census of Retail Distribution, conducted
annually, reports on the size and characteristics of retail
and service outlets; the effective distribution of consumer
products in these establishments by client and competitive

brands, geographic area, store sales volume and other detail.
NATIONAL Total-Market Audit service furnishes the following
information by major brands: consumer sales, dealer purchases, inventories, distribution by store count, distribution
by product sales, out-of-stock, month's supply. These data
are presented for the total United States, major sales districts, city-size, product type and size, type-of-store, size-
of-store, chain vs. independent.

RESTAURANT Product Usage Index, based on a semiannual
survey of commercial eating places, reports on usage of
brands, package sizes, product types for specified products
or product categories. Data are available for five restaurant
types, nine geographic regions, three major metropolitan
areas, four city sizes, or client sales regions.

    Market Research Corporation of America is known primarily
for the data provided by its national consumer panel.   (J 3)

THE NATIONAL Consumer Panel of over 7,500 families
reports weekly on purchases of food, household, drug, textile and other products. Data collected permit analysis of
size, frequency, source of purchase; influence of deals; purchasing by new and repeat customers. Reports show total consumer purchases of the product and by individual brands and
types; number of families buying; purchases per buying
family; average price paid. Data are also available for the
United States, regions, and outlet types and by demographic
characteristics.

METROPOLITAN Supermarket (MSA) and Drug Audit (MDA)
is a quarterly in-store check of products in over 2,000 million dollar supermarkets and in some 1,000 drug stores in 55
key metropolitan areas. This produces data on distribution,
relative stock status and share of assigned shelf space by
brands, price ranges, merchandising effort and similar factors.

THE NATIONAL Menu Census, conducted over a period of a
year at five year intervals, obtains data from a 4,000 family

sample on food consumption and eating habits in and out of the home. Facts, stored on punched cards and magnetic tape, are available in a wide variety and many combinations.

BRAND Rating Index is a media related service of Brand Rating Research Corp. It identifies heavy and current users of product groups and specific brands, describes the demographic characteristics of these users, profiles the specific audiences of magazines, television and radio programs, and newspapers, thereby making it possible to relate media selection to marketing goals and advertising plans. Reported data also permit the study of brand loyalty and the response to new products and premium-priced brands.   (J 4)

Marketing Evaluations, Inc., provides a service, SCAN, on consumer brand attitudes and awareness, advertising awareness, brand purchase, usage and familiarity. Reports, based on monthly studies conducted by mail questionnaire, are available on a national or regional basis, monthly or quarterly.   (J 5)

The computerization of inventory, ordering and billing in food and drug wholesaling has given rise to a number of warehouse withdrawal services. Those listed here are offered by independent research organizations. Others are made available by local distributors and brokers who also offer their facilities for test marketing.

Point-of-Sale Research Co. audits supermarket and drug chain warehouse withdrawals. Its Brand Movement Data Service supplies monthly reports on case movement, retail dollars, promotions, share of market, warehouse inventories for some 6,000 branded items on a local, regional or national basis.   (J 6)

Pipeline Research, Inc. audits the warehouse withdrawals of drug chains and wholesalers. Monthly data are supplied in units and dollars for product brands, sizes, prepacks on a national or individual market area (of which there are 60) basis.   (J 7)

Griffin Publishing Co. , Inc. issues the monthly Griffin
Audit Report based on warehouse shipments of grocery store
products to stores in the Greater Boston television market. Product
data for each category include brand, pack, size, case volume and
percentage of each brand's share of total category.   (J 8)

Product Movement Indices, Inc. , a subsidiary of Market Research Corporation of America, provides warehouse-to-store reports
Product Movement Indices, on grocery products. Weekly data
for each product category show, for every item, type and size within brand by standard metropolitan statistical areas for all or any
combination of cooperating chains or for selected chains on an individual basis. New products are reported as they become available to the consumer, as they enter new market areas, as they enter new chains of divisions or chains. Through the services of its
parent company these studies can be complemented with analytical
in-store checks and consumer purchase information.   (J 9)

Selling Areas-Marketing, Inc. , a subsidiary of Time, Inc. ,
measures warehouse movement of grocery products of food chains
and wholesalers in major television markets. SAMI reports, on
the basis of 4-week periods, brand activity in terms of size, pack,
price, case and dollar volume, item's share of brand and product
category sales, dates of new item introductions.   (J 10)

SPEEData Inc. supplies 13 four-week reports on grocery
store products in 30 market areas. Data include warehouse distribution, inventory and week's supply on hand, weekly case movements, retail dollar volume and share, item rank, gross profit
share and other detail.   (J 11)

Media services, too, are offering an increasing volume of
marketing data as a significant part of their audience measurement
and analysis. Product and brand usage, purchase information, in-

tentions to buy advertised products, demographic characteristics are
included in such studies as the Consumer Market and Magazine Report (Daniel Starch & Staff), Selective Markets and
Media Reaching Them, and A Study of Mass Markets and
the Media Reaching Them (W. R. Simmons & Associates Research
Inc.).

INDUSTRIAL MARKETING SERVICES

Dun & Bradstreet, Inc. , in addition to its financial services,
offers a growing fund of computer-based data for industrial marketing.   (JA 1)

DUN'S Market Identifiers, or DMI service, is a data
bank of 390,000 industrial establishments grouped in four categories: manufacturing; mining; contract construction; transportation, communication and public utility. Each establishment
is "identified" by name, address and some 20 marketing facts
permitting statistical and sales analysis by line of business,
location and size.   Facts and format are available in a number of combinations.

MARKET Penetration Analysis provides data on sales penetration by industries, by customer size groupings, and by geographic areas.   It also supplies selected packages of prospect
cards identifying prospects in a client's customer industries.

VERIFIED Prospect Service is designed to identify verified
prospects for specific industrially consumed products, components, materials, or services.   Information is supplied for
each plant and includes the annual level of purchases of the
product, location where purchases are made, name of purchasing department person handling purchases, frequency of
product purchase, and size of average order, with additional
sales support information available on a custom basis.

MARKETING Information System provides a measurement of
market potential and penetration by states, and by specific
sales districts and individual sales territories.   The service
is available for individual products, or for any combination of

industrially consumed products or components. It shows size
of market and market share by numbers of prospects and customer plants in terms of units or dollars. The analysis is
based on customer sales data, product consumption data by
Standard Industrial Classification code and size of plant, and
DMI statistical data.

Fortune, in cooperation with C-E-I-R Inc., offers an Input/
Output Matrix. The up-to-date model, based on Fortune's forecast of the gross national product and reflecting major technological
changes, shows what each industry in the United States buys from
and sells to every other industry. It reveals not only where the customers are but where the customer's customers are and where com-
peting products are sold. Using this service, industrial marketers
can analyze the current market for a product as well as the probable
market if conditions change in other sectors of the economy. (JA 2)

INDIVIDUAL INDUSTRY AND PRODUCT SERVICES

Specialized industry or product services emanate from a
variety of agencies: single-industry orientated publishers; general
business service firms; trade associations; or, as in the case of the
previously cited Chemical Economics Handbook (see H 7c), from
research institutions. The data supplied are extremely detailed and
serviceable only to the analyst concerned with the particular industry.

Although most publishers in this field limit their services to a
single industry, the following company is notable for the variety of
products covered by its publications.

PREDICASTS, Inc. [Specialized Studies] Cleveland: Predicasts,
Inc. Irregular.   (JB 1)
A series of analytical studies containing historical and projected data on specific industries (e.g. paint, cryogenic gas,
glass fibers, rubber products).

ELECTRONICS Trends. Cleveland: Predicasts, Inc. Quarter-
ly.   (JB 2)

Series of continuing reports for marketing and financial planning based on published information and industry sources. Each
issue explores a special aspect of the industry and contains an
index of published materials.

PAPER Trends. Cleveland: Predicasts, Inc. Quarterly. (JB 3)
Similar in presentation and scope to above item.

PLASTIC Trends. Cleveland: Predicasts, Inc. Quarterly.
Similar in presentation and scope to above item.   (JB 4)

For agricultural marketers, the Farm Journal Research
Service provides a data bank based on the 1964 Census of Agriculture
with comparable figures from the 1959 census.   Information available for various geographic combinations covers all phases of farm
production, equipment, farm and operator characteristics and similar detail.   (JB 5)

In the automotive field, R. L. Polk & Co. compiles new
vehicle (passenger and commercial) sales reports and total registration counts. Statistics are available by state, county, town,
make, model and other detailed breakdowns.   (JB 6)

Construction data are available from several services:

F. W. Dodge Co. (McGraw-Hill Information Systems Co.)
specializes in the collection of data useful in the marketing of building products. It produces, sells and services construction contract
statistics. Data cover public and private contract totals, by type
and number of projects, square feet and dollar value. Possible geographic combinations include counties, metropolitan areas, states,
or individual sales territories. Information is tailored and pack-
aged to fit individual needs. The company publishes Dodge Reports, a news service covering building projects and the organizations planning such construction. Both publications and computer
resources are geared to enable clients to estimate future demand for

their products, improve their marketing and distribution, and increase their sales effectiveness.   (JB 7)

Seymour Kroll & Associates, Inc., consultants to the construction industry, have established an Information Retrieval Center to provide marketing information from secondary sources on the residential, nonresidential, and repair and remodelling segments of the industry.   (JB 8)

A new entrant into the field is Allied Chemical Corp. Its PROJECTRON computerized service, available for 161 cities, projects the number of new homes, apartments and condominiums that will be needed, by price range and rent range, during the next ten years.   (JB 9)

For defense and space marketing, Frost & Sullivan, Inc. offers a complete data collection, processing and retrieval system. On the basis of contract award information, measurements are provided of such indicators as market size, location and penetration; dollar volume; market share; product mix. Additional features are comprehensive analyses of companies, defense agencies, and individual products, systems and industry segments.   (JB 10)

To health and beauty aids manufacturers Towne-Oller & Associates, Inc. offers a selling tool based on a panel of over 20,000 food outlets in 38 major marketing areas. Detailed data are issued in four report forms;   (JB 11)

> The Regular Monthly Sales Report measures an item's position in its category by market, area, and national summary. The Moving Average Report indicates the progress and direction of an item, brand, or category over a current seven month period. The Graphs based on this report depict the dollar sales trends of products within each category and the per cent of market attained by brands within the category. The Sequential Report ranks all items in the health and beauty aid field by dollar volume and unit sales and places them

in their earned position against all HBA products, and in their respective categories. A unique feature of this report is a current listing of items added or deleted by individual toiletry merchandisers and chains.

TEXTILE OR'GANON, a series of monthly statistical bulletins, has a long record of providing essential marketing data to the man-made fiber industry. In addition to regular compilations of data from domestic and foreign sources its issues carry many special features such as a directory of man-made fiber producers and products made, textile fiber end use surveys, reviews of world cotton and wool industries.   (JB 12)

BUSINESS, ECONOMIC AND STATISTICAL SERVICES

Although the business field is well supplied with both service agencies and service publications, only a few have been included in this selected list. These were chosen for their basic usefulness, their general interest in marketing and business research, and as illustrative of the varied nature of this type of source.

Dun & Bradstreet, Inc. specializes primarily in the collection, analysis and publication of credit information and other business data. Its major service is the bimonthly Reference Book which gives the business classification (including the Standard Industrial Classification code), capitalization and credit ratings of about 3 million industrial and commercial enterprises in the United States and Canada. Also available to subscribers is a detailed reports service. Other compilations include: statistics and analyses of business failures; key business ratios in wholesaling, retailing, manufacturing, and construction; a monthly business magazine, Dun's Review; Early Sensitive Indicators of Business Trends, a series of 11 statistical releases on new business incorporations, business failures, bank clearings, building permit values, wholesale commodity and food prices, businessmen's expectations and weekly review of developments in retailing, wholesaling and manufacturing.   (JC 1)

Economic Statistics Bureau of Washington, D. C. issues the
Handbook of Basic Economic Statistics, a monthly, quarterly, and annual service which provides a continuing compendium of
over 1,500 statistical series selected from federal government
sources. Current and historical data include general business indicators; employment and earnings; production, labor productivity
and labor cost; profits and working capital; prices; national product
and national income; and other series useful in economic and market
research. A valuable feature is its detailed subject index.   (JC 2)

Lionel D. Edie & Co. , Inc. , economic consultants and investment counselors, maintains an economic service of major inter-
est to marketing: Edie State Indexes of Manufacturing
Production. These monthly statistical series for durable, non-
durable and total manufacturing are available for all states except
Alaska and Hawaii both on a raw and on a seasonally adjusted basis.
Tabulations are supplemented by periodic updating of chart over-
lays. The period covered by historical data varies for each state.
Each index, comparable in procedure and computation with the
Federal Reserve Board index of industrial production, is a barometer
of local economic conditions and thereby can serve as a guide to
regional sales, distribution, marketing and other business activity.
                                                                (JC 3)

ITT Data Services provides a computer-based sales analysis and forecasting tool called STATUS. Its basic concept is to
compare the trend of some measure of the progress of a firm for
which data are available, such as sales, earnings, or inventories
with the trends of a large group of industry, national, and international statistics including those classified as business cycle indicators. The trends of these time series are compared with the
input data for leads up to fifteen months. The purpose of this comparison is to have the computer select those economic indicators or
statistical time series whose trends correlate historically most
closely with the firm's progress. These indicators are then used to
predict the future trend of the firm in terms of the input data. The

principal output from STATUS is a month-by-month projection of
the input data up to twelve months beyond the point where the input
data ends.   (JC 4)

PREDICASTS, Inc. Growth & Acquisition Guide. Cleveland:
Predicasts, Inc. Monthly.   (JC 5)

> Condenses and analyzes key facts from the publishers' Predi-
> casts (see OA 1) and Funk & Scott Index (see OC 2).
> Acquisition and merger news listed by company, alphabetically
> arranged. Growth products list identifies companies by name,
> address, product, financial data. Industry growth rates, his-
> torical and projected. Growth product forecasts and new prod-
> uct news cited from current press.

S. J. Tesauro & Co. provides correlated tabulations of
housing and population characteristics from the 1960 decennial
censuses in its People and Homes in the American Market.
County reports are bound in individual state volumes. These also
carry state totals. A separate volume provides totals for each of
212 standard metropolitan statistical areas and for the United States
as a whole.   (JC 6)

U. S. Economics Corporation/ The Econometric Institute
Inc. specializes in economic analysis and forecasting - translating
prospective changes in the economy into their likely quantitative effect on specific industries and products. In addition to its custom
studies and services, the company issues periodic forecast reports:
                                                                   (JC 7)

> Monthly forecasts five months ahead by months, five quarters
> ahead by quarters, with a summary analysis of gross nation-
> al product and 27 of its component series, production and its
> major components, and retail trade.
> Topical, self-contained forecasts on timely aspects of the
> economy such as prices, wages, consumer spending, govern-
> ment spending, business profits, capital spending and similar
> subjects.

Semiannual summaries: March edition analyzes the portent of
the President's "State of the Union" and budget messages;
September edition is timed to the corporate budget season.

FINANCIAL SERVICES

This group represents a vast output of economic,financial
and related data issued for the guidance of lay and professional investors. The range is from specific recommendations on individual securities to statistical analyses of companies and industries, as
well as forecasts for these and for the national economy.

Omitting purely investment advisory publications, the services cited below illustrate the encyclopedic scope of directory and
statistical information available and its applicability.

Moody's Investors Service, Inc. publishes a series of five
annual Manuals each supplemented by twice-weekly news issues:
Banks and Finance (including insurance, real estate, investment trusts); Municipals and Governments; Industrials;
Public Utilities; Transportation. Similar information,
varied to fit the type of agency or firm, is given for each listing:
location, history, nature of business, officers, directors, subsidiaries, property, basic financial data and securities information. A
statistical section in each volume serves as a compendium of
pertinent data.   (JD 1)

Standard & Poor's Corp. offers the following services:
                                                        (JD 2)
. . . Corporation Records. Looseleaf.
Revised continuously and updated by daily news bulletins.
Factual information on corporations and their securities
covers: location and history of the company; officers, products, plants, subsidiaries, abstracts of financial statements
and related data.

TRADE and Securities Service.

INDUSTRY Surveys. Looseleaf.

Over 40 "Basic Analysis" sections, each devoted to a major industry group, are revised about once a year and updated by quarterly supplements. In addition to financial information, each section includes detailed industry data culled from a variety of sources, analysis of competitive factors, and outlook statements for the industry and the major companies in it.

STATISTICAL Section. Looseleaf.

A looseleaf volume containing numerous statistical series indicative of general business and basic industries' activity. Current and historical data are arranged in broad industry and economic groups: agricultural products; textiles, chemicals, etc.; metals; building materials; income and trade; production and labor; etc.

THE Outlook. Weekly.
Investment advisory letter.

STOCK Guide. Monthly.
Digest of financial data for quick analysis of common and preferred stocks.

OTHER SERVICES

Marketing has also felt the impact of several new services which give every indication of growing in value and application.

Long-range weather research and forecasting have been used by business enterprises to schedule production, control inventory, estimate sales.

Comparative newcomers are the "marketing mapmakers" -- specialists who apply a blend of market research and the science of geography to store site selection, trading area evaluations, product distribution patterns, for a growing list of business clients.

Equally new are real estate research services who advise

cities, corporations , and developers on what to build, where and
when.

The rise of data processing has been marked by the spread
of its practitioners across the country.   One of the newest services,
it has already added scientific precision to a number of manufacturing and business operations.   Its application to voluminous company
records has produced useful marketing indicators.   With time, better and cheaper hardware will be on the way and, with it, common-
place use of a greater variety and quantity of data in market research, as well as the means for their more sophisticated analysis.

GUIDES TO SERVICES AND FIELD RESEARCH

Published Services

DIRECTORY of Business and Financial Services, 6th ed. , Mary A.
McNierney, ed. New York: Special Libraries Association, 1963.
v, 187 p.   (JE 1)

> Guide to over 1,000 business, economic and financial services
> issued periodically or with regular supplements by some 500
> organizations.   Coverage, frequency, price and address of
> publisher are given for each listing.   Indexed by publisher-
> author-title, and detailed subject.

Firms and Individuals

Practical advice on selecting research service organizations
is given in the following references:

"Evaluating the Quality of Marketing Research Contractors," by
Charles S. Mayer. JOURNAL OF MARKETING RESEARCH, May
1967, p. 134-141.   (JE 2)

> Outlines a rating system for evaluating marketing research
> work done by outside contractors.

USING Marketing Consultants and Research Companies. (Studies in
Business Policy 120). New York: National Industrial Conference

Board, Inc., 1966. 60 p.   (JE 3)

    Describes procedures and criteria for selecting marketing
consultants, marketing research agencies, and researchers.
Offers useful rules of thumb drawn from the opinions and
practices of over 280 cooperating executives.

SELECTING Marketing Research Services, by William C. Gordon,
Jr. (Management aid for small manufacturers 117).   Washington,
D. C.: Small Business Administration, July 1960. 8 p.   (JE 4)

    A step-by-step guide for the selection of outside marketing
research services.

    Detailed information on research organizations, consultants,
interviewing and tabulating firms is included in the following directories. In addition, trade associations, universities and professional societies maintain lists of institutions and individuals engaged in
consulting practice.

BRADFORD'S Directory ... P. O. Box 276, Fairfax, Va.:
Bradford's Directory of Marketing Research Agencies. Biennial.

                                                 (JE 5)

    Lists domestic marketing research firms and consultants
by states, cities and foreign firms by country. Gives detailed information on size and nature of staff, areas of
specialization, scope of operations and services offered.
Includes name, personnel and type-of-service indexes.

GREEN Book: International Directory of Marketing Research
Houses and Services. New York: American Marketing Association
New York Chapter. Annual.   (JE 6)

    Alphabetical list, annotated for specializations. Geographical
index.

ADVERTISING Research Foundation.   Directory of Research
Organization Members.   New York: Advertising Research
Foundation. 1968. 104 p.   (JE 7)

Research member firms briefly described as to facilities and
personnel. Referenced geographically and by type of service.

---Directory of Social Scientists Interested in Motivation Research.
New York: Advertising Research Foundation, 1954. xvii, 143 p.
(JE 8)
Alphabetical list, with geographical index, of psychologists,
sociologists, cultural anthropologists (primarily educators)
interested in motivation research as applied to advertising and
marketing. Information similar to that in companion volume
listed above is given for each individual.

AMERICAN Management Association, Inc. Directory of Consultant Members. (see P 17)

WASSERMAN, Paul, ed. Consultants and Consulting Organizations ... (see P 18)

Foreign
For those concerned with researching foreign markets:

MARKET Research Directory. Le Ruscino, Quai Antoine 1er,
Monaco: John Anns Organization. Annual.   (JE 9)
Listing of research firms and national and international marketing organizations exclusive of those in the United States.
Information limited to address and name of principal executive. United Kingdom listings also show services offered,
names of professional personnel and, in some instances,
clients, size of staff.

ANGEL, Juvenal L. International Reference Handbook of Services,
Organizations, Diplomatic Representation, Marketing and Advertis-
ing Channels. New York: Regents Publishing Co. , Inc. Triennial.
(JE 10)

A useful current source.   For each of over 100 countries,
lists marketing research organizations, advertising agencies,
information centers for the country (both in the United States
and in the country itself), as well as economic and demographic data and general reference sources.

U. S. Bureau of Foreign Commerce.   Directory of Foreign
Advertising Agencies and Marketing Research Organizations
... Washington, D. C.:   Government Printing Office, 1959.
iv, 135 p.   (JE 11)

Although outdated in many details, still useful as a guide. Information was gathered through on-the-spot surveys by the
U. S. Foreign Service. Coverage includes practically all
countries except those in the Soviet bloc, and the United
States and its noncontiguous territories and possessions.
Arrangement is alphabetical by area.   Marketing research
firms, advertising agencies, management consultants, and
other businesses which provide research services are identified by name, address, nationality, area covered, size of
staff, and specialization.

ADVERTISING
MEDIA

Media provide marketing information primarily to inform the advertiser and to promote the medium. Many also offer their clients and prospects advisory services on marketing problems within their geographic or product areas. Thus, for example, media which conduct product surveys, store checks and similar studies may be requested to include specific brands, products, attitude questions, etc., in regularly scheduled field work. Media representatives, too, furnish primarily media information and, at times, parallel marketing information for the medium for which they act as selling organizations.

Published data are usually of two types: digests or compilations of extant information, and presentations of original facts based on independent research. A large proportion of both types, subject as it is to the promotional efforts of the sponsor, of necessity varies in content and, with few exceptions, lacks continuity.

Currently, a new selling tool of marketing usefulness is available to local media, through the research services of <u>Media Survey Inc</u>. From in-store checks of supermarket products, MSI reports bimonthly on stock conditions, shelf locations, price, special displays, product facings -- store-by-store and chain-by-chain, within seven days of the field work. Local media, such as television stations, radio stations and newspapers, subscribe to MSI reports and offer them as a service to their advertisers.

Most media research, however, is produced by the medium's own research department or by outside research organizations working on a contract basis. Highlighted here are the broad categories of continuing marketing data distributed by media. Citations punctuate the typical or the unusual to brief the user on the range of such information. Many of these publications are listed in the guides cited at the end of this chapter. Others can be located by regular scanning of the trade press or by direct approach to the pertinent medium.

The acceptability and usefulness of media reports have been the object of much critical appraisal by marketing men in recent years. Each may be evaluated according to the criteria set forth in the first chapter of this book and particularly in the published guides listed there. With the growing acceptance of such standards, media sources stand in a unique position to offer marketers increasingly valid and valuable data.

NEWSPAPERS AND NEWSPAPER SUPPLEMENTS

Almost every daily paper publishes general marketing information for its city or trading area. Although some reports are more detailed than others, most do provide compilations of data from primary sources on population, income, housing, retail outlets, retail sales, and other market characteristics.

From the larger cities come supplementary releases on car registrations by make, sales of alcoholic beverages, and other statistics.

For some of the largest markets detailed guides are issued from time to time:

BIENNIAL Survey of the Metropolitan Detroit Newspaper Audience. Detroit: Detroit News. Biennial.   (K 1)
     Data on population, households, family characteristics, household activities and possessions.

NEW YORK Market Analysis: New York City and Suburbs Population and Housing. New York: New York Mirror, New York News, New York Times, General Outdoor, 1963. [140] p. maps, tables.
                                                                 (K 2)
     Based on census data and special field work this study includes income information rendered in tabulations and colored maps. A companion volume to the following:

NEW YORK Market Analysis: New York City and Suburbs
Retail Trade. New York: New York Mirror, New York News,
New York Times, General Outdoor Advertising Co. , 1961.
[147] p. maps, tables.

Based on special tabulations supplied by the Bureau of the
Census, data show population and families, number of store
outlets and dollar sales for every major category of retail
trade. New York City is further broken down to 114 neighborhoods each with its own locality map showing primary and
secondary shopping streets.

INSIDE Phoenix. Phoenix, Ariz. : Arizona Republic and Phoenix
Gazette. Annual.   (K 3)

Statistical information on population, education, housing, employment, industry, retail sales.

THE TOP Twenty Markets; Basic Data for America's Largest Trading Area. Philadelphia: Philadelphia Inquirer, 1967. maps. (K 4)

Brief descriptions and maps of area; comparable data on
population, households, retail trade, housing characteristics.

PHILADELPHIA Market/Newspaper Profile. Philadelphia   Philadelphia Bulletin, 1967. 2 vols.   (K 5)

Demographics, product ownership and use, reader data on
the eight-county Philadelphia standard metropolitan statistical
area and the 14-county Greater Philadelphia market.

A number of newspapers sponsor distribution checks and
surveys of brand preferences, product use, buying habits and buying intentions for a broad range of consumer products. Some have
established uniformity in research methods and reporting which add
to the advantages of continuity. The latter type fall into approximately five groups: (K 6)

CONSUMER Analysis studies, patterned on the pioneer Milwaukee Journal survey of that name, are conducted annually.
They cover grocery, drug, home equipment, apparel, auto-

motive and other products. Results for each area are published by the sponsoring newspaper and, in less detail, in
a consolidated report.

TOP Ten Brands surveys, also conducted annually, rank the
leading brands of foods, household products, appliances,
toiletries and other products on the basis of household use.
Individual reports are published for each area; the consolidated report has been discontinued.

CONTINUING Home Audits are published by a growing number
of city dailies. The nature of the product often determines the
frequency of the survey (bimonthly, quarterly, semiannual,
annual). Buying patterns, in many instances documented
with demographic profiles of user households, are reported
for apparel, food, household products, appliances, toiletries,
tobacco products.

Scripps-Howard Newspapers issues a consolidated report
showing product distribution in grocery stores in each of its
markets.

Similarly, the New England Newspapers Advertising Bureau
conducts two retail distribution studies (alcoholic beverages
and grocery store products) in some 50 New England markets
and publishes its findings in consolidated reports.

Occasionally individual newspapers probe beyond brand
preferences and product use into consumer buying habits, psychology
and characteristics and make special presentations of such findings to advertisers and their agencies.

In addition to surveys and trading area data, many newspapers compile route lists. Most common for drug and grocery
stores, these directories are issued as an aid to advertisers' sales-
men in making calls.

Local market data are also available from newspaper representatives, Sunday supplement publishers (e.g., Metropolitan Sunday Newspapers, Inc., This Week Magazine and Parade Publications, Inc.) and newspaper sales/service organizations (e.g., Newspaper 1). Marketing aids from these sources quite often deal with local markets collectively and against a background of national data. Quantitatively, grocery and drug store products receive the greatest emphasis.

For example:

[BIENNIAL Grocery Study] New York: This Week. Biennial. (K 7)
Issued under varying titles, this survey of major food chains, manufacturers, wholesalers and consumers presents statistics and analyses on various aspects of grocery product retailing. Featured prominently are detailed data on the major grocery chains.

MAJOR Market Memo. New York: Newspaper 1. Monthly.   (K 8)
Newsletter reporting on business conditions, media developments, retail changes, spot surveys of new product advertising and new product promotions in newspapers in the organization's 30 market areas.

CONSUMER MAGAZINES

Research aids produced by consumer magazines concern the national market as a whole and its social, economic, geographic characteristics. The greatest number represent one of three general types: marketing guides; surveys; industry or product digests and fact sheets.

Marketing Guides

Statistical studies of the national market usually combine compilations of original data with special tabulations derived from benchmark statistics. Those cited below have been in general use for some time and offer the advantage of continuity. Others, less comprehensive, are issued occasionally and usually in greater numbers in those years when revised benchmark data become available.

HEARST Magazines, Inc. Hearst Trading Area System of
Sales Control. New York: Hearst Magazines, Inc.   (KA 1)
    A series of maps and Buying Power Index studies revised at
irregular intervals:
    CONSUMER Trading Area Map of the United States. 1966. map.
Delineates 580 Trading Areas, economic units whose
boundaries are based on the flow of retail trade, and shows
the Principal Trading Center for each.
    THE Marketing Map of the United States. 1966. map.
Shows the 580 Principal Trading Centers and all towns of 2,500 and
over population within the respective Trading Area lines,
and the 219 SMSA's in outline.
    INDIVIDUAL State Marketing Maps. 1962. 60 maps.
One map for each state and one for each of the first ten
Standard Metropolitan Statistical Areas. On a county background, they show the 580 Principal Trading Centers and
towns of 1,000 and over population within the respective
Trading Areas.
    COUNTY Composition of the 580 Consumer Trading Areas. 1964.
Companion volume to the above. Lists the counties
which make up each Trading Area and, in a second section,
gives an alphabetical listing of counties, by states, indicat-
ing the Trading Area in which each is located.
    Designed for use with the above are the following series of
Buying Power Indexes which show the value of each Area and
Principal Trading Center in terms of its percentage of the
United States total, as well as each one's relative rank and
value compared to the others.
    THE General Market Buying Power Index. 1966.   (KA 1a)
Based on the three factors of income, population and retail
sales, this index is designed to sell products that have mass
appeal.
    THE Home Market Buying Power Index. 1964.   (KA 1b)
For products bought for home use. Based on households,

household income, and retail sales in three store categories.
THE Style and Quality Market Buying Power Index. 1964.

(KA 1c)

Based on factors of concentration of wealth and the appropriate type of retail outlets, this index indicates sales potentials
for class merchandise.
THE Male Market Buying Power Index. 1964.   (KA 1d)
Weighted factors include qualified male population, sporting
goods sales, and TBA sales, to show the male market potential.
BOATING Market Index. 1962.   (KA 1e)
Factors used to establish this index: 1961 reported sales of
retail dealers, marinas and local boat yards; sales of boats,
engines, accessories, supplies, and services. Study also
shows number of dealers and sales in each of the Trading
Areas.

A new series of merchandise-line sales indexes were re-
cently issued:
SALES by Kind of Retail Outlets in the 580 Consumer Trading Areas
of the United States.   New York: Hearst Magazines, Inc., 1967.
5 reports.   (KA 2)
The series comprises the following reports:
Cosmetics, Toiletries and Drugs.
Furniture, Sleep Equipment and Floor Covering.
Groceries and Other Foods.
Major Appliances, Television and Radio.
Women's and Girls' Clothing.
Based on 1963 Census of Business merchandise-line sales
figures updated to 1965.   Each study shows total U. S. retail sales estimates of the merchandise-line group; its dollar
volume by type of retail outlet; the total of the group as well
as a percentage of the U. S.   Data in each report are for
each of the 580 Hearst Trading Areas.

LIFE. A Graphic Guide to Consumer Markets ... New York:

National Industrial Conference Board.   Biennial.   (KA 3)

> Chartbook of major statistical series on population, income,
> expenditures, markets for 14 product groups, etc. , with a
> bibliography of primary sources used. Updated monthly by
> "Consumer Market Statistics" supplied by the National Indus-
> trial Conference Board in its release, Consumer Market
> Indicators. Statistical supplements in alternate years.

SUNSET Western Market Almanac. Menlo Park, Calif.: Sunset.
Annual.   (KA 4)

> General business and marketing facts for seven western states
> and Hawaii.

NEW YORKER. The Primary Markets for Quality Merchandise.   New York: New Yorker Magazine, Inc. , 1966. 68 p.
map.   (KA 5)

> Ranks 40 major and 20 minor areas on the basis of seven
> indexes: retail sales, women's ready-to-wear store sales;
> department store sales; new, price class 4 car registra-
> tions; families with incomes of $15,000 and over, and
> $25,000 and over; character of stores. Statistical data ob-
> tained from published and unpublished government and private
> sources are supplemented by the publication's own field work.

Surveys

Many magazines conduct surveys among their subscribers on
every type of product and service that could be bought by consumers or, in the case of management publications, by businessmen
and their companies.

Along with brand preferences such studies provide more information than newspaper reports on buying influences, place of
purchase, package size, frequency of use, product features liked
and disliked, and related aspects of ownership and purchase. Many
findings are related to reader characteristics and projected to
national totals.

Although numerous, few of these surveys are continuing such as Popular Mechanics' automobile and liquor studies. Some are conducted at two or three year intervals. More frequently, however, a single product or product group is surveyed on a one-time basis, a few of them through subscriber panels such as those maintained by Seventeen, Good Housekeeping and Popular Mechanics.

Retailer and wholesaler studies are less frequent. Notable examples are those of the Drug and Toiletries Trade Marketing Council and of the Food Trade Marketing Council. Both are sponsored by Family Circle for the purpose of researching the marketing and merchandising practices of manufacturers, distributors and retailers in the food and drug-toiletry fields. In-depth studies have been issued on such aspects as retailer policies in marketing frozen foods; food retailer and wholesaler practices in merchandising soft drinks and non-food items; grocer, drug store and wholesaler practices in marketing drug and toiletry products.

Digests and Fact Sheets

Infrequent, but very helpful, are the miscellaneous industry and product digests issued by some of the consumer magazines.

Redbook's series on the young adult market have covered such products as appliances, furniture, toiletries and cosmetics, convenience foods, baby products.

INDICES, the internal house organ of Meredith Publishing Co. (Better Homes & Gardens, Successful Farming), devotes each issue to digests and reproductions of current data on a particular subject or area of interest in consumer or farm marketing.

House & Home presents in Housing Facts and Trends a compendium of basic housing industry statistics gathered from a large variety of private and governmental sources. Over 200 pages of tabular data are supplemented by an eight-page alphabetical subject index.

On a continuing basis, statistical analyses and trend data,

indicative of sales performance and outlook, are issued for selected product groups. Currently available are True's and Newsweek's series of market reports on alcoholic beverage products.

Fact sheets citing national data are issued occasionally as the sponsor's promotional effort warrants. These, however, do not constitute a source for market research unless they present well documented special tabulations of basic statistics not easily available otherwise.

FARM PUBLICATIONS

The output of national farm publications, like that of the regional and state papers, closely resembles the surveys, industry digests and fact sheets issued by consumer magazines.

WHAT's Ahead in Farming. Philadelphia: Farm Journal. Semiannual.

> General outlook on the farming industry, as well as detailed reports from the various farming regions of the country. Also included are special reviews of pertinent trends in various segments of agriculture and farm management.

INDICES. Des Moines: Meredith Publishing Co.
> Digests current consumer and farm data.

Regional and state farm papers offer a variety of data, many with geographical breakdowns and comparisons for their areas, on farm population; equipment saturation; cash income; crop production; acreage harvested; livestock population; etc.

Particularly numerous are surveys of equipment ownership, product use, buying intentions, brand preferences. A large majority of these are one-time studies. Some are repeated at irregular intervals. A few, including the examples listed below, have been published on a continuing basis for some time.

BUYING Intentions of Farm Families in the 8 Midwest States.

Chicago: Midwest Farm Paper Unit. Annual. 7 state reports and summary.

WHAT'S Being Bought ... Spokane. Northwest Farm Paper Unit. Annual.

BUYING Intentions of Colorado Ranch and Farm Families. Denver: Colorado Rancher and Farmer. Annual.

TRADE PAPERS

Hundreds of trade magazines, published by commercial organizations or trade and professional associations, service the nation's economic activities. Each is devoted to a specific industry or business function. Some fields are served by more than one magazine. Each represents a source of marketing information within its area of specialization, particularly useful in researching commercial and industrial market facts.

The editorial content of trade papers and special issues supplied with subscriptions are treated in the chapter on periodicals. However, it is well to note here that in many instances statistical analyses, forecasts and industry reviews, originally published in these magazines, are reprinted for more general distribution among interested marketers. To this the publishers add a tremendous volume of special studies compiled by either their research departments or by their knowledgeable editorial staff.

Among these the most prevalent are industry "studies" which outweigh in number and scope their counterparts supplied by other media. Many are products of original research or of information obtained from private sources. Some are valuable abstracts of benchmark statistics. Others represent "educated guesstimates" of specialists.

In format these report vary from single-page data sheets to voluminous sales and marketing guides. Some are revised at irregular intervals, others are issued regularly -- usually on an annual basis. With the advent of computerization, vast quantities of machine-readable facts are being offered either as substitutes or as data banks complementary to the information issued in printed form.

Like the publications themselves which range through the whole spectrum of commerce and industry, the information supplied is varied: industry censuses indicating branches, primary and secondary producers, plant sizes; number of establishments by geographic, sales volume, employee-size, and other breakdowns; production, shipments, sales; distribution patterns and techniques; consumption, expenditures and needs for supplies, equipment and services; progress reviews, technical developments, expansion plans; economic forecasts, production and sales estimates; short-range projections and long-range forecasts for industries and their markets.

A comprehensive listing would fill a sizeable book. Consequently, the representative selection of continuing publications, including several basics, listed below are designed to illustrate the breadth, scope and variety of such sources. Many others, continuing and one-time, are publicized in the catalogs and bibliographies listed at the end of this chapter and in the editorial content of the press serving the specific industries.

McGraw-Hill Publications, a division of Mc-Graw Hill, Inc., issues some 40 periodicals for business and industry and maintains 17 regional offices to assist businessmen with their marketing problems. Its Department of Economics compiles a variety of data on the developments in and outlooks for various industries and products as well as for the economy as a whole. It also computes a number of indexes of business and industrial activity, costs, prices, production, operating rates and new orders, for product groups and industries, which appear in its business and trade publications. Among its continuing programs: (KB 1)

LABORATORY of Advertising Performance. Looseleaf. Published data and original research feed this service covering some 50 subjects. Although many reports relate to advertising, others give data on selling, distribution and marketing costs, sales methods, input/output of interest to the industrial marketer.

BUSINESS' Plans For New Plants and Equipment. Semiannual.
Reports plans of manufacturing (by industry groups and
regions) and nonmanufacturing businesses. Also includes indexes of industrial capacity by principal categories. The
Spring survey shows actual expenditures for the preceding
year and those planned for the next three years; Fall survey
shows estimated expenditures for the current year, those
planned for the next year and preliminary plans for two years
ahead.

The company has also devised a number of economic indicators covering trends in business and industrial activity, costs,
prices, production, consumption, sales and new orders, as
well as some 130 individual sub-group indexes which appear in
its business and trade publications. It also compiles a variety of data on the developments in and outlooks for various
industries and products as well as for the economy as a whole.

The Chilton Company, another leading business magazine
publisher, offers an assortment of marketing services. Among
these are several industry censuses which illustrate the sophisticated information provided industrial marketers by leading business
magazines: (KB 2)

The Iron Age Census of U. S. Metalworking, updated
annually and completely revised every three years, provides,
on punched cards or computer tape, full information on metalworking plants - their location, principal products by 6-digit
SIC code, production operations performed, employment size,
state and county code. A printed version, Master List of
Metalworking Plants, presents the same plant data in two ar-
rangements: alphabetically by state and by primary product
6-digit SIC code. A statistical summary of the census is
published in the Metalworking Marketguide, a national and
state analysis of plants by product, employee-size, production
operation.

Similar in scope and detail is the Electronic Engineer's

Census of the Electronic Market.

Distribution Manager maintains a Census of Freight Producers which identifies the pertinent establishments and their department managers by name and title.

In the retail field the Hardware Age Census enumerates independent hardware outlets selling hardware and allied product lines, classifies them by 4-digit SIC, by sales-size and location.

Like Chilton, the Penton Publishing Company produces an impressive amount of industrial market data.   (KB 3)

To its advertisers Steel offers a data-bank service based on its Continuing Census of Metalworking Plants.   Location, product classification, employment and metalworking operations and other information are provided on IBM cards; statistical analyses in published form.   Metalworking facts and figures, a financial analysis of the steel industry, and the Metal Selector (a product directory of ferrous and nonferrous metals and alloys) are published annually in the magazine itself.

Its Foundry magazine publishes a foundry directory, a marketing guide to the metalcasting industry (both at two-year intervals) and an inventory of foundry equipment (quadrennially).   In the Design Engineer Census, Modern Design provides a geographic analysis of the original equipment market by 4-digit SIC number, number of design engineers and total number of employees;   a checklist of the major types of engineered products in the market; a county outline map showing the geographic concentrations of the establishments that comprise the OEM.   The data are cumulated annually and published biennially.

MACHINERY.   Geographical Pattern of the Metalworking Market.
New York: Machinery.   Triennial.   (KB 4)

Geographical distribution of shipments of cutting and forming types of machine tools.

SERVICE Job Analysis.   Chicago, Hunter Publishing Co. , 1966.
Irregular.   (KB 5)

> Statistical data on the automotive aftermarket.

MOTOR Age.   Automotive Marketing Guide,   7th ed.   Philadelphia: Chilton Co. , Inc. , 1965. 135 p. maps, tables.   (KB 6)

> Data on automotive wholesale and retail market. Revised
> periodically.

METAL Products Manufacturing.   Annual Statistical Review.
Elmhurst, Ill. : Dana Chase Publications, Inc. Annual.   (KB 7)

> Shipments and/or factory sales of fabricated metal products
> such as appliances, plumbingware and business machines.

MODERN Medicine.   Medical Market Guide.   Minneapolis:
Modern Medicine. Irregular.   (KB 8)

> State and county data on drug stores, physicians, hospitals,
> physician purchases, hospital purchases, prescription sales,
> total ethical sales.

SUPERMARKET News.   Distribution of Food Store Sales ...
New York: Supermarket News. Annual.   (KB 9)

> Number of stores and share of the market accounted for by
> chains, voluntary and cooperative groups and leading inde-
> pendents in over 200 markets.

PROGRESSIVE Grocer's Marketing Guidebook. New York: Progressive Grocer, 1967. 700 p. maps.   (KB 10)

> First edition of statistical and directory information on the
> grocery industry.   In addition to national data, covers 83
> major markets with county figures on population, households,
> food store sales (total, per capita and per household), number
> of food stores and supermarkets.   Also, for each market,
> gives information on major distribution centers, including
> company data, key personnel, buyers and buying practices,
> warehouse locations and sales, stores served.

DRUG News Weekly.   The Drug Store Market - USA.   New

York: Drug News Weekly.   Irregular.   (KB 11)

For 50 leading markets gives number of stores and percentage of sales done in each market by chains and independents,
and information on specific chains and independent wholesalers,
including the number of stores and sales volume.   A large
section contains a compilation of information and statistics
from the Bureau of the Census and other governmental and
private sources.

Surveys sponsored by trade papers fall into two general
groups.   Those conducted among industry executives probe expenditures and buying influences, patterns and needs for a variety of
supplies, equipment and services.   Dealer, wholesaler, distributor
surveys produce "statistical profiles" covering such activities as
products handled; sales volume; buying, selling and servicing practices; budget allocations; and, in certain instances, customer needs,
buying habits and characteristics.

In addition a number of publications issue house organs or
newsletters on industry trends and marketing developments.   Many
provide mailing list services and aid on individual problems, including the mounting of field surveys.

AIR MEDIA

Coverage maps, audience characteristics studies and other
media tools outnumber the marketing materials issued by broadcasting systems and stations.

Trading area information, drawn from standard statistical
sources and tailored to station coverage, is usually available from
the individual broadcasters, from the networks and from station
representatives for the markets covered by their systems.   Occasional surveys, showing product and brand acceptance in their
areas, are issued by some of the radio and television stations.

Among the more sophisticated marketing tools used by air
media are the previously mentioned Media Survey, Inc. reports

and the computerized Marketing Information Bank which supports the sales effort of Group W stations. MIB, fed by reports from 500-family panels in each of the network's markets, supplies product buying and usage data, including demographics on users, brand and private label preferences, loyalty, shopping habits.

On the whole, however, the product/brand, marketing and area data produced by this medium are considered of limited usefulness by many researchers. It has been pointed out that they lack frequency and the standardization necessary for inter-market comparability and that this type of information is relatively easy to obtain elsewhere. Consequently, it is to be expected that stations will continue to channel their rather limited research budgets into media evaluation and selection projects.

GUIDES TO MEDIA SOURCES

AVAILABLE Market Data. Advertising Age. Chicago: Advertising Publications, Inc. Annual feature of an April or May issue.

(KC 1)

A comprehensive annotated bibliography of research and promotional publications recently issued, or planned, by various media. List is classified by national, regional-local, farm, distribution, industrial, professional, Canadian and international markets. Items are coded for 10 types of data contained.

MARKET Information Guide. Industrial Marketing. Chicago: Advertising Publications, Inc. Annual feature of a fall issue.

(KC 2)

Industry market data materials available mostly from trade publications are grouped under broad industry classifications.

BUREAU of Advertising of the American Newspaper Publishers' Association. Research Studies and Reports Published by Newspapers in the United States from August, 1966 through December 1967. New York: Bureau of Advertising,

ANPA, 1968. 47 p.   (KC 3)

Enumerates contents of Consumer Analyses, Top Ten Brands
surveys, Continuing Home Audits, as well as of special subject, audience and market studies.

MAGAZINE Advertising Bureau of Magazine Publishers Association,
Inc.   Bibliography of Consumer Magazine Research, 2d
ed. New York: Magazine Advertising Bureau, 1967. 11 p.   (KC 4)

Product, readership and other research studies of its member magazines arranged in 18 subject categories.

---Sources of Consumer Magazine Information, 2d ed. New
York: Magazine Advertising Bureau, 1965. 16 p.   (KC 5)

Sources of advertising, marketing and audience information
arranged in seven subject groups.

MARKETING Information Guide. (see QB 1)

WHAT'S New in Advertising and Marketing. (see QB 2)

STANDARD Rate and Data Service. Skokie, Ill.: Standard Rate and
Data Service, Inc. Monthly, quarterly or semiannual depending on
edition.   (KC 6)

Primarily a media service giving rates, circulation, dis-
counts and related information.   Issued in a series of ten
editions each devoted to a specific advertising medium.   The
Consumer Magazine and Farm Publications Rates
and Data and Business Publication Rates and Data
editions provide brief descriptions of editorial content, scope
and objectives.   The latter also presents a geographical and
industry analysis of subscribers and identifies feature issues,
special issues and semiannuals, annuals and biennials published by the business and trade press.   Useful for locating
media sources of marketing information. (See also NE 4)

In addition, many individual publishers supply lists of their research materials. A particularly extensive and well indexed compilation:

MARKET and Media Index ... New York: Chemical Engineering, 1967. 45 p. (KC 7)

> A classified, annotated list of the magazine's research reports and basic articles which provide marketing information in the chemical process industries. Detailed subject index.

BUSINESS
FIRMS

Many private business organizations provide a rich source of information. Much of it originates in the course of the firm's own business activity and is offered free for the asking to customers and prospective clients. In a few instances companies commercialize the results of their compilations and research.

Brokerage houses and investment bankers issue industry studies, company analyses and prospectuses. Local and regional data, as well as individual assistance, may be obtained from banks, railroad industrial departments and utilities interested in expanding business activity in their areas. Commodity exchanges supply commodity prices and trading volume. Manufacturers and other business enterprises compile statistics and conduct original research principally to guide their own development or to service the interests of their clients.

A certain amount of such intramural information, statistical and analytic, is issued in house organs, newsletters, and special reports for limited or general distribution. The groups cited below represent an assortment of publications indicative of the data available from these and similar organizations.

PRODUCT AND COMPANY INFORMATION

Despite the number of commercially published product and company directories, detailed research, particularly in the industrial field, relies to a great extent on company-issued information.

Product Literature

Company product catalogs, specification sheets, sales literature, technical bulletins, as well as advertisements in trade and technical journals, provide considerable detail on product properties, end uses and applications.

Some of this literature is available from local distributors. Much of it may be requested directly from the companies themselves which can be identified in business and product directories and catalog services. Many firms maintain mailing lists for such materials. Journals publish articles and announcements on new developments in processes and products. Both means can be used to maintain a current flow of this type of information.

Corporate Literature

House organs, too, are an excellent source for learning about a company's products, research activities, expansion plans. More than 4,000 corporations, mostly manufacturers, issue such magazines and newsletters. But service firms, too, are represented. Well known to marketers, for example, is the Nielsen Researcher which covers many aspects of marketing food and drug products.

The other large source of company information is the financial report. Issued by publicly owned firms, these annual and quarterly documents vary in scope and detail. Many, however, provide in text a corporate profile of progress and plans unavailable in the services which abstract from them only the basic directory and financial facts. Closely related to financial reports are the prospectuses issued by investment banks and brokerage houses whenever corporations call upon their services for public financing. Uniform in format and disclosure, prospectuses present in detail the company's history, product line, purposes for financing, management profiles and balance sheet data.

A selection of useful house organs may be made from the directories listed at the end of this chapter. Financial reports are mailed regularly to stockholders and, upon request, to interested individuals and organizations. A microfiche and microcard service, for annual reports only, is provided by Godfrey Memorial Library for corporations listed on the New York, American and Canadian

Stock Exchanges.   Prospectuses are advertised in the business press.
A favorite medium is the Wall Street Journal.   Since a
limited stock is printed, it is advisable to request them on the day
of announcement.

Advisory Literature

As every investor knows, a large amount of corporate and
product literature is digested and evaluated in the research departments of large brokerage houses and investment banks.   Thus these
firms, in turn, provide company analyses based on information
from corporate and other sources.

INDUSTRY INFORMATION

Brokers, banks, manufacturers and service organizations
also publish a surprising number and variety of industry facts and
aids.   Probably the most generally known are the industry appraisals issued by the major security dealers.   Other publications may
be categorized loosely as advisory, statistical and marketing.   The
following examples have been selected to illustrate each type.

Advisory

Many house organs and newsletters, including those issued
by service firms, some advertising agencies and research organizations, are advisory in nature.   Bank letters, too, although pre-
dominantly devoted to business conditions, carry articles on trends
in specific industries.

GREY Matter. New York: Grey Advertising, Inc. Monthly.
    Advertising, merchandising, marketing, business conditions.

NIELSEN Researcher.   Chicago: A. C. Nielsen Co. Irregular.
    Distribution and marketing.

PETROLEUM Situation. New York: Chase Manhattan Bank. Monthly.

Review of demand, supply, inventory and prices in relation to current marketing situation.

TRAVEL Report. New York: Kelly, Nason, Inc. Monthly.
Digest of news, facts and research materials of current interest to travel industry executives.

Statistical

AMERICAN Telephone and Telegraph Co. The World's Telephones. New York: American Telephone and Telegraph Co. Annual.
Statistics on number of telephones in all countries and all principal cities of the world. Includes data on private and government operation, number of conversations, telephones per 1,000 population.

LAVENTHOL, Krekstein, Horwath & Horwath. Hotel Operations. New York: Laventhol, Krekstein, Horwath & Horwath. Annual.
Current and trend data on room sales and rates, occupancy, operating and financial ratios.
Annual operating ratio studies are also published by the company for motor hotels, restaurants, curb-service drive-ins, country clubs, city clubs, Florida hotels, Puerto Rico hotels.

ELI LILLY & Co. Lilly Digest. Indianapolis, Inc.: Eli Lilly & Co. Annual.
Average operating costs and ratios for over 2,500 retail pharmacies classified by sales size and prescription volume.

METROPOLITAN Life Insurance Co. Statistical Bulletin. New York: Metropolitan Life Insurance Co. Monthly.
Vital statistics data and trends based on published and intramural research. Annual index cumulated decennially.

ROBERT MORRIS Associates. Annual Statement Studies. Philadelphia: Robert Morris Associates. Annual.

> Composite or "average" balance sheets and income statements
> for over 200 different lines of business -- manufacturers
> wholesalers, retailers and services.

NATIONAL Cash Register Co. Expenses in Retail Businesses.
Dayton: National Cash Register Co. Irregular.

> A compilation from various trade sources of operating ratios
> for some 65 types of retail and service outlets. The com-
> pany also maintains a Merchants Service to assist retailers
> with their business problems.

Marketing

A large amount of research is sponsored by manufacturers
for their own guidance in product development and in market planning. Some findings are published primarily to promote the end
use of the company's products among their industrial customers,
retailers and other interested marketers. As evidenced by the
examples cited, these studies differ considerably from those produced by media.

THE AMERICAN Tobacco Co. A New Look at Cigarette and
Related Tobacco Products Merchandising in Supermarkets.
New York: The American Tobacco Co., 1966. 27 p.

> Report on the merchandising methods of stores falling above
> and below the average in sales of tobacco products.

COMMERCIAL Credit Co. Consumer Buying Prospects. Baltimore: Commercial Credit Co. Quarterly.

> A new quarterly survey developed for the company by the
> National Bureau of Economic Research and the U. S. Bureau
> of the Census. It obtains probability judgments from house-
> holds regarding future purchases of automobiles, houses, in-
> dividual appliances and furniture. The data are processed by

the quarterly's editors, a panel of outstanding economists, to develop expected total consumer demand in units and in dollar totals.

E. I. du Pont de Nemours & Co. through its various divisions has issued surveys on the distribution and acceptance of aerosol products; impulse buying of major categories of supermarket products and the characteristics of the supermarket shopper; buying habits of motorists in service stations including types of gasoline and motor oil purchased, make and model of cars serviced, use of credit cards.

Jones & Laughlin Steel Corp. studies and reports on the market for aerosol products and on consumer attitudes toward bedding.

LEVER Brothers Co. McKinsey-Lever Promotion Study: Four Keys to Managing Grocery Advertising and Display Programs More Effectively. New York: Lever Brothers Co.,
1965. 48 p. illus.

---Increasing Distributor Profits on Soaps and Detergents. New York: Lever Brothers Co., 1964.

MARPLAN. The Decade of Incentive. New York: Marplan. Annual.

Economic, marketing, advertising, media review and forecast.

OWENS-Corning Fiberglas Corp. Report on Home Buyer's Preferences. Toledo: Owens-Corning Fiberglas Corp. [1967] unpaged.

Survey of about 10,000 new home buyers. Probes satisfaction with present homes and changes looked for in the purchase of new ones.

THE PILLSBURY CO. Frozen Baked Foods; the View Today.

Minneapolis: The Pillsbury Co. , 1966.   34 p.

> Discusses new opportunities and new requirements in bakery operations and management.

An instance of a cooperative project is the National Travel Market Survey conducted at intervals since 1955 by the University of Michigan Survey Research Center under the sponsorship of a number of commercial organizations.   One study, for example, underwritten by Boeing, General Electric, General Motors, Port of New York Authority and United Air Lines, gathered data on the demographic and economic characteristics of air and overseas travelers.   Another, sponsored by the Federal Aviation Agency, General Motors, Greyhound, Hertz, Port of New York Authority, and Time, detailed the attitudes toward travel and various modes of transportation.   Reports such as these are not always available for general distribution.

BUSINESS CONDITIONS

Bank and brokerage newsletters offer a continuing source on economic conditions and the business and political climate affecting them.   Large banks in major metropolitan areas provide economic analyses of national scope.   Others are a good source for regional and local information.

National

CHASE Manhattan Bank.   Business in Brief.   New York: Chase Manhattan Bank. Bimonthly.

> Notes on current business developments and review articles on economic factors in the news.

CLEVELAND Trust Co.   Business Bulletin.   Cleveland: Cleveland Trust Co. Monthly.

> Evaluation of business conditions.

FIRST National City Bank.   Monthly Economic Letter.   New

York: First National City Bank. Monthly.

   Comment and analysis of all phases of the economy and current business developments.

MORGAN Guaranty Trust Company of New York. Morgan Guaranty
Survey. New York: Morgan Guaranty Trust Company of New York
Monthly.

   Articles and statistics on business and financial conditions.

PRUDENTIAL Insurance Company of America. Economic Forecast.
Newark, N. J.: Prudential Insurance Company of America. Annual.

Regional/Local

FIRST National Bank of Hawaii. Economic Indicators. Honolulu: First National Bank of Hawaii. Monthly.

   Statistics on economic and business activity for the state.

   ---HAWAII in [year] Honolulu: First National Bank of Hawaii.
Annual.

   Review of economic and business conditions.

FRANKLIN National Bank of Long Island. Statistical Abstract
of Nassau and Suffolk Counties. Franklin Square, N. Y.:
Franklin National Bank of Long Island [1962] 320 p. charts, maps.

   Data on population, including income, education, religious
   and political affiliation; manufacturing, trades and services,
   construction; natural resources, communication, transportation; etc.

VALLEY National Bank. Arizona Statistical Review. Phoenix:
Valley National Bank. Annual.

   Facts on population, tourist trade, business activity.

SERVICES

In addition to publications many firms offer advice and assistance on many aspects of business.

Suppliers of packaging equipment and materials maintain laboratories for testing their products and customers' package designs. Many manufacturers offer marketing help, as well as technical assistance, to their clients.

Banks are a good source for unpublished credit information, and data on business conditions and local industries. One large bank, as a service to its retail clients, initiated a program of /reporting monthly department store sales in the New York area to replace the data discontinued by the Federal Reserve Bank. Others maintain special departments to service particular industries.

Railroads and utilities offer assistance for plant locations through their industrial and area development activities. For example:

DATA on Cities of Michigan. Jackson, Mich. : Consumers Power Co. , 1967. [150] p.

GUIDES TO BUSINESS FIRM SOURCES

There are many area, industry and product directories which can be checked for the names of companies that can supply the kind of information and advice discussed here. These can be supplemented by the following references:

U. S. Business and Defense Services Administration. Data Sources for Plant Location Analysis. Washington, D. C. : Government Printing Office, 1959. p. 38-41.   (L 1)

Includes a brief directory of railroad industrial departments.

Haight Hill Co. , on the basis of a survey, has compiled the names of commercial banks who have local market data and information on the type of statistics collected.

Publications of business firms are announced in the trade press and listed in the regular bibliographies of marketing materials. The best guides to house organs, however, are the two directories listed below:

GEBBIE House Magazine Directory. Sioux City, Ia.: House Magazine Publishing Co., Inc. Triennial.   (L 2)

SCIENCE-Technology House Journals. [New York] Special Libraries Association San Francisco Bay Region Chapter [1967] unpaged.   (L 3)
    List of company-issued house organs available in the libraries
    of the San Francisco Bay Region Chapter. Includes only those
    publications which contain informative technical articles on re-
    search and development.

DIRECTORIES
AND MAILING 'LISTS

DIRECTORIES

Directories constitute a unique group. Compiled and published by a variety of agencies, public and private, they serve a dual purpose. Some, like the directories of services, associations, periodicals, and specialists, are guides to information and as such are listed in the chapters relating to those sources. The larger number, however, are marketing tools - - aids in the identification of prospective customers and in the direction of sales strategy for a wide variety of goods and services.

The type of information in these directories varies from simple name and address listings to complex analyses of company operations and detailed product classifications. Coverage, too, ranges from multi-industry compilations to lists of specific commodities; from comprehensive enumeration of local residents and enterprises to selective or topical lists of national scope.

For practical use a selected number of general purpose, national directories are grouped here in two categories: biographical and business. Familiarity with the content and special features of these, and of the local and specialized directories, indicates, however, a usefulness beyond such precise classification. Thus, too, often overlooked in the search for specifics is the ubiquitous telephone directory and the equally common and useful city directories.

Telephone Directories

Alphabetical and classified subscriber directories for every community serviced are frequently updated and easily available from the local telephone companies. Collections of out-of-town directories are often maintained by local telephone offices, public libraries or chambers of commerce. Particularly useful are the classified sections not only for their specific product and business listings but also for the advertisements elaborating on the products and services of local firms.

City Directories

City directories, usually compiled by private companies specializing in this type of publication, are available for all but the largest metropolitan areas on a current basis, annual or biennial. Standard information includes names of residents with telephone, address, occupation and home ownership indicated; local businesses classified by type of activity; government officials and other city information. Businesses arranged by street address and special listings of manufacturing firms are frequent features.

City directories may be purchased from their publishers or consulted at the local public library. Also, the Association of North American Directory Publishers maintains over 1,000 City Directory Libraries, usually at local chambers of commerce, where publications of its members are available for brief reference.

Biographical Directories

Biographical dictionaries of prominent men and women such as Who's Who in America and its companion publications are universally familiar. Two general directories of business executives are listed below. Local and regional directories in this category are comparatively few. Numerous, however, are the specialized directories of trade and professional people. Many are issued by commercial publishers, some as rosters of trade and professional societies. Some associations provide lists of conference attendees which lack biographical detail but are a particularly good source of prominent and active professionals. Executive listings are also commonly included in firm and product directories.

WHO'S Who in Advertising, 1st ed.; edited with an introduction by Eldridge Peterson ... New York: Who's Who in Advertising, Inc.,

1963. 1,275 p.   (M 1)

The only directory devoted to biographies of executives engaged in advertising, marketing, media, art and related activities. A company index lists individuals by current business affiliation.

WORLD Who's Who in Commerce and Industry. Chicago: Marquis Who's Who, Inc. Biennial.   (M 2)

Biographical sketches of prominent businessmen, here and abroad. Company-executive index.

U. S. Congress. Official Congressional Directory. Washington, D. C.: Government Printing Office. Published for each session of Congress.   (M 3)

Outlines the organization and membership of the legislative, executive and judicial branches of the federal government. Particularly useful for its detailed roster of committees and congressmen who, in many instances, are the only source of supply for copies of certain bills, congressional documents, hearings and reports.

POOR'S Register of Corporations, Directors and Executives, United States and Canada. New York: Standard & Poor's Corp. Annual.   (M 4)

Primarily a directory of corporate personnel updated by three quarterly supplements. Company listings give home office, officers, principal products, number of employees and, in many instances, annual sales. Standard Industrial Classification numbers and a product breakdown into 900 groups in the industry section permit further identification of firms' activities. Executive index includes brief biographies and intercorporate affiliations. The Geographical Index is published separately.

Business Directories

Information on products and firms, helpful in locating mar-

kets for goods and services as well as sources of supply, is inter-
woven in numerous general and specialized business or trade directories: purchasing directories or buyers' guides; general industrial
directories - - national, state, local; directories of given manufacturing or business lines.

Nor is business directory information limited to simple listings of company and product names. Commonly included are data
on employment, plant location and capacity, executive personnel,
and equipment, as well as general statistics for the industry.

Although many product and special industry directories are issued by commercial publishers, an even larger number are compiled
by trade journals servicing the particular field. These are distributed as special issues to subscribers or sold independently. Regional
and local directories of manufacturers are usually compiled by state
or local government agencies, by chambers of commerce, and by
university bureaus of business research. Some national or local
publications of all types in this group are also issued by trade associations.

Route lists of retailers and wholesalers are ordinarily provided as a service to advertisers by newspapers in many large cities.
These directories, arranged by street address in a sequence convenient in guiding a salesman's calls, are most numerous for drug
and grocery outlets.

Some generally useful business directories are listed below.
Others may be located through the bibliographies and guides given
at the end of this chapter.

Business Directories: Products

MACRAE'S Blue Book. Chicago: MacRae's Blue Book Co.   (MA 1)
Annual.

> Primarily a purchasing guide for engineering, production and
> purchasing executives. Manufacturers are listed alphabetical-
> ly under specific product headings. Contains a trade name
> index and an alphabetical company index which shows products,
> addresses, and invested capital ratings.

THOMAS Register of American Manufacturers. New York: Thomas
Publishing Co. Annual.   (MA 2)

>   Directory of manufacturers and suppliers classified by product
>   and arranged geographically. Gives addresses and capital rat-
>   ings. Company, trade name, and product category indexes.

   In addition to product directories, catalogs of individual suppliers are collected and distributed in published or, more recently,
in microimage form. The major microfilm catalog files cited below,
like the printed product directories and buying guides, indicate two
approaches, industry by industry (e. g. , Sweet's, CSMF, VSMF) and
all manufacturing industries (e. g. , Thomas).

SWEET'S ... Catalog Services. New York: F. W. Dodge. Annual.
                                                               (MA 3)

>   Basically these are bound volumes of manufacturers' catalogs
>   assembled in product groups for use by industrial purchasers.
>   Each set is indexed under manufacturers' names, products or
>   services, and trade names. Sets, issued in two series, are
>   grouped as follows:
>   Sweet's Industrial Catalog Services
>   Plant Engineering Catalog File
>   Manufacturing Engineering Catalog File
>   Product Design Catalog File
>   Interior Design Catalog File (In preparation)
>   Sweet's Construction Catalog Services
>   Architectural Catalog File
>   Industrial Construction Catalog File
>   Light Construction Catalog File
>   Other catalog files, standards and specifications are
>   available in microimage or printed form.

THOMAS Micro-Catalogs (TM-C). New York: Thomas Publishing
Co. Annual with mid-year supplement.   (MA 4)

>   Technical product information in vendors' catalogs reproduced
>   on microfiche alphabetically by vendor name. Cross-indexed

by product classification in a product index.

VSMF (Visual Search Microfilm File). Englewood, Colo.: Information Handling Services, Inc. Triennial.   (MA 5)

  Catalog data, specifications, drawings and test reports on parts, materials, services and equipment are issued in 16mm microfilm cartridge form in two editions: Defense Products Edition and OEM Design Edition for commercial and industrial products. The Vendor Selector Edition provides data on the capabilities, facilities, finances and personnel of all manufacturers of defense, commercial and industrial equipment. Service includes a product-company index.

CSMF (Chemical Specifications Microfilm File) Englewood, Colo.: Information Handling Services, Inc. Quarterly.   (MA 6)

  Catalog pages and other technical data on equipment, materials, services and capabilities used in the chemical, petrochemical and refining industries are grouped and indexed by specific product group, category and types. Published in 16mm microfilm cartridge form.

Business Directories: Plants

  Plant directories are available in three forms: custom computer printouts from data banks maintained by services and some directory publishers; multi-industry plant directories which cover major manufacturing companies; single-industry plant directories such as the Metalworking Directory listed below. In seeking the single-industry type, major trade papers as a source should not be overlooked.

FORTUNE. Plant and Product Directory. New York: Time, Inc. Biennial.   (MA 7)

  Includes the top 1,000 manufacturing firms. The company section lists plants under their parent companies, which are alphabetically arranged, and shows plant locations and products of each company and each plant. The geographical section lists

plants by state and county, enumerates all products manufactured at the plant, and gives approximate employment to
indicate plant capacity. In the product section, plants are
listed by industry in 5-digit SIC order with a product index.
Information includes parent company and division, SIC
number of each product, approximate employment.

KEY Plants. New York: Market Statistics, Inc. Triennial.   (MA 8)
Contains all manufacturing plants with 100 or more employees.
Each listing contains plant name, address (including county),
4-digit SIC number, employment to nearest 100 and name of
parent company where applicable. Arranged in two ways: by
4-digit SIC code; by state, county within state, and 4-
digit SIC within county. Data also available on punched
cards for customized printouts from Market Statistics, Inc.

METALWORKING Directory   New York: Dun & Bradstreet, Inc.
Annual.   (MA 9)
Lists some 35,000 plants and 1,800 metals distributors geographically, by product line, alphabetically. Statistical summary shows number of plants by line of business and by number of employees in each county. Directory information includes plant personnel, employment, primary and secondary
products, operations and processes performed, raw materials
purchased.

Business Directories: Companies

MILLION Dollar Directory. New York: Dun & Bradstreet, Inc.
Annual with twice yearly supplements.   (MA 10)
For businesses with a net worth of $1 million and over, shows
nature of enterprise, range of sales volume, number of employees, 4-digit SIC code, names of officers and directors.
Section II classifies the companies geographically; Section III
lists them by type of business (Standard Industrial Classification numbers). Section IV is an alphabetical list of officers
and directors and their company affiliations. Interim informa-

tion on unlisted companies is available upon request.

MIDDLE Market Directory. New York: Dun & Bradstreet, Inc.
Annual.   (MA 1)
    Includes companies with net worth of $500,000 to $1,000,000.
    In nature of information and in arrangement (by name, geo-
    graphical location and type of business) it resembles the
    Million Dollar Directory listed above.

    Although many business and product directories include data
on company capitalization, employment and other indicators of size
and financial status, the following two are special purpose compilations of large firms identified and ranked by various factors.

FORTUNE Directory. The 500 Largest U. S. Industrial Corpora-
tions and the 50 Largest Banks, Merchandising, Transportation,
Life-Insurance, and Utility Companies. New York: Time, Inc.
Annually in mid-June issue.

---200 Largest Foreign Industrial Corporations. New York: Time, Inc.
Annually in mid-September issue.   (MA 12)
    Ranked rosters of these seven business groups give head-
    quarters location and data on sales, assets, net profit, in-
    vested capital, and other financial information. Publication
    dates vary slightly.

NEWS Front. ... Leading U. S. Corporations. New York: Year
Incorporated. Annual (?)   (MA 13)
    Included are publicly owned and privately held companies (manu-
    facturers with sales of $1 million and over; service firms with
    100 plus employees) classified by 3-digit SIC categories and
    ranked by sales or revenues. Also shown are share of market
    employees, number of plants, earnings, and other financial
    data. The whole is indexed alphabetically and geographically.
    Further analyses appear regularly in the monthly magazine.
    Published and a large amount of unpublished detail is available

on punched cards, tape and printouts.

More detailed data on the organization, finances, and credit ratings of individual 'companies (also available from local banks) are published by such service as Moody's, Standard & Poor's, Dun & Bradstreet.

Closer study of a business enterprise, if it is a publicly owned corporation, may call for an analysis of such primary sources as annual reports and proxy statements.

Bibliographies and Guides: Comprehensive

KLEIN, Bernard. Guide to American Directories. New York: Klein and Co. Triennial.   (MB 1)

> Gives publisher, address, contents, and price for each directory. Arrangement is by some 250 business, industry and professional groups with alphabetical title index.

TRADE Directories of the World. Queens Village, N. Y.: Croner Publications. Monthly looseleaf service.   (MB 2)

> Some 1,500 directories are arranged by title under country of publication. Citations include pagination, frequency, scope, price, name and address of publisher. Indexed by country, and trades and professions.

U. S. Small Business Administration. National Directories for Use in Marketing. (Small Business Bibliography no. 13). Washington, D. C.: Small Business Administration. Irregular.   (MB 3)

> A subject indexed list of some 100 directories with emphasis on those businesses which buy goods for resale. Introductory text suggests sources for locating other directories, national and local.

Many directories and their scheduled publication dates are included in

SPECIAL Libraries Association. Guide to Special Issues ...
(see NE 5)

STANDARD Rate & Data Service, Inc. Business Publication
Rates and Data (see KC 6)

      Newly published national, regional, general, and specialized
trade directories are listed regularly in Marketing Information
Guide.
                                         (MB 4)

PUBLIC Affairs Information Service Bulletin indexes separately
published works in all fields as well as directory features of magazines and other publications. The annual volume provides a convenient cumulative list.
                                         (MB 5)

BUSINESS Periodicals Index cites separately, or under specific
subject, those directories which appear in the magazines covered
by the service.
                                         (MB 6)

Bibliographies and Guides: Specialized

AMERICAN Telephone & Telegraph Co. Telephone Directory
Price List. New York: American Telephone & Telegraph Co.
Approximately annual.
                                         (MB 7)
      Section 1 groups geographically Bell System and most inde-
      pendent company directories published in the United States and
      Canada. Localities not having directories of their own are
      cross-referenced to the directory in which their listings ap-
      pear. Symbols indicate the availability of white pages, yel-
      low pages and month of publication. Section 2, similarly ar-
      ranged but giving less detail, lists directories published out-
      side the United States and Canada.

ASSOCIATION of North American Directory Publishers. Catalog
of City, County and State Directories Published in North America.
New York: Association of North American Directory
Publishers. Annual.
                                           (MB 8)

Arranged by states and provinces (Canada) each directory is coded for special features, frequency of publication and name of publisher, and is indexed for geographical coverage. Included are listings of both member and nonmember publishers.

CHAMBER of Commerce of the United States. Sources of State Information and State Industrial Directories. (see FA 3)

E-D Index of Free-Listing Directories. Chicago: Engel-Dow Sales Methods Division, Thomas Tobias Engel, Inc. Triennial.   (MB 9)

Classifies by trade several hundred industrial directories and buyers guides which accord free listings for products and services. Each listing gives name of directory, publisher's address, frequency and publication dates, industry and markets served, contents, circulation, closing dates and listing information.

DIRECTORY of Commercial Directories and Annual Publications. New York: William Dogan Annual Publications Associates, 1968. 116 p.   (MB 9a)

Classified list of annual buyers' guides and directories that accept advertising. Title and SIC number indexes.

BRITTON, Hugh, et al. Industrial Directories. Chicago: American Marketing Association, 1963. xii, 63 p.   (MB 10)

Guide to state industrial directories compiled by the AMA Industrial Directories Committee. It is divided into two parts. The first reports on the content, format and methods of compilation of current directories; provides a checklist of evaluation criteria; and, as a guide to publishers, suggests improvements in content and arrangement. The second part cites an industrial directory for each state, where available, or a statement of publication plans for those states for which no directories exist. Each directory listed is accompanied by information on the name and address of publisher, price, frequency, dates of latest and forthcoming editions, format, sources of

data used, method of obtaining the information, and prospective changes.

MAILING LISTS

Directories and original records are the primary sources used
in the compilation of specialized mailing lists for all lines of businesses and all types of individuals. The lists are of two general
types. Mail order lists consist of names that originated in sales
or responded to promotion appeal mailings similar to those of the
list buyer. Compiled lists consist of names, individual or corporate,
culled from a variety of sources to tap a specific market.

The quality and selectivity of mailing lists have always been
of major consideration to list buyers. Both are becoming more at-
tainable through new developments in the industry. Professional
auditing of mailing lists is provided by the Audit Bureau of Marketing Services, an affiliate of the Audit Bureau of Circulations. The
report format was established in cooperation with the Direct Mail
Advertising Association. Audited data include breakdowns by basic
list categories, geographical distribution, sex and source of names,
and also provide data on the extent of duplication and deliverability.

Greater selectivity is possible through the application of
electronic data processing. A leader in the industry estimates that
about 10,000 of the 500,000 lists used are computerized and that the
number will double every three years or so. Such automation offers list buyers the prospect of a highly sophisticated product almost continuously current. Already available are businesses by
SIC classifications, sales size, geographic location; individuals by
age, sex, occupation, spending for air transportation, travel, department store purchases.

The Donnelley Quality Index, for example, electronically
maintained by The Reuben H. Donnelley Corp., is a blend of its
automobile owner list and other sources. Coded to census tracts
and such consumer characteristics as educationsl level, income,
family size, housing, families with children, it is one of the company's precisely tooled prospect lists. Others developed by the
firm's marketing division are the Donnelley Suburbia Index of fami-

lies in quality urbanized areas and the Donnelley Home Improvement and Upkeep Index, available on a service basis only, of home re-modeling and modernization prospects.

Some mailing list houses offer national or local lists in a limited number of lines. A number of large firms maintain a wide variety of mailing lists and issue catalogs of those readily avail-able. Since these price lists indicate the number of names per list and are often revised annually, they also serve as useful guides to the number of prospective customers.

All mailing lists, ready-made or custom compiled, are either sold or rented. In the latter case, the mailing house itself addresses, inserts and posts the outgoing literature. As a rule, these services are also available for lists sold. In addition, some houses offer to supply copy, design and production facilities for the mailing piece themselves.

Trade journal publishers, trade and professional associations, newspapers, magazines, chambers of commerce are also useful sources of mailing lists and mailing list services.

Although not the best substitutes, current catalogs of general-line houses and the classified telephone directories may be used for lack of the following guides.

DIRECTORY of Mailing List Houses. New York: B. Klein and Co. Biennial.   (MC 1)

> For more than 1,000 brokers, compilers and list houses, ar-ranged geographically, gives founding year, types of lists and services offered, name of manager and address. Alphabetical subject index refers to companies by their city listing. Re-vised approximately every two years.

STANDARD Rate and Data Service. Direct Mail Lists Rates and Data. Skokie, Ill.: Standard Rate & Data Service, Inc. Semiannual with updating bulletins.   (MC 2)

> Business, consumer and farm lists classified and indexed by industry, product or consumer demographics. In addition to description of list, reports list source, size, rental rate,

delivery time, how list is cleaned and maintained. Also contains brokers and custom compilers sections.

U. S. Small Business Administration. National Mailing-List Houses. (Small Business Bibliography no. 29). Washington, D. C.: Small Business Administration. Irregular.   (MC 3)

General-line and limited-line houses are listed separately. Each entry includes address and description of lists and services offered. Also includes suggestions for building and maintaining mailing lists.

PERIODICALS

Up-to-date facts are a prime necessity.

The business sections of such newspapers as The New York Times report local and national events of business significance as they occur. In addition, they publish review articles on individual products and industries from time to time. More detailed, and equally timely, are the business dailies, Wall Street Journal and Journal of Commerce.

Supplementing the currency and straight reporting of the daily press is the interpretative reporting of periodicals with their deeper, more analytic, more specialized coverage.

New developments of interest to marketers range through many areas, from new product announcements to basic research techniques and methodology. The mainstream of such information courses through a great variety of periodicals whose responsiveness to trends in the field creates a constant flux in their editorial content. Thus, the current focus on marketing has been reflected not only in the introduction of new periodicals but also in a significant shift of editorial emphasis to this subject, particularly by the business and trade press.

Consequently, each practitioner must select and update his own reading list on the basis of the timeliness and editorial policy which would supply him with the coverage necessary for his immediate needs or for research on specific problems.

Grouped below are those periodicals which offer a continuing flow of marketing information and only a sampling of specialized magazines. A larger selection of the latter is available in the directories cited at the end of this chapter.

Statistical magazines of federal agencies, newsletters of banks and services, periodicals issued by colleges and universities, research institutions and other corporate bodies have been treated

in the chapters devoted to these sources. Further information on
such publications can be located in the directories and catalogs
covering those organizations.

TABLES OF CONTENTS

Compilations of photographically reproduced tables of contents of various journals have been current for some years in the scientific field. Their purpose is to present to the busy reader a compact overview of articles appearing in selected periodicals pertinent to the subject field. Listed below is the first such publication for the businessman.

TABLES of Contents. Princeton, N. J.: Marketing Communications
Research Center. Monthly.   (N 1)
> Tables of contents of current issues of selected marketing
> and advertising publications from the United States, Canada
> and England.

PROFESSIONAL JOURNALS

JOURNAL of Marketing. Chicago: American Marketing Association.
Quarterly.   (NA 1)
> Leading journal devoted exclusively to all phases of marketing.

JOURNAL of Marketing Research. Chicago: American Marketing
Association. Quarterly.   (NA 2)
> Initiated in 1964 as a medium for technical articles on mar-
> keting research.

Research methods and techniques, statistical and technical
problems of survey research, developments in sociology and applied psychology, and allied areas of interest to marketing are covered in a number of journals. Most of these are issued by professional societies and have been included in the descriptions of the respective associations. Among them, for example, are the following:

JOURNAL of Advertising Research. New York: Advertising Research Foundation. Quarterly.   (NA 3)

PUBLIC Opinion Quarterly. Princeton, N. J.: Princeton University Press. Quarterly.   (NA 4)

AMERICAN Economic Review. Evanston, Ill.: Northwestern University. 5/yr.   (NA 5)

JOURNAL of the American Statistical Association. Washington, D. C.: American Statistical Association. Quarterly.   (NA 6)

JOURNAL of Applied Psychology. Washington, D. C.: American Psychological Association. Bimonthly.   (NA 7)

AMERICAN Sociological Review. Washington, D. C.: American Sociological Association. Bimonthly.   (NA 8)

BUSINESS MAGAZINES

BUSINESS Week. New York: McGraw-Hill. Weekly.   (NB 1)
Articles on industries, individual companies, technological advances, new product developments, and national events of interest to business management; special reports on regional business conditions; monthly data on personal income by states; findings of McGraw-Hill economic research projects.

DUN'S Review. New York: Dun & Bradstreet, Inc. Monthly. (NB 2)
Covers new advances in business and industry. Publishes Dun & Bradstreet data on business failures; operating ratios; survey-based quarterly forecasts, including a Sales Optimism Index of manufacturers, wholesalers, and retailers for sales, profits, prices, inventories, and employment.

FORTUNE. New York: Time, Inc. Monthly.   (NB 3)
Detailed, analytic treatments in nontechnical language of economic and marketing factors, industries and individual

companies; comprehensive series on timely topics including consumer and capital goods markets; assessments of current business conditions and estimates of capital requirements based on original research.

HARVARD Business Review. Boston: Harvard University Graduate School of Business Administration. Bimonthly.   (NB 4)

Presents analytic articles, authored by academic and business specialists, on all phases of business management, including marketing.

NATION'S Business. Washington, D. C.: Chamber of Commerce of the United States. Monthly.   (NB 5)

Mainly of interest for its occasional forecasts of general business conditions and individual industry outlooks.

NEWS Front. New York: Year Incorporated. Monthly.   (NB 6)

Business magazine notable for its annual analyses: 1,000 leading United States manufacturers; 500 leading United States nonmanufacturers; best managed United States corporations; 1,000 leading foreign corporations; R&D expenditures of leading United States corporations. Keyword index of major articles (January issue).

Although directed at investors, financial magazines such as Forbes and Barron's publish value background material, not available elsewhere, on industries, companies and products.

NEWSLETTERS

National Affairs

AMERICAN Letter. Washington, D. C.: Whaley-Eaton Service. Weekly.   (NC 1)

Covers Washington political and economic developments.

KIPLINGER Washington Letter. Washington, D. C.: The Kiplinger

Washington Editors, Inc. Weekly.   (NC 2)

   Analyses and some forecasting of political and economic
   events.

KIPLINGER Tax Letter. Washington, D. C.: The Kiplinger Washington Editors, Inc. Biweekly.   (NC 3)

   News and advisory service on federal tax legislation and administration.

REPORT for the Business Executive. Washington, D. C.: National Research Bureau, Inc. Weekly.   (NC 4)

   Interpretative service on Washington developments affecting
   all phases of business.   Brief comments on business indicators, national economy, taxation, labor, international affairs.

Individual Industries

   Unlike the national newsletters, many of those serving individual industries tend to report facts rather than to interpret or
predict the news. Their format, however, and timeliness relate
them more to this category than to services which place a greater
emphasis in reference use.

In agriculture:

DOANE'S Agricultural Report. St. Louis: Doane Agricultural Service, Inc. 3/month.   (NC 5)

   Reports on all phases of farm management and farm economics including price forecasts.

KIPLINGER Agricultural Letter. Washington, D. C.: The Kiplinger
Washington Editors, Inc. Biweekly.   (NC 6)

   Forecasts, advice, and interpretation of political and economic news of interest to farmers.

For the automobile industry:

WARD'S Automotive Reports. Detroit: Ward's Automotive Reports.
Weekly.   (NC 7)
> News, statistics and forecasts of United States and Canadian
> industry production and sales.

For the chemical and allied industries:

CHEMICAL Horizons Reports. New York: Chemical Horizons, Inc.
Weekly.   (NC 8)
> Issued in two editions: North American and Overseas. Brief
> abstracts of trade journal articles of current interest to
> chemical marketing and sales executives.

SEARCH: CPI Marketing and Statistics. Fort Lee, N. J.: Compendium Publishers International Corp. Monthly.   (NC 9)
> One of 19 services each of which is devoted to a segment of
> the chemical or allied product industry. Presents digests of
> articles from the business and trade press. Cumulative in-
> dex.

For the petroleum industry:

PLATT'S Oilgram News Service. New York: McGraw-Hill, Inc.
Daily.   (NC 10)
> News of all segments of the oil industry for a management
> audience.

PLATT'S Oilgram Price Service. New York: McGraw-Hill, Inc.
Daily.   (NC 11)
> Reports prices and news of industry and government actions
> affecting them.

Of multi-industry interest:

NEW Products Digest.   New York: Batten, Barton, Durstine &
Osborn Information Center. Monthly.   (NC 12)

Consumer and industrial products and services classified by
broad industry groups. Each entry gives product's name,
manufacturer, size, price and other detail. Alphabetical
product/service name index and company name index in each
issue.

TRADE PUBLICATIONS

Much marketing information appears in the numerous magazines which service the individual industries and trades. Scope and
editorial coverage expand in direct relationship to the specialized
interests of each magazine's audience.

Some publications support their own research programs and
report statistical data on the products and services of their industries
as regular features of their editorial content. Larger projects are
incorporated in special issues distributed regularly to subscribers.
A number of such compilations serve as basic handbooks in their
respective industries and in market research.

In all cases, editorial staffs, well versed in their highly
specialized fields, can supplement published data with information
drawn from experience.

Advertising and Marketing

General advertising magazines carry news and articles on
marketing developments, plans and case histories, and announcements of research sources as they become available. Much of
their material is topical and pertinent to the study of individual
products, companies and industries.

ADVERTISING Age. Chicago: Advertising Publications, Inc. Weekly.
(ND 1)

Timely and broad news coverage of all events of interest to
marketers as well as advertisers.

INDUSTRIAL Marketing. Chicago: Advertising Publications, Inc.
Monthly.   (ND 2)

News and articles directed to advertising and marketing executives in business and industry. A Spring issue carries a list of business publications and a Fall issue a section on marketing information available from industrial media.

MARKETING/Communications. New York: Decker Communications, Inc. Monthly.   (ND 3)

Formerly Printers' Ink. News reports and basic articles on current developments in the advertising, merchandising, and marketing of consumer and industrial goods and services. Provides bibliographies and reprints of articles on all topics covered by the magazine.

MARKETING Forum. New York: Bardo Publications, Inc. Bimonthly.   (ND 4)

Feature articles of interest to industrial marketers.

MARKETING Insights. Chicago: Advertising Publications, Inc. Weekly during the school year.   (ND 5)

For college students and teachers in marketing, advertising and journalism. Editorial content represents the application of marketing principles by practitioners.

SALES Management. New York: Sales Management, Inc. 27/yr.
                                                                  (ND 6)

Informative articles on all phases of marketing, selling and distribution.

More specialized publications in this field offer occasional articles and case histories of general marketing interest.

Other Industries

Industry trade journals are one of the most important information sources available, particularly to the industrial market researcher. Their awareness of trends generally precedes actual events. It also permits them to forecast the effect of technological progress and economic conflicts on products and industries. Advertisements in these magazines, as mentioned previously, are important indicators of product properties, end uses and applications as well as of new developments. Regular issues, in many instances, carry current statistics compiled by trade associations, government agencies and, in some cases, by their own research efforts. Comprehensive data are usually featured annually in the magazine or published separately. In addition to these statistical factbooks, trade papers issue handbooks, manuals and by far the largest proportion of all buying guides and directories published.

A brief sampling, purely illustrative, follows:

Frozen Food Age section on institutional marketing
Food Topics study of "consumer expenditures" for food store products.
Drug Topics similar study for drug store products.
Modern Brewery Age Blue Book
Merchandising Week statistical issue on household appliance market
Variety Department Store Merchandiser "Profit Engineering Study"
Automotive News Almanac
National Petroleum News Factbook
Chemical and Engineering News facts and figures issue
Electronic Buyers' Guide
Modern Plastics Encyclopedia
Machine Design fastening and joining reference issue
Industrial Research yearbook and buyers' guide

DIRECTORIES OF PERIODICALS

N. W. AYER & Son's Directory of Newspapers and Periodicals. Philadelphia: N. W. Ayer & Son, Inc. Annual.   (NE 1)
    Gives names of editor and publisher, address, date estab-

lished, frequency, and circulation. Titles are arranged by
city of publication under state. Alphabetical and classified
subject indexes.

ULRICH'S International Periodicals Directory ... New York: R. R.
Bowker Co. Triennial with supplements.   (NE 2)
  Over 25,000 periodicals published around the world are
  grouped by detailed subjects arranged alphabetically. In addition to the regular directory information such as price, address, frequency, etc., each entry indicates the presence of
  abstracts, bibliographies, statistics and other editorial features; name of editor; services which abstract or index it.
  Title-Subject index.

THE Standard Periodical Directory. New York: Oxbridge Publishing
Co., Inc. Annual with supplements.   (NE 3)
  Arranged by numbered subject categories which are indexed
  alphabetically. For each title gives name and address of
  publisher, name of editor, editorial coverage, frequency and
  other detail. Title index.

STANDARD Rate and Data Service. Skokie, Ill.: Standard Rate &
Data Service, Inc. Monthly, quarterly or semiannual depending on
edition.   (NE 4)
  To be listed in this service a periodical "must carry a significant amount of national advertising which is sold through
  advertising agencies." Full directory information given in the
  detail necessary for media buying. Periodical editions are:
        Business Publication Rates and Data. Monthly.
        Consumer Magazine and Farm Publication Rates and Data.
            Monthly.
        Newspaper Rates and Data. Monthly.
        Weekly Newspaper Rates and Data. Semiannual.
            This edition also includes shopping guides.
  For additional detail see KC 6.

GUIDE to Special Issues and Indexes of Periodicals, ed. by Doris B.
Katz, et al. New York: Special Libraries Association, 1962. vi,
125 p.   (NE 5)

Alphabetical listing of 799 consumer, trade and technical periodicals showing for each the availability of advertiser and editorial indexes, and "specials")i. e. , special sections, features
and/or issues). Detailed subject index.

STATISTICAL and Review Issues of Trade and Business Periodicals.
Boston: Harvard University Graduate School of Business Administration, Baker Library. Irregular.   (NE 6)

Special issues with approximate date of publication listed under
magazines arranged alphabetically by title. Subject index.

NATIONAL Directory of Newsletters and Reporting Services, 1st ed.
Detroit: Gale Research Company, 1966. 252 p.   (NE 7)

Approximately 1,500 publications of associations, commercial
and research organizations grouped in 12 subject categories.
For each newsletter or service gives name of issuing body and
editor, frequency, subscription rate, sc pe and content. Subject index.

ABSTRACTS
AND INDEXES

The major difference between abstracts and indexes is that abstracts present the basic contents of a publication in brief form whereas indexes cite only its title (verbatim or in meaningful phrases), author, publisher, date and paging. Consequently, abstracts, if topically arranged or subject indexed, are more immediately informative than indexes.

Many publications are planned and produced to fill the precise function of abstract or index. Others, however, elude such categorical classification.

In marketing, there is a dearth of both types of bibliographic tools. Cited here, therefore, in addition, are annotated bibliographies and other substitutes issued on a continuing basis. To accommodate the broad scope of marketing, abstracts, indexes and "substitutes" from the allied sciences and other subject fields are included as well. Applying formal definitions loosely, these publications are classed on the basis of their applicability. Those which cite or describe contents are listed as abstracts; those lacking this feature are grouped with indexes.

ABSTRACTS

In general, literature abstracts are brief summaries of current articles, books, pamphlets, and are published for the benefit of workers in a particular subject or in a particular field. Each carries complete bibliographic identification for easy reference to the original source. Arrangement and/or indexing provide a detailed subject approach.

Some abstracts appear as regular features of professional journals. Others, assembled and issued in periodical format by pro-

fessional societies or commercial publishers, are usually distributed
on a subscription basis and are generally referred to as abstract
journals or abstract services.

A small number of such services in the field of marketing have
come and gone. Currently available are the sources grouped below.
Those devoted to marketing literature in particular precede a number of services whose coverage encompasses areas of general and
specialized interest in marketing and market research.

Omitted are abstract features of periodicals in allied fields.
These, as well as other abstract journals, can be found by checking Ulrich's.

Marketing Abstracts

MARKET Research Abstracts. London: The Market Research Society.   Semiannual.   (O 1)
   Abstracts from British and American periodicals selected
   from the fields of research, statistics, psychology, sociology,
   economics, marketing, advertising and business management.
   Arranged by broad subject groups with specific subject index.

MARKETING Abstracts. Journal of Marketing.   Chicago: American Marketing Association.   Quarterly.   (O 2)
   Signed reviews of significant marketing articles culled from a
   broad list of business and trade periodicals and other publications. Included are occasional studies by government agencies
   and business organizations.   Listing is under 22 general subjects arranged alphabetically.

LEGAL Developments in Marketing.   Journal of Marketing.
Chicago: American Marketing Association. Quarterly.   (O 3)
   Abstracts of legislation and litigation arranged under specific
   topics with full citations to the Commerce Clearing House
   Trade Regulation Reporter and other sources.

MARKETING Information Guide.   (see QB 1)

General Business and Industry "Abstracts"

PREDICASTS. Cleveland: Predicasts, Inc. Quarterly; Annual cumulative summary.   (OA 1)

From some 250 publications this service abstracts all forecasts for general economic indicators, industries, products
and services.   Each abstract gives forecast's effect on other
products; base period, short and long range data; document
source. Arrangement is by modified 5-digit SIC code.
Another section presents composite forecasts (medians of published forecasts adjusted to form a consistent pattern) for some
160 economic and industrial series.

EXPANSION and Capacity Digest. Cleveland: Predicasts, Inc.
Quarterly; April issue is 12-month cumulative.   (OA 2)

Data on existing and projected capacities, expansions and
capital spending of industries and individual producers from
trade, business, financial and government press. Arranged
in two sections: 1) by industry, tabular form shows product,
SIC number, producer, plant location, in-place capacity, expansion and its cost, date and page of publication used as
source; 2) alphabetical company list gives expansion and
capacity news followed by citation of information source.

WORLDCASTS. Cleveland: Predicasts, Inc. Quarterly.   (OA 3)

Published in two editions, regional and product. Information
is almost the same in both editions which differ principally
in their arrangement. Each edition is also available by
specific region or product category. Sources of information
and presentation similar to those above.

Individual Industry Abstracts

The long tradition of abstracting scientific chemical literature has carried over into the business aspects of the industry.
Listed here are several services published specifically to aid the
marketer in chemical and allied fields. Excluded are the many sci-

entific and technical abstracting services which, too, are significant tools for industrial market researchers. These, however, can be easily identified in Ulrich's.

CHEMICAL Horizons Intelligence File. New York: Chemical
Horizons, Inc. Biweekly.   (OA 4)
> Current abstracts of market data from trade and business press and conference reports supplied on 3x5 cards indexed for product, company and geographic location.

CHEMICAL Horizons Information Fulfillment Service. New York:
Chemical Horizons, Inc.   (OA 5)
> An inquiry service which supplies back files or a continuing supply of abstracts on specified items of chemical market information. Coverage dates back to 1963 and is based on the company's Intelligence File service.

CHEMICAL Market Abstracts. New York: Foster D. Snell, Inc.
Monthly.   (OA 6)
> Abstracts articles in professional and trade journals, government reports, house organs, company annual reports, etc. Arrangement is by product groups each subdivided by such headings as acquisitions, consumption, imports, mergers, new products, production, uses. Two detailed indexes in each issue: monthly index for the current issue; cumulative index for the calendar year through current issue.

PLASTICS Industry Notes. Washington, D. C.: American Chemical
Society. Weekly.   (OA 7)
> Abstracts, from business and technical-business magazines, classified by subjects: production/consumption, prices, marketing/sales, plant expansion, finance, new products/uses, corporate news, state-of-the-art surveys, etc.

Allied Discipline Abstracts

INTERNATIONAL Abstracts in Operations Research. Baltimore:

Operations Research Society of America. Bimonthly.   (OB 1)

> Covers all aspects of operations research -- theory, hardware, software, applications in specific lines of commerce and industry.

JOURNAL of Economic Abstracts. Cambridge, Mass.: Harvard University, Littauer Center. Quarterly.   (OB 2)

> The first issue was dated January 1963. Publication is under the auspices of the American Economic Association acting as agent for the cooperating economic associations and contributing journals, American and foreign. Abstracts, written in most cases by the authors of the articles, are limited to about three hundred words. Arrangement is by broad subject. Author index.

PSYCHOLOGICAL Abstracts. Washington, D. C.: American Psychological Association. Monthly.   (OB 3)

> Covers a broad range of psychological research with frequent references to publications of value in market research. Brief subject index; author index.

SOCIOLOGICAL Abstracts. New York: Sociological Abstract, Inc. 7/yr. plus annual cumulative index.   (OB 4)

> In addition to sociology, abstracts cover methodology, research technology, statistical methods, communications and related subjects. Author index.

Inter-disciplinary Abstracts

DISSERTATION Abstracts. (see GB 1)

INDEXES

The search for current data can be greatly expedited by the knowledge and use of specialized and general indexes.

Actually there is no one, continuing, comprehensive index of marketing literature. For current information it is necessary to refer to the collective indexes of the business press. These cover many publications but, of necessity, not in exhaustive detail. Many individual magazines either publish their own editorial indexes or maintain them on cards as a service to their staff and readers. (Published indexes of this sort are noted in the Guide to Special Issues and Indexes of Periodicals (see NE 5)). Many large city dailies, too, maintain either unpublished indexes or "morgues" which are clippings of their news stories filed by subject.

A rather recent development is the continuing indexes to specific types of facts (such as forecasts, mergers) and guides to statistical data published on a continuing basis by sources within and for a particular industry.

Not usually classed with the traditional indexes are the index features of annuals, bibliographies, guides, publications catalogs and checklists. In marketing, however, these "disguised" indexes are important keys to facts and figures. Those of general interest are listed here. Others, more specialized, are covered in the publications grouped in the chapter on Research Aids.

Like periodicals, some of the other types of materials have their own indexes. These may be continuing such as the indexes to theses and Federal Reserve Bank bulletins, or one-time, such as the special indexes to some of the decennial censuses. Both types are highly specialized and are grouped with the sources to which they pertain.

Marketing

INDEX. In U. S. Business and Defense Services Administration. Market Information Guide. Washington, D. C. : Government Printing Office. Monthly, cumulated quarterly for the year to date.

(OC 1)

Devoted exclusively to marketing materials, this is the most comprehensive index available to the books, pamphlets, special articles, government documents and other publications selected for listing and annotated in the monthly issues of the Guide.

Business Press
<u></u>

 For lack of a single index covering all marketing literature, general business literature indexes are used extensively.

FUNK and Scott Index of Corporations and Industries. Cleveland: Predicasts, Inc. Weekly; cumulative to monthly and annual. (OC 2)
> Indexes primarily financial and business news appearing in over 200 business and trade periodicals and services. Industries, products, processes, are grouped by Standard Industrial Classification in one of two sections. The other indexes news of publicly and privately owned corporations by name of company. Serves as basis for the publisher's Growth & Acquisition Guide (see JC 5).

NEW York Times Index. New York: The New York Times Co. Semi monthly; cumulated annually.   (OC 3)
> Detailed name and subject index gives exact date, page and column references. Brief contents notes amplify the entries. Annual edition is illustrated with maps, diagrams and photos.

WALL Street Journal Index. New York: Dow Jones & Co., Inc. Monthly.   (OC 4)
> Arranged in two sections: corporate news alphabetically by firm name; general news by subject. Brief summaries accompany index entries.

BUSINESS Periodicals Index. New York: H. W. Wilson Co. Monthly except July; cumulative to annual.   (OC 5)
> Detailed subject index to over 150 trade, business and industry magazines. Also cites, separately or by subject, directory issues of magazines covered by the service.

PUBLIC Affairs Information Service Bulletin. New York: Public Affairs Information Service. Weekly; cumulative to annual. (OC 6)
> A selective, alphabetical subject index to books, pamphlets,

reports, government documents, directories, periodical
articles published in English throughout the world. Covers
public affairs, economic and social conditions with emphasis
on the factual and statistical.

Technical Press

Research on scientific and technological aspects of a business
problem often requires the use of more specialized indexes. Those
listed here were selected because they and the publications they index are most generally available in company and public libraries.

BIOLOGICAL & Agricultural Index. New York: H. W. Wilson Co.
Monthly, except September; cumulative to annual.   (OC 7)
Subject index to 148 periodicals in the fields of agricultural
chemicals, agricultural economics, agricultural engineering,
agriculture and agricultural research, animal husbandry, dairy-
ing and dairy products, ecology, feeds, forestry and conservation, horticulture, nutrition, plant science, poultry, soil science, veterinary medicine and related subjects.

APPLIED Science & Technology Index. New York: H. W. Wilson
Co. Monthly, except August; cumulative to annual.   (OC 8)
Subject index to approximately 225 periodicals in the fields of
aeronautics, automation, chemistry, construction, electricity
and electronics, engineering, geology and metallurgy, industrial and mechanical arts, machinery, physics, telecommuni-
cation, transportation, and related subjects.

Statistics

The lack of a continuing index to statistical data is in some
measure compensated for by two features of the annual Statistical
Abstract of the United States: the minutely detailed subject "Index" to its statistical tables, and the bibliographic "Guide to
Sources of Statistics" (see QA 11).   (OD 1)

WASSERMAN, Paul, et al, eds. Statistical Sources, 2d ed.
Detroit: Gale Research Co. , 1965. 387 p.   (OD 2)

>   Dictionary arrangement of some 8,000 specific topics show-
>   ing for each those publications and/or government or private
>   agencies which provide statistical data.

PREDICASTS (see OA 1)

EXPANSION & Capacity Digest (see OA 2)

WORLDCASTS (see OA 3)

SOURCES of Commodity Prices, compiled by Paul Wasserman.
New York: Special Libraries Association, 1960. 170 p.   (OD 3)

>   Alphabetical list of more than 6,800 commodities showing for
>   each the title of the periodical publishing the price, market
>   or markets in which price is effective, and the frequency with
>   which prices appear in the periodical (American and Canadian).

Statistics: Government Data

>   Bibliographies and guides, and the indexed and classified
> catalogs of government agencies (listed in the last chapter) are ex-
> cellent supplements to the publications cited here.

U. S. Bureau of the Census. Directory of Federal Statistics
for Local Areas ... (see FB 5).

---Directory of Federal Statistics for States, 1967
(see FA 5)

ANDRIOT, John L. Guide to U. S. Government Statistics,
3rd ed. , rev. & enl. McClean, Va. : Documents Index, 1961. 402
p.   (OD 4)

>   Publications, ranging from one-table releases to compendia,
>   are arranged by departments and agencies. Each annotated

entry gives frequency, availability, "keep" and "discard" nota-
tions indicating the existence of these data in other sources.
Alphabetical subject index codes each publication for 26 types
of statistics and for frequency of data.

INDEX to Reports by Subjects. In U. S. Bureau of the Census.
Bureau of the Census Catalog. Washington, D. C.: Government
Printing Office. Quarterly; cumulative to annual.   (OD 5)
    Detailed alphabetical subject index to all of the Bureau's re-
    ports listed in the particular issue.

INDEX to Reports by Geographic Areas. In U. S. Bureau of the
Census. Bureau of the Census Catalog. Washington, D. C.:
Government Printing Office. Quarterly; cumulative to annual.
                                                            (OD 6)
    This is an alphabetical subject index in six sections: cities;
    counties; standard metropolitan statistical areas; states;
    census regions/divisions; outlying areas of the United States.
    Covers those Bureau reports listed in the particular issue.

Statistics: Individual Industries

    The works cited below were specially compiled as keys to the
statistical sources of individual industries. Similar references are
to be found in the bibliographic guides grouped in the last chapter.

SOURCES of Insurance Statistics, Elizabeth Ferguson, ed. New
York: Special Libraries Association, 1965. 192 p.   (OD 7)
    Index to statistics published regularly by commercial firms,
    insurance organizations and some state and federal agencies.
    Each part (Health, Life, and Property/Liability) divided into
    United States and Canadian sections. Arranged by subject,
    references identify source and frequency of data, and the peri-
    od of time the statistics cover.

SOURCES of Petroleum Marketing Statistics. (Publication no. 1548).

New York: American Petroleum Institute, 1963. xvii, 114 p. (OD 8)
  Primarily a bibliography of current publications which contain
  data on petroleum, natural gas and related industries. Arrangement is alphabetical by name of issuing agency within each of
  five sections: federal agencies; state agencies; petroleum
  trade associations, organizations and publishers. For each
  publication gives title, frequency and release date, time lapse,
  and precise description of data covered. Its detailed subject
  index provides a finding guide to the statistics of the subject
  area covered.

U. S. Sources of Petroleum and Natural Gas Statistics, compiled
by Margaret M. Rocq. New York: Special Libraries Association,
1961. vii, 94 p.   (OD 9)
  Alphabetical subject index of products and facilities showing
  type of statistical information, geographical area, period
  covered, and source. Indexing was limited to data released
  currently in American publications at regular intervals.

U. S. Business and Defense Services Administration. Chemical
Statistics Directory, No. 3. Washington, D. C.: Government
Printing Office [1964] iii, 195 p.   (OD 10)
  Prepared in cooperation with the Chemical Marketing Research
  Association. Indexes statistics in federal publications issued
  during 1960-61. Commodities in SIC group 28, their raw
  materials and certain minerals are listed alphabetically and
  coded for source and type of data (14 types). The continuing
  nature of many of the sources cited makes this index a useful
  guide to current data.

---U. S. Government Statistical Publications for the Food Industries, Listing and Index ... Washington, D. C.: Department of
Commerce, 1955. ii, 22 p.   (OD 11)
  Statistical publications (relating to food, tobacco, fats and
  oils) of ten government agencies are listed by originating
  agency and by industry groups. Part III classifies these pub-

lications by type of data provided and codes each to ten broad product groups.

---SOURCES of Statistical Data: Textiles and Apparel. Washington, D. C.: Government Printing Office. August 1968. 36 p.

(OD 12)

Covers statistical sources of the federal government, international organizations and other miscellaneous bodies.

INFORMATION CENTERS
AND SPECIALISTS

Publications, information and advice are available through a number of channels, many of them close at hand, and are often free for the asking.

LIBRARIES

Numerous public and college libraries maintain excellent collections of business information. In the larger institutions these materials are serviced by special departments. Smaller libraries can obtain publications which they lack through interlibrary loan.

Required to be open to the public without charge are some 600 U. S. Depository Libraries located in every state, District of Columbia, and Puerto Rico. These are college and public institutions which, under provisions of the law, have been designated to receive and maintain certain series of federal government publications. Since each library selects publications of interest to its community, not all federal publications are equally available in all Depositories. The system is administered by the Superintendent of Documents (Washington 25, D. C.) who also issues two periodically revised lists which can be used to determine Depository facilities in specific areas:

LIST of Depository Libraries.... Washington, D. C. Superintendent of Documents. Annual. (P 1)

> Arranged alphabetically by state and alphabetically by city under each state. This list also appears in each September issue of the Monthly Catalog of United States Government Publications (see QB 3).

LIST of Classes of United States Government Publications Available
for Selection by Depository Libraries. Washington, D. C. : Superintendent of Documents. Annual.   (P 2)

> Series titles are grouped by names of issuing agencies and
> their subordinate divisions.

Although many public and college libraries and more than one
half of the U. S. Depository Libraries maintain complete files of
the major censuses, the Bureau of the Census, itself, has designated over 100 institutions as Census Depository Libraries.   These
do not coincide with those in the U. S. Depository system.   Each
of these libraries receives reports of the major censuses, as well
as reports in the Bureau's current statistical programs. Series
consisting of many individual reports for small areas are offered
for selection. In many cases, these libraries elect to receive only
reports for areas within the home state and nearby states.   Space
limitations, clientele, and other factors influence not only the volume but also the length of time these materials are retained.   A
six-page list, "Census Depository Libraries," is available from the
Bureau of the Census.

Special libraries, in general, are those which exist to implement the activities of private business organizations - - commercial firms, chambers of commerce, trade associations.   Their
reference collections cover the organizations' primary and allied
subject areas in depth with a variety of documentation forms ranging from books to unpublished materials. Also included in this
group are libraries open to the public whose general or departmental collections fall within the definition of subject specialization.
Many libraries of both types offer services to the businessman.
However, practical considerations of limited space and staff, and
the frequent complexity of the research project would suggest a
preliminary contact by phone or letter as a matter of good policy
for the best results. Although there is no list of market research
libraries per se, collections of such data can be located through the
directories listed at the end of this chapter.

In view of the growing interrelation of technology and business, the services of the National Referral Center for Science and Technology could be very helpful in industrial research. Operated by the Library of Congress with the support of the National Science Foundation, the Center is a clearinghouse designed to make information resources known to the country's scientists and engineers and to assure the fullest possible utilization of these resources. It does not answer technical questions directly but refers inquirers to the organizations, institutions, or individuals capable of furnishing the material or information desired.

FIELD OFFICES OF FEDERAL AGENCIES

Publications for distribution and consultation, as well as libraries, information and advice, are available through a network of field offices supported by a number of federal agencies.

The most extensive system is maintained by the Department of Commerce with field offices in the 42 cities listed below. Here ready access is provided to the publications and services of the Bureau of the Census, Business and Defense Services Administration, and other departmental units. Each office maintains a reference library of private as well as official materials and acts as sales agent for numerous government publications relating to business. Its field personnel is available for individual service on specific problems.

Albuquerque, New Mexico

Anchorage, Alaska

Atlanta, Georgia

Baltimore, Maryland

Birmingham, Alabama

Boston, Massachusetts

Buffalo, New York

Charleston, South Carolina

Charleston, West Virginia

Cheyenne, Wyoming

Chicago, Illinois

Cincinnati, Ohio

Cleveland, Ohio

Dallas, Texas

Denver, Colorado

Des Moines, Iowa

Detroit, Michigan

Greensboro, North Carolina

Hartford, Connecticut

Honolulu, Hawaii

Houston, Texas

Jacksonville, Florida

Kansas City, Missouri

Los Angeles, California

Memphis, Tennessee

Miami, Florida

Milwaukee, Wisconsin

Minneapolis, Minnesota

New Orleans, Louisiana

New York, New York

Philadelphia, Pennsylvania

Phoenix, Arizona

Pittsburgh, Pennsylvania

Portland, Oregon

Reno, Nevada

Richmond, Virginia

St. Louis, Missouri

Salt Lake City, Utah

San Francisco, California

Santurce, Puerto Rico

Savannah, Georgia

Seattle, Washington

In addition, several hundred chambers of commerce, manufacturers' associations and similar groups are official Cooperative Offices of the Department of Commerce whose publications they receive and maintain for consultation. Problems beyond their resources are referred to the nearest field office.

Regional offices of the Bureau of Labor Statistics are located in eight cities:

Atlanta, Georgia	Kansas City, Missouri
Boston, Massachusetts	New York, New York
Chicago, Illinois	Philadelphia, Pennsylvania
Dallas, Texas	San Francisco, California

Each distributes its own regional office materials and certain national publications of the Bureau.

Similarly, regional materials of the Board of Governors of the Federal Reserve System are offered through the Publications Offices of the following twelve Federal Reserve Banks. These also distribute some of the Board's publications, other than subscription items.

Atlanta, Georgia	Minneapolis, Minnesota
Boston, Massachusetts	New York, New York
Chicago, Illinois	Philadelphia, Pennsylvania
Cleveland, Ohio	Richmond, Virginia
Dallas, Texas	St. Louis, Missouri
Kansas City, Missouri	San Francisco, California

Research departments of the Banks are staffed with personnel conversant with the Board's national and regional data output. And each of the twelve maintains a library whose reference collection includes not only the Board's publications but also a wide selection of sources on domestic business and economy.

The Department of Agriculture maintains field offices and staff in support of its many local programs. Generally a limited selection of its "national" publications is available for distribution at these locations as well as from state extension officers usually located at the state colleges. Agricultural experiment stations and state agricultural colleges distribute their own reports.

The Small Business Administration maintains field offices where small firms are encouraged to seek individual assistance in the solution of marketing and distribution problems. Regional offices maintain reference libraries of publicly and privately published materials of possible value to the small businessman.

Albuquerque, N. Mex.	Los Angeles, Calif.
Anchorage, Alaska	Louisville, Ky.
Atlanta, Ga.	Lubbock, Tex.
Augusta, Maine	Madison, Wis.
Baltimore, Md.	Marshall, Tex.
Birmingham, Ala.	Miami, Fla.
Boise, Idaho	Minneapolis, Minn.
Boston, Mass.	Montpelier, Vt.
Casper, Wyo.	Nashville, Tenn.
Charlotte, N. C.	New Orleans, La.
Chicago, Ill.	New York, N. Y.
Clarksburg, W. Va.	Newark, N. J.
Cleveland, Ohio	Oklahoma City, Okla.
Columbia, S. C.	Omaha, Neb.
Columbus, Ohio	Philadelphia, Pa.
Concord, N. H.	Phoenix, Ariz.
Dallas, Tex.	Pittsburgh, Pa.
Denver, Colo.	Portland, Ore.
Des Moines, Iowa	Providence, R. I.
Detroit, Mich.	Richmond, Va.
Fargo, N. D.	St. Louis, Mo.
Hartford, Conn.	Salt Lake City, Utah
Hato Rey, P. R.	San Antonio, Tex.
Helena, Mont.	San Diego, Calif.
Honolulu, Hawaii	San Francisco, Calif.
Houston, Tex.	Seattle, Wash.
Indianapolis, Ind.	Sioux Falls, S. D.
Jackson, Miss.	Spokane, Wash.
Jacksonville, Fla.	Syracuse, N. Y.
Kansas City, Mo.	Washington, D. C.
Little Rock, Ark.	Wichita, Kans.

DIRECTORIES OF INFORMATION CENTERS AND SPECIALISTS

To be supplied with current data on specific industries, products or trading areas frequently requires recourse to library resources, appropriate trade associations, government agencies, chambers of commerce, media research centers and other sources and to their knowledgeable personnel. All of these can be identified through a number of directories. Of those enumerated in preceding chapters several are repeated here for emphasis and to supplement the list of general and specialized guides to information centers and specialists.

Directories: Comprehensive

KRUZAS, Anthony T. , ed. Directory of Special Libraries and Information Centers, 2nd ed. Detroit: Gale Research Co. , 1967. 3 vols.   (P 3)

Vol. 1 arranges over 10,000 entries in two sections (U. S. and Canada) by name of supporting organization - business, governmental, institutional. Information for each unit includes names of key personnel; size, subject and composition of collection; serial publications issued; extramural services provided. Subject index. Vol. 2, Geographic-Personnel Index, in one section, lists alphabetically all library personnel named in the first volume and, in a second section, provides a geographic guide to the organizations covered by the main directory. Vol. 3, New Special Libraries, an interedition service to be published every six months, is planned to update the basic volume.

AMERICAN Library Directory. New York: R. R. Bowker Co. Biennial.   (P 4)

This state-city listing includes special libraries, notes subject collections of general libraries and indicates federal document depositories. Since ephemeral format characterizes much of the business literature, number of volumes held should not be taken as a final criterion of scope.

SUBJECT Collections ... New York: R. R. Bowker, Co.   Irregular.
(P 5)

This companion volume to the American Library Directory is a "guide to special book collections and subject
emphases as reported by university, college, public, and
special libraries in the United States and Canada." Under each
detailed subject, arrangement is alphabetical by state, city and
name of collection.   In addition to the library, its address
and name of librarian, some indication is given as to the extent and character of the collection, reproduction facilities.
restrictions on use of the materials.

RESEARCH Centers Directory (see GA 1)

U. S. Library of Congress. National Referral Center for Science
and Technology.   A Directory of Information Resources
in the United States: Social Sciences. [Washington, D. C.:
Government Printing Office] October 1965.   224 p.   (P 6)

Describes more than 600 information resources including university research bureaus, libraries, professional societies,
federal and state government offices and other organizations
with specialized interests.   Each resource is described in
terms of subject coverage, collections, services and publications.   Subject index, organization index.

---A Directory of Information Resources in the United States:
Physical Sciences, Biological Sciences, Engineering. [Washington,
D. C.: Government Printing Office] January 1965.   352 p.   (P 7)

Companion volume, providing similar information, to the
above.

---A Directory of Information Resources in the United States:
Water. [Washington, D. C.: Government Printing Office] September
1966.   v, 248 p.   (P 8)

Alphabetical by name of organization. For each gives: address and telephone number; areas of interest; holdings of
library or special collections of materials; publications issued;
information and other services available.

Directories: Federal Sources

U. S. Bureau of the Budget. Statistical Services of the United States
Government. (see C 1)

---Federal Statistical Directory. Washington, D. C.: Government
Printing Office. Biennial.   (D 9)

> List of professional, technical and administrative personnel
> engaged in the planning, operation and dissemination activities
> of the federal statistical programs. Arranged by agencies and
> their constituent units. For each individual gives building,
> room location and telephone number. Updated by personnel
> news published in the Statistical Reporter (see C 2).

U. S. Library of Congress. National Referral Center for Science and
and Technology. A Directory of Information Resources in the United
States: Federal Government. Washington, D. C. [Government
Printing Office] June 1967. vii, 411 p.   (P 10)

> More than 1,600 federal government and government-sponsored
> information resources concerned with science (including social
> sciences) and technology are described in terms of areas of
> interest, holdings, publications and information services.
> Organization index; subject index.

U. S. Department of Agriculture. How to Get Information from the
U. S. Department of Agriculture. Washington, D. C.: Department of
Agriculture. Irregular.   (P 11)

> Brief listing of departmental units and their informational
> personnel.

---Directory of Organization and Field Activities of the Department
of Agriculture. Washington, D. C.: Government Printing Office.
Irregular.   (P 12)

> Shows the organizational structure of the Department of Agri-
> culture; explains briefly the multiple activities of its agencies
> and offices; gives names of its executive personnel.

Directories: State and Local Sources
DIRECTORY of Interstate Agencies. (see F 1)

WORLD WIDE Chamber of Commerce Directory. (see FA 4)

U. S. Congress. Joint Economic Committee. A Directory of Urban
Research Centers ... (see FB 2)

THE Municipal Year Book. (see FB 4)

CHAMBER of Commerce of the United States. Sources of State Information and State Industrial Directories. (see FA 3)

ASSOCIATED University Bureaus of Business and Economic Research. Directory. (see GC 1)

U. S. Department of Agriculture. Directory of State Departments of
Agriculture. Washington, D. C.: Department of Agriculture. Approximately biennial.   (P 13)

> Lists addresses and telephone numbers of state marketing
> service agencies and names of key officials of state depart-
> ments of agriculture.

---Professional Workers in State Agriculture Experiment Stations
and Other Cooperating State Institutions. Washington, D. C.:
Government Printing Office. Annual.   (P 14)

> Lists specialists in marketing.

Directories: Associations

Associations and their personnel constitute a combined resource of information centers and specialists. Membership rosters
and headquarters staff can also suggest names of experts willing to
offer assistance and advice. The two major directories for this
kind of search are:

ENCYCLOPEDIA of Associations.   (see IB 1)

AMERICAN Marketing Association.   Membership Roster.   Chicago:
American Marketing Association.   Irregular.   (P 15)
Arranged in three sections: biographical detail by name of
individual; individuals by name of employer; individuals
by city under state.

Directories: Media

Marketing data compiled by media are seldom available in
general libraries. They must be obtained directly from the sponsor's advertising or promotion department or from his sales representative. For this purpose the following source is particularly
useful.

STANDARD Rate and Data Service.   Skokie, Ill.:   Standard Rate
and Data Service, Inc.   Monthly, quarterly or semiannual depending on edition.   (P 16)
Service in ten editions of which newspaper, consumer and
farm magazine, and business publications issues are most
useful in locating media personnel (editors, advertising
managers, sales representatives) acquainted with specific
products, industries, and markets.

Although Ayer's and Ulrich's lack the specialized information of the above listed publication, they are more generally available and can be used to the same end.

Directories: Consultants

Information on specialists and services for developing data by field research is provided in the directories listed in the chapter on services.

AMERICAN Management Association, Inc. Directory on Consultant Members. New York: American Management Association, Inc. Approximately biennial.   (P 17)

Association members listed by field of consultancy and coded for specific services.

WASSERMAN, Paul, ed. Consultants and Consulting Organizations ... Ithaca, N. Y.: Cornell University Graduate School of Business and Public Administration [1966] viii, 386 p.   (P 18)

Descriptive detail on about 2,612 firms and individuals. In three parts: alphabetically arranged profiles; cross index of subjects, a subject approach to content, and a key to locations of foreign offices of firms; alphabetical index of individuals.

RESEARCH AIDS

The reference aids included in this chapter are those commonly used as selection tools. These are the bibliographies, guides, catalogs, checklists and other, less formal media, applicable in creating and maintaining, preferably on a day-to-day schedule, a basic body of published facts.

Criteria of usefulness are the timeliness, accuracy, scope, bibliographic detail and annotations provided by each aid. Subject arrangement and subject indexing contribute to expeditious fact finding and back checks in special project research.

The group detailed here includes not only the traditional bibliographic tools but also a selection of publications whose special features constitute important segments in the pattern of marketing documentation and whose variety is indicative of the "scatteration" of such information.

Although comprehensive bibliographies, guides and catalogs are superior to selected lists in the overall approach to marketing information, the latter when cited in textbooks, at the ends of chapters and in the footnotes of reference works should not be overlooked.

The index and abstract features of bibliographic guides, as discussed in the chapter on abstracts and indexes, also can be used in search projects. If published on a continuing basis, these guides and the current press constitute excellent selection and current awareness sources.

BIBLIOGRAPHIES AND GUIDES

Marketing bibliographic tools are a comparatively recent offshoot of business literature. Somewhat more numerous, even now, are the general guides and bibliographies of business data as a whole. Many pamphlets and a number of books have been written for the lay researchers and businessmen concerned with extracting factual information from the increasing accumulation of business literature. In addition to these manuals, practically every bibliography compiled from the general business or economic aspect of a specific industry or trade includes references to publications important in marketing research.

As for the bibliographic guides themselves, valuable as they are for general orientation, they quickly lose their currency with the passage of time. Consequently, periodically revised guides and continuing catalogs, checklists, indexes and abstracts offer more precise tools for the location of current information. Such, moreover, is the interrelation of these groups that all must be considered in the search for pertinent publications or for the facts themselves.

In using this manual, therefore, it would be advisable to check its index where the references listed here are supplemented by those to more specialized bibliographic-type publications classed throughout the chapters with the sources to which they pertain.

Marketing

Although a number of excellent bibliographies are available on the general and specific aspects of marketing, comparatively few deal with statistical research sources exclusively.

Most comprehensive, encompassing the output of public and private agencies, are the following:

CARPENTER, Robert N. Guidelist for Marketing Research and Economic Forecasting. (Research Study 50). New York: American Management Association, 1966. 112 p.   (Q 1)

Annotated listings of information sources are grouped as follows: guides and bibliographies; published data based on plans, projections and forecasts; annual and periodic statistical summaries; maps and market guides; data on production of goods and services; population, labor force, and income;

customer buying habits; data on business financial activities
and distribution costs; other data sources; organization studies.
Special emphasis has been put on providing leads to sources.
Index is by broad subjects.

GUNTHER, Edgar and Goldstein, Frederick A. , comps. Current
Sources of Marketing Information.   (AMA Bibliography
Series, no. 6). Chicago: American Marketing Association, 1960.
119 p.   (Q 2)

> This annotated bibliography is "arranged according to a logical
> sequence of marketing activities." Particularly extensive are
> the sections on regional data, and industries and trades.   With
> few exceptions publications issued prior to 1954 have been
> omitted.   Author index.

Although theses and dissertations, university research, and
the serial publications of bureaus of business research are seldom
included in these comprehensive guides, their contents are accessible through the guides listed in the chapters dealing with these
sources.

Marketing: Topical

> Topical guides and bibliographies are valuable for their in-
depth treatment of specific subjects.   Thus they can be used for
general orientation as well as in the search for specific facts.

AMERICAN Marketing Association.   Bibliographies Series.
Chicago: American Marketing Association.   (Q 3)

> To date the following titles have been issued in this series.
> No. 1, Current Sources of Information for Market Research.
> 1954.
> No. 2, A Basic Bibliography of Marketing Research. 1963.
> No. 3, Discount Selling, Retail Price Cutting, and Resale
> Price Controls, 1956.

No. 4, A Basic Bibliography on Industrial Marketing. (Revised edition in preparation)

No. 5, A Bibliography on New Product Planning. 1966.

No. 6, Current Sources of Marketing Information. 1960. (A revised and enlarged edition of No. 1.)

No. 7, A Basic Bibliography on Mathematical Methods in Marketing. 1962.

No. 8, Marketing Management: Annotated Bibliography. 1963.

No. 9, Automatic Merchandising. 1964.

No. 10, An Annotated Index to Proceedings. 1966.

No. 11, Physical Distribution and Marketing Logistics: An Annotated Bibliography. 1966.

No. 12, A Bibliography on Personal Selling. 1966.

No. 13, Marketing in Canada. 1967.

No. 14, A Basic Bibliography on Experiments in Marketing. 1968.

No. 15, Quantitive Methods in Marketing. 1968.

U. S. Bureau of the Census. Guide to Industrial Statistics ... [Washington, D. C.] Government Printing Office [1964] iv, 60 p. illus.   (Q 4)

Brief guide to industrial data in major censuses and other statistical sources. Illustrated with sample table excerpts and detailed description of contents.

U. S. Business and Defense Services Administration. Data Sources for Plant Location Analysis. Washington, D. C.: Government Printing Office, 1959. iv, 42 p.   (Q 5)

Annotated bibliography of statistical sources, public and private, arranged by subjects important to systematic area studies.

---A Guide to Negro Marketing Information. Washington, D. C.: Government Printing Office, September 1966. v, 50 p.   (Q 6)

Contains a selected annotated bibliography; statistical summary of population, consumption and income characteristics;

directory of national Negro business associations; directory of
Negro newspapers and national magazines; and a list of pre-
dominantly Negro colleges and universities.

---Measuring Markets ... (see FA 12)

---Measuring Metropolitan Markets ... (see FB 3)

---Personal Income, a Key to Small-Area Market Analysis.
(see FB 10)

AEROSPACE Industry Information Sources. New York: Aviation Week
& Space Technology, n. d. 31 p.   (Q 7)
    Publications and information sources arranged in 20 detailed
    subject groups. Each reference clearly annotated. Publica-
    tion dates lacking in many citations.

DIRECTORY of Marketing Information on the Chemical Process
Industries. New York: Chemical Engineering, 1966. 98 p.   (Q 8)
    Basic bibliography of books, periodicals, directories, sta-
    tistics, research materials and other sources. General
    references followed by those for 18 consuming industry seg-
    ments are arranged in two sections, domestic and internation-
    al.   Final chapters deal with media and basic marketing texts.

Government Publications

ANDRIOT, John L. Guide to U. S. Government Serials and
Periodicals ... McLean, Va.: Documents Index. Annual (?)

                                                                  (Q 9)
    The definitive work on continuing federal government publica-
    tions. Titles are arranged alphabetically under issuing agency.
    Among the vast amount of detail supplied for each publication
    are: beginning dates, frequency, availability (free or priced),
    purpose and audience as defined by the agency, description of
    contents, recurring features, relationship to other publications,

special issues, historical supplements. Planned to be issued
annually,with supplements and with author, title,and subject indexes.

General Business

COMAN, Edwin T. Sources of Business Information [2nd] rev.
ed. Berkeley, Calif.: University of California Press, 1964. xii,
330 p.   (QA 1)

A guide for businessmen, seasoned and novice. Arrangement
of the material reflects basic businesses and business functions as well as the optimum method of locating desired information. Annotated lists of textbooks, periodicals, directories and other publications are accompanied by commentary
on the subject and sources and by helpful suggestions for con-
ducting the search.

MANLEY, Marion C. Business Information; How to Find and
Use It [1st ed.] New York: Harper, 1955. svi, 265 p.   (QA 2)

The current value of this manual on the practical application
of business facts lies in the first part which offers a guide
to the origin and uses of various types of business information. The second part is a selective bibliography of standard
reference sources arranged by subject.

WASSERMAN, Paul. Information for Administrators ...
Ithaca, N. Y.: Cornell University Press, 1956. 375 p.   (QA 3)

Comprehensive, descriptive treatment of business publications
and services, and of their issuing agencies. Compiled from
the point of view of the informational needs of business
management, it covers many sources of value to marketing
men.

General Business: Topical

MANAGEMENT Information Guide Series. Detroit: Gale Research
Co.   (QA 4)

Some of the titles pertinent to industrial research:

Real Estate Information Sources. 1963.

Building Construction Information Sources. 1964.

Textile Industry Information Sources. 1964.

Standards and Specifications Information Sources. 1965.

Public Utilities Information Sources. 1965.

Transportation Information Sources. 1965.

Business Trends and Forecasting Information Sources. 1965.

Packaging; a Guide to Information Sources. 1967.

U. S. Small Business Administration. Small Business Bibliography [series] Washington, D. C.: Small Business Administration. 75 titles revised irregularly. (QA 5)

Publications and information sources, governmental and private, are covered in each bibliography. Some of the titles directly relating to marketing:

No. 4, New Product Development and Sale.

No. 9, Marketing Research Procedures.

No. 10, Retailing.

No. 12, Statistics and Maps for National Market Analysis.

No. 13, National Directories for Use in Marketing.

No. 16, Store Location.

No. 34, Distribution Cost Analysis.

No. 49, Warehousing.

No. 55, Wholesaling.

No. 67, Manufacturers' Agent.

No. 68, Discount Retailing.

Finance

U. S. Bureau of International Commerce. Sources of Credit Information on Foreign Firms for United States Firms Trading, Investing or Manufacturing Abroad. Washington, D. C.: Government Printing Office, 1967. 108 p. (QA 6)

Metallurgy

GIBSON, Eleanor B. and Tapia, Elizabeth W. , eds. Guide to
Metallurgical Information, 2d ed. (SLA Bibliography no. 3)
New York: Special Libraries Association, 1965. xviii, 222 p.(QA 7)
> Annotated references to worldwide sources of information on
> all aspects of metallurgy. Among the topics covered: trade
> associations, government agencies, indexes, directories,
> handbooks, specifications, statistics. Five indexes: Personal
> author Organization, General title, Serial title, Subject.

Transportation

U. S. Congress. House. Committee on Post Office and Civil Service. Subcommittee on Census and Government Statistics. Improving Federal Transportation Statistics ... Washington,
D. C.: Government Printing Office, 1962. xii, 89 p. (87th
Congress, 2d Session, House Report no. 1700)   (QA 8)
> This report discusses in detail the transportation statistics
> currently compiled by government agencies, the, at that
> time, proposed census of transportation, and areas of infor-
> mation requiring improvement. Its value lies in its exact
> citations, its selected bibliography of official and other sour-
> ces, and in its subject index.

BLAISDELL, Ruth F. , et al. Sources of Information in Transportation. Evanston, Ill.: The Transportation Center at Northwestern University, 1964. 262 p.   (QA 9)
> Statistical, economic and regulatory sources of information
> on highways, motor carriers, metropolitan transportation,
> railroads, pipelines, merchant marine, inland waterways,
> air transportation, and missiles and rockets.

CURRENT Literature in Traffic and Transportation. Evanston, Ill,;
The Transportation Center at Northwestern University. Monthly.
                                                            (QA 10)

Covers foreign and domestic periodicals, books, research reports, government publications.

Statistics

GUIDE to Sources of Statistics. In, U. S. Bureau of the Census.
Statistical Abstract of the United States. Washington,
D. C.: Government Printing Office. Annual.   (QA 11)
> Included in each edition under a slightly varying title, this
> bibliography of some 40 pages classifies primary, and select-
> ed secondary and nonrecurring statistical publications by sub-
> ject and cites Abstract sections where data from these
> sources appear.

PRINCIPAL Statistical Publications of Federal Agencies. In U. S.
Bureau of the Budget. Statistical Services of the United
States Government. Washington, D. C.: Government Printing
Office. Irregular.   (QA 12)
> Interim editions of this chapter issued in mimeographed form.

Packaging

U. S. Business and Defense Services Administration. Sources of
Information on Containers and Packaging. Washington
D. C.: Government Printing Office, 1965. 21 p.   (QA 13)
> Publications and sources of information pertaining to manu-
> facturing techniques, research and development, uses, dis-
> tribution, production and trade statistics. Arranged in six
> sections: federal government publications, nongovernment
> publications, sources of technical information, directories,
> periodicals, trade associations and other groups. No subject
> index.

CATALOGS AND CHECKLISTS

Catalogs and checklists are useful primarily as aids in
selecting and acquiring current marketing materials as they become
available. If well indexed they can also serve to locate specific

publications applicable to immediate research projects.

In the following group, those covering all types of market data publications precede a number of special purpose lists.

Comprehensive

U. S. Business and Defense Services Administration. Marketing Information Guide. Washington, D. C.: Government Printing Office. Monthly.   (QB 1)

Most comprehensive source for all kinds of governmental and nongovernmental publications issued currently in the field of marketing. Books, surveys, reports, directories, ephemeral materials, etc., are well annotated and arranged by broad subjects and marketing functions. Subject index in each issue is cumulated quarterly for the calendar year to date.

WHAT'S New in Advertising and Marketing. New York: Special Libraries Association Advertising Division. 10/yr.   (QB 2)

Subject catalog of publications available from a variety of sources. Each issue carries a prepublication column on forthcoming materials. Particularly useful for ephemeral and media sources.

Special Purpose: Media

AVAILABLE Market Data. Advertising Age. (see KC 1)
MARKET Information Guide. Industrial Marketing. (see KC 2)

Special Purpose: Federal Publications

Since not even the comprehensive Marketing Information Guide lists all of the many federal government publications supplying valuable research data, it is necessary to have recourse to the catalogs and checklists published by the agencies themselves. These provide the broader coverage, greater detail and timeliness often lacking in selective lists.

Virtually every United States government department and

bureau issues some sort of publications list. Enumerated here are catalogs and checklists of those agencies whose programs produce a large number and variety of general purpose statistics and reports. Not included in the group below are similar lists of agencies whose programs produce data of a more special interest type. Such catalogs are available upon request from the individual agencies.

U. S. Superintendent of Documents. Monthly Catalog of United States Government Publications. Washington, D. C.: Government Printing Office. Monthly.   (QB 3)

> According to law, the Library of the Division of Public Documents of the Government Printing Office receives one copy of each publication produced by any branch or bureau of the United States government. On this basis it compiles this most comprehensive listing of federal government publications. Each issue lists, by agency, every printed and processed publication (except administrative and confidential) published the preceding month. Entries include bibliographic detail but not content annotations. For each it indicates whether the publication is available for sale, distributed by the issuing unit, published for official use only, sent to federal Depository Libraries. Monthly issues include a detailed subject-title index. A cumulative annual index is published in the December issue and a list of Depository Libraries in September. On a highly selective level it is supplemented by the following checklist:

---Selected United States Government Publications. Washington, D. C.: Superintendent of Documents. Biweekly.   (QB 4)

> Annotated list of predominantly recent publications issued for sale by various federal agencies. Useful as a checklist of major reports issued by agencies whose catalogs are not updated at frequent intervals.

CHECKLIST of Congressional Hearings. Washington, D. C.: Bernan Associates. Approximately weekly.   (QB 5)

Published Congressional hearings are listed by committee
with brief annotations of contents and directions for ordering.

U. S. Department of Agriculture. List of Available Publications of
the United States Department of Agriculture. (List no. 11) Washington, D. C.: Government Printing Office. Annual. (QB 6)
Titles are classified by 18 broad topics. Detailed subject
index to titles, not contents.

---Bimonthly List of Publications and Motion Pictures. Washington, D. C.: Department of Agriculture. Bimonthly. (QB 7)
Annotated publications list arranged by series type. Good
for market studies issued by this department.

U. S. Agricultural Economics. Periodic Reports of Agricultural
Economics, Economic Research Service, Statistical Reporting
Service. Washington, D. C.: Agricultural Economics. Annual.
(QB 8)

---Checklist of Reports Issued by the Economic Research Service
and the Statistical Reporting Service. (Series AE-CL). Washington, D. C.: Department of Agriculture. Monthly. (QB 9)
Includes studies and reports of agricultural experiment stations.

U. S. Consumer and Marketing Service. Federal-State Market
News Reports -- a Directory of Services Available. (C & MS 21).
Washington, D. C.: Consumer and Marketing Service, 1966. 39 p.
(QB 10)

---Available Publications of USDA's Consumer and Marketing
Service (Except Market News Reports). (C & MS 53). [Washington,
D. C.] Consumer and Marketing Service, 1967. 19 p. (QB 11)

U. S. Department of Commerce. United States Department

of Commerce Publications, a Catalog and Index. Washington, D. C.: Government Printing Office, 1952. xv, 795 p.(QB 12)
   Arrangement is by issuing units within the Department. More
   than 300 pages are devoted to a detailed subject index. Updated by annual supplements and the Checklist cited below.

 ---Business Service Checklist. Washington, D. C.: Government
Printing Office. Weekly.   (QB 13)
   Lists publications and press releases of the Department and
   its subordinate agencies.

U. S. Bureau of the Census. Catalog of United States
Census Publications, 1790-1945. Washington, D. C.: Government Printing Office, 1950. x, 320 p.   (QB 14)
   Arranged in two sections: decennial census publications grouped
   chronologically other than decennial census publications similarly grouped under major subject. Entries are annotated and
   indexed. Supplemented by the following:

U. S. Bureau of the Census. Bureau of the Census Catalog.
Washington, D. C.: Government Printing Office. Quarterly cumulative to annual; monthly supplements.   (QB 15)
   Divided into two parts. Part I presents annotated listings
   of all reports issued by the Bureau arranged under administrative divisions; selected publications of other agencies; ap-
   pendixes listing reports of major censuses, current related
   surveys, and other special series or one-time publications as
   well as statements on various statistical programs of the Bureau.   Part II lists material available on computer tape and
   punchcards, special tabulations provided on a cost basis, and
   other unpublished data. Subject and geographical indexes in
   each issue. The Monthly Supplement is a current, unannotated list of all Bureau reports except those issued on a
   regular monthly and quarterly basis.

U. S. Bureau of International Commerce. Checklist [of] Inter-

National Business Publications. Washington, D. C.: Bureau of
International Commerce. Semiannual.   (QB 16)

> Federal publications of interest to international business and
> marketing.

U. S. Department of Labor. Publications of the United States
Department of Labor, Subject Listing. [Washington, D. C.:
Department of Labor] Annual.   (QB 17)

> Classified by broad subjects. Each edition covers a 5 1/2
> year period.

---New Publications. Washington, D. C.: Department of Labor.
Monthly.   (QB 18)

> Unannotated checklist of selected publications, issued by the
> constituent bureaus of the Department, classified by broad
> subjects.

U. S. Bureau of Labor Statistics. Publications of the Bureau of
Labor Statistics, 1886-1967; Numerical Listings, Annotations,
Subject Index. (Bulletin 1567). Washington, D. C.: Government
Printing Office [1968] v, 156 p.   (QB 19)

---BLS Reports (Nos. 1-200) ... Washington, D. C.: Bureau of
Labor Statistics, 1961. 16 p.   (QB 20)

> Reports published since February 1953 are classified by
> subject and listed numerically.

---Catalog of Publications ... Washington, D. C.: Bureau of
Labor Statistics. Semiannual.   (QB 21)

> Entries are annotated and classified by subject. Includes
> all publications issued by the Bureau and its regional
> offices. Also notes reports in progress and important
> articles in the Monthly Labor Review.

Special Purpose: State Publications

Lists of state publications are available from the individual state libraries, archivists or other state agencies.   However, the following catalog may be used as a nearly complete general guide:

U. S. Library of Congress. Monthly Checklist of State Publications. Washington, D. C.:   Government Printing Office. Monthly.   (QB 22)

Unannotated catalog, arranged by state, of all state documents received and recorded by the Library of Congress.   Publications of associations of state officials and regional organizations are grouped in a special section.   For periodicals only the first number of each volume is noted.   Annual subject index.

CURRENT PRESS

Catalogs and checklists, however, can be used more effectively against a background of business and industry trends.   And it is the press - the newspapers and magazines of business and industry - which supplies current awareness of events and developments and provides the perspective which directs the successful selection of specific sources for current or future use.   Editorial content of periodicals has been treated in a preceding chapter.   Reviewed here are the features which, in addition to news notes, make them a useful complement to other selection tools.

Judged by the measure of timeliness, newspapers, particularly the business sections and advertising columns, offer immediate reporting on current studies of general interest.   Unlike news notes, however, feature stories in the daily press are more likely to cite data of indeterminate vintage from sources not always clearly identified.

Advertising and marketing magazines, on the other hand, offer timeliness and scope as indicated by the special columns each one features:

ADVERTISING Age. Chicago: Advertising Publications, Inc.

Weekly.   (QC 1)

> News announcements of privately published books, studies,
> research materials.

MARKETING/COMMUNICATIONS. New York: Decker Communications, Inc. Monthly.   (QC 2)

> "Critique." Book reviews.

> "Media Marketing." Lists pamphlets, research and promotion-
> al materials.

SALES Management. New York: Sales Management,Inc. 27/yr.
                                                 (QC 3)

> "Books." Brief review column of books and basic studies.

> "SM Digest of Articles ... from Business and Academic
> Journals." Several lengthy abstracts of special interest to
> marketing appear in each column. Citations omit paging of
> the originals.

> "Sales Aids from Advertisers." Annotated list of booklets and
> samples described in recent Sales Management advertise-
> ments.

> "Worth Writing For." Annotated list of market and media
> studies.

MEDIA/SCOPE. Skokie, Ill.: Standard Rate & Data Service, Inc.
Monthly.   (QC 4)

> "Media/Market Studies." Annotated list of reports available
> from media, services, trade associations and other sources.

> "New Books." Book reviews.

INDUSTRIAL Marketing. Chicago: Advertising Publications, Inc.
Monthly.   (QC 5)

"IM Factfile: Marketing Information." Lists free current publications pertinent to the marketing of industrial products.

"IM Factfile: Books." Reviews of books and special reports.

JOURNAL of Marketing. Chicago: American Marketing Association. Quarterly.   (QC 6)

"Book Reviews." Detailed, authoritative, signed reviews.

"Legal Developments in Marketing" (see O 3) and "Marketing Abstracts" (see O 2), as noted previously, report on business, trade and legislative publications.

JOURNAL of Advertising Research. New York: Advertising Research Foundation.   Quarterly.   (QC 7)

"Federal Statistics in Advertising." Well documented reviews of marketing data in new reports, analyses of information provided by basic statistical series, market research articles based on federal statistics.

"Research in Review." Detailed staff reviews of research in advertising, marketing, and the allied sciences published in books, business and professional journals, government reports, and monographs.   Publications reviewed are listed by author in the "Reviews" section of the Journal's annual index.

"Briefly Noted." Short reviews of books, articles, government publications, and monographs in the general rather than the specifically research area of the subjects cited above. Similarly indexed as the feature above.

"Publications Received." Unannotated acquisitions list of consumer surveys, media and market studies, books, reference works, government publications.   Many studies are listed under the name of the research firm which conducted the field work.

JOURNAL of Marketing Research. Chicago: American Marketing
Association. Quarterly.   (QC 8)

"Book Reviews." Lengthy, signed reviews of academic works,
reference tools and popular books bearing on all aspects of
marketing.   Supplemented by an unannotated checklist, "Publications Received."

APPENDIX
STATE STATISTICAL ABSTRACTS

The following list, with slight adaptations, is a reprint of the "Guide to State Statistical Abstracts" published by the Bureau of the Census in the 1967 edition of the Statistical Abstract of the United States (Washington, D. C.: Government Printing Office, 1967. p. 997-1000).

As noted there: This bibliography includes the most recent state statistical abstracts published since 1960 plus those now in preparation that will be issued in late 1967 or early 1968. When a statistical abstract does not exist for a particular state, a near equivalent has been listed, wherever possible. For some states two or more such publications have been listed. All sources contain, under one cover, statistical tables on a variety of subjects for the state as a whole, its component parts, or both. The page numbers given for publications cited as "In process" are approximate.

ALABAMA
ECONOMIC Abstract of Alabama.   University, Ala.:   University of Alabama Bureau of Business Research, 1966.   200 p.   (R 1)

ALASKA
ALASKA's Population and Economy -- Regional Growth, Development and Future Outlook.   In Statistical Handbook, vol. 2. Juneau, Alaska: Department of Commerce, 1962.   229 p.   (R 2)

ARIZONA
ARIZONA County Base Book [4th ed.] Tucson, Ariz.:   University of Arizona Division of Economic and Business Research, 1962. 59 p.
(R 3)

ARIZONA Statistical Review. Phoenix, Ariz.: Valley National Bank.
Annual.   (R 4)

ARKANSAS

ARKANSAS Almanac, 10th ed., 1968. Little Rock: Arkansas Almanac, Inc. 320 p. (In process)   (R 5)

CALIFORNIA

CALIFORNIA Statistical Abstract. Sacramento, Calif.: Department
of Finance. Annual.   (R 6)

COLORADO

COLORADO Year Book. Denver, Colo.: State Planning Division.
Triennial.   (R 7)

CONNECTICUT

CONNECTICUT Market Data. Hartford, Conn.: Connecticut
Development Commission. Annual.   (R 8)

DELAWARE

THE Delaware Economy, 1939-1958. Newark, Del.: University of
Delaware Bureau of Economic and Business Research, 1961. 95 p.
                                                     (R 9)

FLORIDA

FLORIDA Statistical Abstract.   Gainesville, Fla.:   University of Florida Bureau of Economic and Business Research.
Annual.   (R 10)

GEORGIA

GEORGIA Statistical Abstract.   Athens, Ga.:   University of
Georgia Bureau of Business and Economic Research.
Biennial.   (R 11)

HAWAII

THE State of Hawaii Data Book; A Statistical Abstract. Honolulu: Department of Planning and Research, 1967. 66 p.   (R 12)

IDAHO

IDAHO Statistical Abstract. Moscow, Idaho: University of Idaho Bureau of Business and Economic Research, 1966. 286 p. (R 13)

ILLINOIS

COUNTY Data Sheets. Springfield, Ill.: Department of Business and Economic Development, 1966. unpaged.   (R 14)

INDIANA

STATISTICAL Abstract of Indiana Counties. Indianapolis, Ind.: Indiana State Chamber of Commerce, 1963.   (R 15)

IOWA

CITY and Community Measurement; A Statistical Reference for 20 Iowa Cities, 7th ed. Sioux City, Iowa: City Council, 1965. 152 p.   (R 16)

KANSAS

KANSAS Statistical Abstract, 1967. Lawrence, Kans.: University of Kansas Center for Regional Studies, 1968. 76 p.   (R 17)

KENTUCKY

DESKBOOK of Kentucky Economic Statistics, 7th ed. Frankfort, Ky.: Department of Commerce, 1968. 31 p.   (R 18)

LOUISIANA

STATISTICAL Abstract of Louisiana, 2d ed. New Orleans: Louisiana State University Division of Business and Economic Research, 1967. 374 p.   (R 19)

MAINE

THE Maine Handbook; A Statistical Abstract, 1st ed. Augusta, Me.:
Department of Economic Development, 1967. 200 p. (In process)

(R 20)

MARYLAND

STATISTICAL Abstract. Annapolis, Md.: Department of Economic
Development, 1967. 169 p.   (R 21)

MASSACHUSETTS

FACTS Book. Boston: Department of Commerce and Development,
1967. unpaged.   (R 22)

MICHIGAN

MICHIGAN Statistical Abstract.   East Lansing, Mich.:
Michigan State University Bureau of Business and Economic
Research. Biennial.   (R 23)

MINNESOTA

A STATISTICAL Profile of the State of Minnesota, 4th ed. Saint Paul:
Department of Economic Development, 1966. 43 p.   (R 24)

MISSISSIPPI

ECONOMIC Highlights of Mississippi.   Jackson, Miss.:
Mississippi Research and Development Center, 1966. 41 p. (R 25)

HANDBOOK of Selected Data for Mississippi. Jackson, Miss.:
Mississippi Research and Development Center, 1967. variously
paged.   (R 26)

MISSOURI

DATA for Missouri Counties. Columbia, Mo. : University of
Missouri Extension Division, 1964. looseleaf.   (R 27)

MONTANA

THE Montana Almanac; Statistical Supplement, 1962-63. Missoula, Mont.: Montana State University, 1962. 110 p.   (R 28)

NEBRASKA

STATISTICAL Abstract of Nebraska. Lincoln, Neb.: University of Nebraska Bureau of Business Research, 1967. (In process)   (R 29)

NEVADA

COMMUNITY Profiles. Carson City, Nev.: Department of Economic Development, 1967. 184 p.   (R 30)

NEW JERSEY

COUNTY Data Sheets. Trenton, N.J.: Department of Conservation and Economic Development, n.d. 92 p.   (R 31)

> Includes data for 1950-1958.
> SUPPLEMENTS for 1958-60, 1960-62, 1962-64. 48 p. each.
> COUNTY Summary. 1964, 1965, 1966. 6 p. each.

THE New Jersey Almanac, 2d ed., 1966-67. Cedar Grove, N. J.: The New Jersey Almanac, Inc. 768 p.   (R 32)

NEW MEXICO

THE STATE'S Economy in 1966. In New Mexico Business, vol. 20, no. 3, March 1967. Albuquerque, N. M.: University of New Mexico Bureau of Business Research. 77 p.   (R 33)

NEW YORK

NEW YORK State Annual Summary of Business Statistics, 1958-1966. Albany, N. Y.: Department of Commerce, 1967. 28 p.   (R 34)

NEW YORK State Business Fact Book ... Albany, N. Y.: Department of Commerce.   (R 35)

Part 1, Business and Manufacturing.   Quinquennial.

Part 2, Population and Housing.   Decennial.

Separate sections published for the state and each of its 12 economic areas.

NEW YORK State Statistical Yearbook, 1967.   Albany, N. Y.:
Division of the Budget, 1968. 253 p.   (R 36)

NORTH CAROLINA

NORTH CAROLINA County Data.   Winston Salem: Wachovia Bank
and Trust Co. , 1966. 301 p.   (R 37)

NORTH DAKOTA

NORTH DAKOTA Growth Indicators, 5th ed. , 1967-68. Bismarck,
N. D.: Economic Development Commission, 1967. 40 p.   (R 38)

OHIO

STATISTICAL Abstract of Ohio, 1st ed. , 1960. Columbus, Ohio:
Department of Industrial and Economic Development, 1960. 239 p.
                                                            (R 39)

OKLAHOMA

OKLAHOMA Data Book, 1966. Norman, Okla.: University of Oklahoma Bureau of Business Research, 1966. 152 p.   (R 40)

OREGON

OREGON Economic Statistics, 1967. Eugene, Ore.: University of
Oregon Bureau of Business and Economic Research, 1967. 82 p.
                                                            (R 41)

PENNSYLVANIA

PENNSYLVANIA Statistical Abstract. Harrisburg, Pa.: Bureau of
Publications, Department of Property and Supplies. Annual. (R 42)

RHODE ISLAND

RHODE ISLAND Basic Economic Statistics, No. 11. Providence,
R. I.: Rhode Island Development Council, 1967. 130 p. (In
process)   (R 43)

SOUTH CAROLINA

GENERAL Statistics of South Carolina. Columbia, S. C.: University of South Carolina Bureau of Business and Economic Research,
1965. 58 p.   (R 44)

SOUTH DAKOTA

SOUTH DAKOTA Economic and Business Abstract, 1939-1962.
Vermillion, S. D.: University of South Dakota Business Research
Bureau, 1963. 263 p. (Bulletin no. 79)   (R 45)

TENNESSEE

[TENNESSEE Statistical Abstract] 1st ed. Knoxville: University of
Tennessee Bureau of Business and Economic Research, 1967. 350
p. (In process)   (R 46)

TEXAS

TEXAS Almanac, 1968-69. Dallas, Tex.: Dallas Morning News,
1967. 704 p.   (R 47)

UTAH

STATISTICAL Abstract of Government of Utah, 1965 ed. Salt Lake
City, Utah: Utah Foundation, 1965. 104 p.   (R 48)

A STATISTICAL Abstract of Utah's Economy, 1964. Salt Lake City,
Utah: University of Utah Bureau of Economic and Business Research, 1964. (Studies in Business and Economics, vol. 24, no.
3)   (R 49)

VERMONT

AN Audit of Vermont; A Statistical Summary of Selected Recent
Economic Changes. Montpelier, Vt.: Central Planning Office, 1963.
11 p.   (R 50)

VIRGINIA

STATISTICAL Abstract of Virginia. Charlottesville, Va.: University of Virginia Thomas Jefferson Center for Studies in Political
Economy, 1966.   (R 51)

WASHINGTON

RESEARCH Council's Handbook, 2d ed., 1964-65. Olympia, Wash.:
Washington State Research Council, 1964. 650 p.   (R 52)

WEST VIRGINIA

COUNTY Study Data Book; Measures of Social Change in West
Virginia. Morgantown, W. Va.: West Virginia University Agricultural Experiment Station, 1961. 96 p. (Bulletin no. 464)   (R 53)

WEST VIRGINIA Statistical Handbook, 1965. Morgantown, W. Va.:
West Virginia University Bureau of Business Research, 1964. 165
p. (Business and Economic Studies, vol. 9, no. 1)   (R 54)

WISCONSIN

FACTS for Industry. Madison, Wis.: Department of Resource
Development, Division of Economic Development, 1964. 171 p.
                                                                                   (R 55)

WISCONSIN Blue Book, 1966. Madison, Wis.: Legislative Refer-
ence Bureau, 1966. 850 p.   (R 56)

WYOMING

WYOMING Statistical Abstract. Laramie, Wyo.: University of

Wyoming Division of Business and Economic Research, 1967. (In process)   (R 57)

About the Index

The indexing has been based upon the text, titles and annotations (which are by no means exhaustive contents listings). Consequently, this index is not a definitive key to all the data actually covered by all the sources cited.

Three types of entries have been used.

Primary emphasis is on specific subject entries. These cover all basic sources cited and, in generic terms, those which have been listed as examples of specifics.

Name entries have been made for all government agencies; for publishers who may be construed as or, in effect, are authors of their works; for nongovernmental authors, editors and compilers; for all public and private organizations with the exception of those cited as illustrative examples or covered by adequate subject or generic terms.

Title entries have been used most sparingly because their length, lack of mnemonic distinctiveness and constant variation, particularly in continuing publications, limit their usefulness as a research aid.

In cross references, entries referred to, when not alphabetical, are listed in the order of closest relationship to the term referred from.

For optimum guidance it is advisable to check subject entries from the most specific through the most general before consulting the generic terms.

Publications and a number of descriptive citations have been coded (e. g. , CA3, E11, etc.) to permit precise referencing to the specific items on a page. General text and statements are referred to by page numbers. In the index, page number precedes code number references. Arrangement within each group is in the order of appearance in the text.

To facilitate the location of coded items in the text the following conspectus relates code number categories to the book pages on which they appear.

Code Number Group	Book Page	Code Number Group	Book Page	Code Number Group	Book Page	Code Number Group	Book Page
A	16-18	E	88-93	H	184-191	M	249
		EA	94-103			MA	250-25
B	21-23	EB	103-115	I	192-194	MB	255-25
BA	23-26	EC	115-119	IA	195-196	MC	259-26
		ED	120-121	IB	198		
C	28-29	EE	122-127			N	262
CA	30-36	EF	127-138	J	201-204	NA	262-26
		EG	139-140	JA	205-206	NB	263-26
D	40-41	EH	141-143	JB	206-209	NC	264-26
DA	42-45	EI	144-151	JC	209-211	ND	267-26
DB	46-53	EJ	151-154	JD	212	NE	269-27
DC	53			JE	214-217		
DD	54-58	F	160			O	273
DE	62	FA	161-164	K	219-222	OA	274-27
DF	64	FB	165-168	KA	223-225	OB	276
DG	66-69			KB	229-233	OC	277-27
DH	69-77	G	172-179	KC	234-236	OD	279-28
DI	78-79	GA	180				
DJ	80-86	GB	180-182	L	245-246	P	284-28
DK	86-87	GC	183				290-29

Code Number Group	Book Page
Q	297-300
QA	301-304
QB	305-310
QC	310-313
R	314-322

Index

A

Abstracts 272-276, EI51, QB1, QC3
  guides to sources of NE 2
Accidents and injuries 127, 140, EC5, EE1-EE2
Accounts, Bureau of 141
Acquisitions see Distribution and acquisition of publications;
  Mergers and acquisitions
Addresses (street) see Directories; Mailing lists
Advertisements, telephone directory 248
Advertising, Bureau of 196, KC3
ADVERTISING AGE KC1, ND1, QC1
Advertising Research H1
  institutions H2

  periodicals NA3
  standards and evaluation A2-A9
Advertising Research Foundation H1
  publications A2, JE7-JE8
    JOURNAL OF ADVERTISING RESEARCH H1, QC7
Advice see Experts; Consultants; Services
Advisory Council on Federal Reports 37
Aerospace industry see Markets--military
Aged see Markets--old-age
Agencies
  federal
    advisory bodies to 36-39, 93
    directories of C1, C5, M3, P9-P10
    field offices 286-289, EE12
    libraries 286-289
    organization C1, C5, M3
    statistical programs 27-28, 36-39, C1-C4, EF24, QA8
    statistical types 27-28, C1
  interstate 159, F1
  state and local 155-157
    directories of FA1-FA3, FA6, FA8, P13-P14
Agricultural Economics (agency) 94
  publications 94-101
    catalogs QB8-QB9
Agricultural economics (subject) EA4, EA 10
Agricultural experiment stations EA9, EA 42
  publications 156

Agricultural Experiment Stations (Cont.)
    catalogs QB 9
Agricultural products (see also Crops; Livestock; CENSUS OF
    AGRICULTURE; and individual products) EA1-EA3, EA12, EA16
    COLD STORAGE REPORT EA7
    marketing EA4, EA10, EA13, EA15, EA38-EA39, EA41-EA42, I8
    prices EA2-EA3, EA5, EA8, EA13, EA15
    production EA2-EA3, EA8, EA16, EA36
Agricultural Research Service 102
Agricultural Stabilization and Conservation Service 102
Agriculture (see also CENSUS OF AGRICULTURE; Markets--farm)
    93-103, BA6, EA34
    area data
        county BA4, DA1 (v. 1, 4, 5 pt. 2-3), EA34
        metropolitan area EA34
        state economic area EA 34
        state 156, DA1 (v. 1-5 pt. 2, v. 5 pt. 4), DA2, EA3, EA5, EA8,
        EA11, EA34
        regional DA1 (v. 2-3), DA2, EA5, EA11, EA18, EA34
        Guam DA1 (v. 1)
        Puerto Rico DA1 (v. 1)
        Virgin Islands DA1 (v. 1)
    BALANCE SHEET OF AGRICULTURE EA37
    census data DA1
    compendia EA1-EA3
    employment and wages, EA6, EA33
    farm level-of-living indexes EA34
    farm life EA42
    farm management EA17, EA35-EA36
    farmer cooperatives EA43, EH9
    finance DA1 (v. 5 pt. 4), EA11, EA18, EA35, EA37
    forecasts EA12-EA30, NC6
    guides to
        experts P11-P14
        statistics CA8
    income BA4, EA2-EA3, EA14
    labor EA6, EA33
    periodicals EA9-EA10, EA38, EA41
        newsletters NC5-NC6
    population BA4, DH13, EA31-EA32
    services JB5
Agriculture, Department of 93-94, EF22
    field offices 288
    methodology CA8
    organization P11-P12
    publications 93-103, CA8, P11-P14
        catalogs QB6-QB7
Air Media (see also Media)
Air transportation EG1-EG3, EJ9
Aircraft EG1, EG3
Alabama (see also State data) G1-G2, R1
Alaska (see also State data) R2
Albuquerque G37

Alcohol, industrial   EH7
Allied Chemical Corp.   JB9
American Association for Public Opinion Research   IA4
American Association of Advertising Agencies   196
    publications   A3-A6
American Chemical Society   194
American Economic Association   39, IA1
    publications   OB2
AMERICAN ECONOMIC REVIEW   GB7, NA5
American Management Association, Inc.   H6
    publications   P17, Q1
American Marketing Association   39, I1
    publications (see also JOURNAL OF MARKETING; JOURNAL OF
      RESEARCH)   A1, FA11, JE6, MB10, P15, Q2-Q3
American Newspaper Publishers' Association see Advertising, Bur-
    eau of
American Psychological Association   IA5, NA7, OB3
American Samoa   D2, DH1 (v.1), DH12
American Sociological Association   IA6, NA8
American Statistical Association   38, FB7-FB8, IA2, NA6
Andriot, John L.   OD4, Q9
Angel, Juvenal L.   JE10
Anns, John   JE9
Annual reports   88, 198, 238, 255
Antitrust and Monopoly, Subcommittee on   DD4
Apparel   EF19, OD12
APPLIED SCIENCE AND TECHNOLOGY INDEX   OC8
Area data see Local data; Census tract data; City block data; Con-
    gressional districts; Postal zone data; Central business district
    data; City data; County data; Metropolitan area data; Standard
    consolidated areas; State economic area data; State data; Economic
    subregion data; Federal Reserve District data; Regional data;
    and these headings as subdivisions under specific subjects.
Area studies see Market studies--area
Arizona (see also State data)   G3-G5, R3-R4
Arkansas (see also State data)   G6-G7, R5
Associated Business Press, Inc.   196, GC1-GC2
Associated University Bureaus of Business and Economic Research
Association of Industrial Advertisers   197, H2
Association of National Advertisers, Inc.   197, A7-A8
Association of North American Directory Publishers   248, MB8
Associations   192-199
    advertising   196-197, I8
    advisory work of   37, 38-39
    commerce and industry   159
    directories of   198, 248, IB, JE9
    field research   I5
    marketing   I1-15 I7-I11
    media   196
    professional   192-196
    trade   196-198, 269, 287
Atlanta   G14
Atlases see Maps and atlases

Audit Bureau of Circulations 258
Audit Bureau of Marketing Services 258
Audits and Surveys Co. J2
Automobiles see Motor vehicles
Automotive Market Research Council I9
AYER (N.W.) & SON'S DIRECTORY OF NEWSPAPERS AND
    PERIODICALS NE1

B

Balance of payments EB23
Bank letters see Newsletters
Bank Public Relations and Marketing Association I10
Banks and banking EH11, EI1, EI3, EI5, EJ13-EJ14, JD1
    deposits BA6
        by counties and metropolitan areas EI4
    state data 157
Beer EH7
BernanAssociates QB5
Bibliographies (see also Catalogs) FA7, QA1-QA4
    federal publications C5, Q9, QA12
    market data GB4, Q1-Q3, Q6, QA5
        industrial Q4-Q5, Q7-Q8, QA4, QA7-QA10, QA13
BIOLOGICAL & AGRICULTURAL INDEX OC7
Births EC3, EC5
    area data
        city EC2-EC3
        county EC2
        metropolitan area EC2
        state EC3
Blaisdell, Ruth F. QA9
Blocks, city see City block data
Board of Governors of the Federal Reserve System (see also
    Federal Reserve Banks)
    methodology and manuals CA22, EI1
    publications 144-147
Boats 140, EG6-EG7
BOOK OF THE STATES FA1
Book Reviews QC2-QC8
BRADFORD'S DIRECTORY OF MARKETING RESEARCH AGENCIES
    JE5
Brand names see Trade names
Brand preferences see Surveys
BRAND RATING INDEX J4
Britton, Hugh MB10
Budget, Bureau of the 27, 37, EF22
    publications 89, C1-C2, CA2-CA3, CA6, E6, P9
Budget, family EF8.1
Budget, federal E3-E5
Bulletins see Newsletters
Bureau of _____ see next most significant term (e.g. Census,
    Bureau of the)
Bureaus, governmental see Agencies

Bureaus, university
    directories of GA1, GC1
    publications 171-172, 179
        bibliographies of GA1-GA2, GC2
        indexes (subject) to GA2, GC2
        periodicals G1-G63, GC1
        state statistical abstracts 314-322
Bureaus of business and economic research see Bureaus, university
Bus transportation DF1 (v. 4), EJ10
Buses see Motor vehicles
Business and Defense Services Administration 103-104, 105, 286
    publications 103-107, DD11, EB31, FA12, FB3, FB10, L1,
        OD10-OD12, Q5-Q6, QA13
Business conditions see Economic conditions
Business cycles B8, EJ3, H4
Business Economics, Office of 107-109, B5-B6
Business failures JC1, NB2
Business firm publications 237-244
BUSINESS HORIZONS 179
Business incorporations, new JC1
Business indicators see Economic indicators
Business magazines see Magazines--business; Magazines--trade
BUSINESS PERIODICALS INDEX MB6, OC5
Business services H7b-c, JC1, JC4-JC5
Buyers' guides see Directories
Buying habits and practices see Surveys

Buying power (see also Income--consumer)
    area data
        city BA1
        county BA1
        metropolitan area BA1, KA1a-e, KA5
        state BA1

C

C-E-I-R, Inc. JA2
Cable communications EJ12
California (see also State data) G8-G9, R6
Canal Zone DH1 (v. 1), DH12
Capital expenditures DB10, OA2
    manufacturing industries DD1-DD2, DD10
    mineral industries DE1
    plant and equipment 109, EI40, KB1
Carpenter, Robert N. Q1
Catalogs (see also Bibliographies; Directories) 304
    federal publications 112, DJ1, E7, QB3-QB21
    mailing lists 259
    manufacturers' products MA3-MA6
    market data publications KC1, QB1-QB2, QC1-QC5, QC7-QC8
        industrial KC2, KC7
    state publications FA6, FA8, FA11, QB22
    surveys KC3
Census, Bureau of the 40-41

Census, Bureau of the (Cont.)
    advisory bodies to 37-39
    methodology and manuals CA9-CA17, DH11
    publications 40-87, B1-B4, B7-B8, CA4-CA5, CA7, CA9-CA17,
      EJ3, FA14-FA15, FB1, FB5, Q4
    catalogs DJ1, GB14-QB15
    in field offices 286
    in libraries 285
    indexes (geographic) to DH6-DH8, OD6
    indexes (subject) to DH7-DH8, OD5-OD6
    unpublished data D1, DH7-DH8, DJ1
Census Statistics, Subcommittee on 36
Census divisions see Regional data
CENSUS OF AGRICULTURE DA1-DA2
    methodology and manuals CA15
CENSUS OF BUSINESS DB1-DB6
CENSUS OF COMMERCIAL FISHERIES DC1
CENSUS OF GOVERNMENTS DG1
CENSUS OF HOUSING DH3-DH5
    indexes to DH8
    methodology and manuals CA13-CA14, CA16-CA17
CENSUS OF MANUFACTURES DB5-DB6, DD1-DD5
CENSUS OF MINERAL INDUSTRIES DB5-DB6, DE1
CENSUS OF POPULATION DH1-DH2, DH5
    indexes to DH6-DH7
    methodology and manuals CA11-CA14, CA16-CA17
CENSUS OF TRANSPORTATION DF1
Census regions see Regional data
Census tract data
    from mailing list houses 258
    housing DH5, EF16
    income of families and individuals EF16
    labor force EF16
    methodology and manuals CA10
    population DH5, EF16
    unemployment EF16
CENSUSES OF BUSINESS, MANUFACTURES, MINERAL INDUSTRIES
    DB5
CENSUSES OF POPULATION AND HOUSING DH5
    methodology and manuals CA13-CA14, CA16-CA17
Central business district data
    retail trade DB1 (v. 3)
    sales, retail DB12
Chamber of Commerce of the United States 158, FA3, NB5
Chambers of commerce 157-158, 287
    directories of FA4
Charted data see Graphic statistics
Checklists see Catalogs
Chemical Marketing Research Association I7, OD10
Chemicals EB3, EI30, H7c-d, OD10, Q8
    industry newsletters OA4-OA6
    marketing abstracts NC8-NC9
Chilton Co. KB2

Citation of references 20
City block data
    housing DH3 (v. 3)
City data (see also Local data; Metropolitan area data; Market
    studies--area; Surveys--consumer)
    births EC2-EC3
    compendia B3, BA1-BA5, FB4
    construction DI1, DI5, DI7-DI8
    consumer expenditures, income and savings EF18
    deaths EC2-EC4
    department store sales DB12
    divorces EC2-EC3
    economic conditions 158
    education EC12
    employment and payrolls DG1 (v. 3; v. 6 pt. 1, 4: v. 7), DG11
    governments DG1 (v. 1-2, v. 4 pt. 3, v. 7), DG10, JD1
    guides to DH6, FA4, FA14, FB2, FB4, FB6, FB8
    housing BA5, DH3 (v. 1-4), DH4, EF16
    income
        consumer spendable BA4
        effective buying BA1-BA3
    indexes (subject) to EI12, OD6
    manufacturing industry DD1 (v. 3)
    marriages EC2-EC3
    motor vehicle registrations BA4-BA5
    population BA1, BA4-BA6, DH1 (v. 1-2), DH14, EF16, FA14
    prices, consumer EF5-EF6
    retail trade BA5, DB1 (v. 2-3)
    sales, retail BA1, BA4-BA5, DB11
    service trade DB1 (v. 7)
    water supply EE25-EE27
    wholesale trade DB1 (v. 5)
City directories 248
City governments see Governments
Civil Aeronautics Board EJ9
Classifications 29
    commodity 82-83, CA2, DD5
    demographic CA11-CA12, CA20
    geographic CA6-CA7, CA13-CA14, CA19
    industrial CA2-CA3, CA11-CA12, DD5
        guides to CA1, CA4-CA5
Cleaning and dyeing plants DB1 (v. 6)
Clearinghouse for Federal Scientific and Technical information 128
Climate (see also Weather) EB46
    local data EB47
    state data EB44-EB45
    regional data EB44
Clothing see Apparel
Coal Research, Office of EE22
Coast Guard see United States Coast Guard
COLD STORAGE REPORT EA7
Colleges and universities (see also Agricultural experiment stations;
    Bureaus, university; Research centers; Theses) 169-170

Colleges and universities (Cont.)
    publications 169-179, EI61
        bibliographies of GA2
        indexes (subject) to GA2
        periodicals G1-G63
Colorado (see also State Data) FA6, G10, R7
Coman, Edwin T. QA1
Commerce, Department of EF22
    cooperative offices 287
    field offices 286-287
    publications 103-115
        bibliographies and catalogs QB12-QB13
Commerce, foreign see Foreign trade
Commerce and industry associations 159
Commercial Fisheries, Bureau of 123-124, DC1, EE12
Commercial standards see Standards and specifications
Commissions 90
Committees see Congressional committees; next most significant
    term in specific name
Commodities (see also Agricultural products; Minerals and mineral
    products; and individual products and industries)
    classification schedules 82-83, CA2, DD5
    directories of 250, M4, MA1-MA2, MA7-MA9
    foreign trade 82-83, 84-85, D3, DJ2, DJ5-DJ14, EB7, EB32
    guides to sources on OD8-OD12
    market research services J1-J11, JB11
    market studies 179, CA23, EB33, EI31, EI51
    prices EF5, EF8-EF10
        guides to OD3
    surveys K5-K6
Commodity Exchange Authority EA45
Commodity exchanges 237, EA45
Companies see Corporations
Compendia B1-B2, B5-B9, JC2
    agricultural data EA1-EA3
    area data
        congressional district B4
        city B3, BA1-BA5, FB4
        county 179, B3, BA1, BA4
        metropolitan area 179, 219, B3, BA1-BA4, EB5, K1-K4,
            KA1
        state 156, 179, B3, BA1, BA4, KA4, R1-R15, R17-R57
        regional 171, B3, BA1
    industry data 197, 269, EB6, JD2, KB2-KB11
    market data
        business and industrial 226-227, 267, BA6
        consumer 219, 226-227, BA1-BA6, EB5, K1-K4, KA1, KA3-
            KA4
        farm 226, 227, BA4, EA1
        negro BA7
Comptroller of the Currency EH11
Conference Board see National Industrial Conference Board
Congress 90-93, M3

Congressional committees   90
  advisory work of   36, 93
  publications   90-93, C3, QA8
    bibliographies and catalogs   E7, QB5
Congressional districts   CA7
  compendia   B4
  population   DH1 (v. 1)
Connecticut (see also State data)   R8
Construction   EB4, EF21, H4b, JB7-JB8, QA4
  area data
    local   DG13
    metropolitan area   EB4
    state   DG13
  census data   46
  value of new   DI4
Consultants (see also Experts)   169, H7
  directories of   JE5-JE9, JE11, P17-P18
  selection   JE2-JE4
Consumer
  expenditures   EF18-EF19, H5j
  finances   EI6-EI7
  markets see Market studies--consumer; Markets; and specific
    topics and geographic areas
Consumer and Marketing Service   101
  publication catalogs   QB10-QB11
Consumer Price Index   131, EF5, EF8
  city data   EF5
  metropolitan area data   EF5
Contract awards   EB1
Controller see Comptroller
Cooperative State Research Service   EA42
Cooperatives   DB3
  farmer   EA43, EH9
Copper   EB3
Corporations   NB6
  COUNTY BUSINESS PATTERNS   D2
  directories of   JD1-JD2, M2, M4, MA1-MA2, MA10-MA13
  finance   238-239, 255, JC1, JD1-JD2
    federal agency data   EI20-EI21, EI40-EI41
  foreign, guides to   QA6
  income tax returns   DB6 (pt. 3), EH8-EH10
  ranked by size   MA12-MA13
CORPORATIONS AND INDUSTRIES, FUNK AND SCOTT INDEX OF
  OC2
Corps of Engineers   139-140, 152
Cost of living see Budget, family; Prices--consumer
Cotton   DA10-DA13, EA19
Council of Economic Advisers   89, EF22
  publications   E1, E6
COUNTY BUSINESS PATTERNS   D2
County data (see also Local data; Market studies--area)
  agriculture   BA4, DA1 (v. 1, 4, 5 pt. 2-3)
    farm level-of-living indexes   EA34

County data (Cont.)
bank deposits EI4
births EC2
compendia 179, B3, BA1, BA4
construction DI1, DI5
deaths EC2
divorces EC2
drainage DA1 (v. 4)
employment and payrolls D2, DG1 (v. 3; v. 6 pt. 1, 4; v. 7), EB22
governments DG1 (v. 1-2; v. 4 pt. 2, 4; v. 5, 7), DG10, DG14, JD1
guides to DH6, FA14, FB10
housing DH3 (v. 1), ED4-ED5, JC6
income
consumer BA1, BA4
farm BA4
personal, guides to FB10
indexes (subject) to OD6
irrigation DA1 (v. 5 pt. 2)
manufacturing industry D2, DD1 (v. 3), DD3, DD10
marriages EC2
methodology and manuals CA14
mineral industries DE (v. 2), EE1-EE2
motor vehicle registrations BA4
population BA1, BA4, DH1 (v. 1-2), DH14, FA14, JC6
retail trade DB1 (v. 2)
sales, retail BA1, BA4
service trades DB1 (v. 7)
wholesale trade DB1 (v. 4-5)
County governments see Governments
Crampon, L. J. FA6
Credit EI1, QA6
consumer EI8-EI11
ratings JC1, MA1-MA2
Crops 95, 96, EA3, EA8
CURRENT INDUSTRIAL REPORTS DD11

D

Dairy Products 96, EA20, EA25
DATRIX GB3
Deaths EC3-EC5
city data EC2-EC4
county data EC2
metropolitan area data EC2
state data EC3
Defense, Department of 151-152
Definitions see Terminology
Delaware (see also State data) R9
Department of _____ see next most significant term (e. g.
Commerce, Department of)
Department stores

operating ratios 170
sales
    central business district data DB12
    city data DB12
    metropolitan area data DB12
    standard consolidated area data DB12
Departments, government see Agencies
Direct Mail Advertising Association 258
Directories (see also Route lists) 247-256
    agencies
        federal C1, C5, M3, P9-P10
        interstate F1
        state and local FA1-FA3, FA6, FA8, P13-P14
    associations 198, 248, IB1, JE9
    bibliographies and guides to FA3, KC6, MB1-MB10, NE5
    biographical JE8, M1-M2 M4, P15
    chambers of commerce FA4
    city 248
    collections for consultation 158, 247, 248
    commercial and industrial 158, 171, 250, 269, H7d, MA1-MA2
    commodities (see also Catalogs--of manufacturers' products) 250,
        269, M4, MA1-MA2, MA7-MA9
    consultants JE5-JE9, JE11, P17-P18
    corporations JD1-JD2, M2, M4, MA1-MA2, MA10-MA13
    executives JD1-JD2, M1-M2, M4, MA10-MA11
    experts 198, FA1, FA4, FB8, IB1, M1, P9, P11-P14
    foreign trade EB34-EB35
    government officials 248, C5, FA1, FB4, M3, P9, P13
    information centers GA1, JE10, P3, P6-P8, P10
    libraries P4-P5
        depository P1
            census 285
        special P3, P5-P8, P10
    mailing lists MC1-MC3
    manufacturers 156, 248, 269, JA1, KB2-KB3, MA1-MA9
    market research firms and services JE5-JE7, JE9-JE11, P15,
        P17-P18
    media P16
    periodicals KC6, ND2, NE1-NE3, NE5-NE7
        special issues KC6, NE5-NE6
    research institutions FB2, GA1
    services JE1, JE5-JE8, NE7
    social scientists JE8
    standards and evaluation MB10
    standards and specifications EI50, EJ1-EJ2
    standards organizations EB50
    telephone 247-248, MB7
    trade names MA1-MA3
    university
        bureaus GA1, GC1
        research centers FB2, GA1
Diseases EC4-EC5
Dissertations see Theses

Distilled spirits EH7
Distribution (see also CENSUS OF BUSINESS; Surveys)
Distribution and Acquisition of publications
   agricultural experiment station 288
   business firm 238-239
   federal government 40-41, 146, 286, 288, M3, QB3
   media 294
   theses GB1
   trade association 197
   university research 170
Distribution checks see Services--market research; Surveys
District of Columbia see State data
Diversification, industrial DB6 (pt. 1)
Dividends 109, EH8
Divisions, census see Regional data
Divorces EC3, EC5
   city data EC2-EC3
   county data EC2
   metropolitan area data EC2
   state data EC3
Documents Index OD4, Q9
Dodge (F. W.) Co. JB7
Donnelley (Reuben H.) Corp. 258
Drainage DA1 (v. 4)
Drivers EG4
Drugs 218
   syndicated service data J1-J7, JB11
Dun & Bradstreet, Inc. JA1, JC1, MA9, MA11
DUN'S REVIEW NB2
Dyeing Plants DB1 (v. 6)

E

Econometric Institute, Inc. JC7
ECONOMIC ALMANAC B9
Economic conditions E1, H4-H5, H7
   area data
      local G1-G63
      city 158
      state 156, 158, G1-G63
      Federal Reserve District 146-147
      regional G1-G63
   forecasts 170-171, H4a, H8, JC1, JC7, NC2
   newsletters 243-244, NC1-NC4
   periodicals G1-G63, H5a, NB1-NB2
   trends B7
Economic Development Administration 112
Economic indicators B8, E6, EI2, EJ3, H4a, H5g-h
Economic Progress, Subcommittee on 92
Economic research
   abstracts EI61, OB2
   associations IA1, IA3
   business magazines NB1, NB3

institutions H4-H5, H7-H8, H11
   periodicals B6, C2, H5a, c, f; H7a, IA2-IA3, NA5-NA6
   universities 169-171, EI61, GA2
Economic Research Service 94, 95
   publications 96-101
     catalogs EA9, QB8-QB9
Economic Services H8, JC2-JC3, JC7
Economic Statistics, Subcommittee on 36, 92
Economic Statistics Bureau of Washington, D. C. JC2
Economic subregion data
   housing DH3 (v. 6)
   population DH1 (v. 1-2)
Edie (Lionel D.) & Co. , Inc. JC3
Editor & Publisher MARKET GUIDE BA5
Education DH1, DH10, EC1, EC10, EC12-EC14, EF16
   forecasts EC11
   school systems DG1 (v. 1, 4 pt. 1)
Education, Office of 118-119
Electric Power EJ11
Electric utilities see Public utilities
Electricity EA46
   prices, metropolitan area data EF7
Electronics JB2
Employment (see also Hours and earnings; Labor; Occupations)
   DH1, EC21, EF11, EF13, EF35
   area data
     local EF36
     city DG1 (v. 3; v. 6 pt. 1, 4; v. 7) DG11
     county D2, DG1 (v. 3), EB22
     metropolitan area D2, DG1 (v. 3), EF12-EF13, FB9
     state economic area D2
     state D2, DG1 (v. 3, 6 pt. 1, 4), DG11, EB22, EF12-EF13, EF37,
       FA13
     regional EB22, EF37
     American Samoa D2
     Guam D2
     Puerto Rico D2
     Virgin Islands D2
   farm EA6, EA33
   forecasts EF23, EF36, NB2
   governments DG1 (v. 3; v. 6 pt. 1, 4; v. 7), DG11
   guides to statistics EF17, EF25, FA13, FB9
   industry (see also CENSUS OF MANUFACTURES, etc.) 137, EB22,
     EF23, EF37
     defense EJ3
     mineral EE1-EE3
   work stoppages 127
Employment Security, Bureau of
   methodology and manuals CA19-CA21
   publications 137-138
Enterprise Statistics series B7-B8, D3, DB6
Executives, directories of JD1-JD2, M1-M2, M4, MA10-MA11
Experts (see also Consultants; Government officials; Unpublished

Experts (Cont.)
    data) 15, 20
    directories of 198, FA1, FA4, FB8, IB1, M1, P9, P11-P14
    types
        business firm 237, 244-245
        chamber of commerce 158
        federal 150, 286-289, P11-P14
        media 218, KB1
        state and local 156
        trade magazine 267
Exports see Foreign trade

F

F & S INDEX OF CORPORATIONS AND INDUSTRIES OC2
FARM INDEX EA2, EA9
Farm Journal Research Service JB5
Farmer Cooperative Service EA43
FATS AND OILS SITUATION EA21
Federal Aviation Agency 139
Federal Communications Commission EF1
Federal Deposit Insurance Corporation EJ12
Federal government (see also Governments; Markets--governmental;
    Markets--military)
    agencies see Agencies-- federal; and names of specific units
    balance of payments EB23
    budget E3-E5
    finances EH1-EH4
    internal revenue collections EH5-EH7
    officials see Government officials--federal
    purchasing see Purchasing
    taxes NC3
Federal Highway Administration 139-140
Federal Home Loan Bank Board EJ14
Federal Housing Administration 120-121
Federal Power Commission EJ11
Federal Reserve Banks (see also Board of Governors of the Federal
    Reserve System) 144, 288, EI5
    publications 146-147
FEDERAL RESERVE BULLETIN EI1
Federal Reserve District data 146-147
Federal Statistics Users' Conference 39
Federal Trade Commission 147-148
Federal Water Pollution Control Administration 116, EE24
FEED SITUATION EA22
Ferguson, Elizabeth OD7
Field research see Market research
Finance company consumer credit EI9, EI11
Financial press 264
Financial ratios see Operating ratios
Financial reports see Annual reports
Financial services JC1, JD1-JD2
Fiscal Service 141

Fish and Wildlife Service 123-124
Fisheries and fishery products EE10-EE14
   census data DC1
Florida (see also State data) G11-G13, R10
Food 218, EA2, EA16, K7, OD11
   prices EA15-EA16
      city data EF6
      metropolitan area data EF6
   syndicated service data J1-J11
Forecasts and forecasting QA4
   abstracts OA1, OA3
   agricultural EA12-EA30, NC6
   economic and business 170-171, H4a, H8, JC1, JC4-JC5, JC7,
      NC2
   education EC11
   employment EF23, EF36, NB2
   housing construction JB9
   income BA1
   indexes (subject) to OA1, OA3
   industry 137, 197, 198, 269, EB2-EB3, EF20, EF22-EF23, EG3,
      H7b, KB1
   inventories NB2
   population BA1, BA4   DH12, FA14
   prices NB2
   sales 197, BA1, NB2
   services 213, H7b, H8, JB1, JB9, JC3-JC4, JC7, OA1
   travel EJ6
   weather 213, EB43
Foreign Commerce, Bureau of 109, JE11
Foreign Service (U.S.) EB33
Foreign trade 79-80, 82-83, 84-85, 103-104, 105, DJ2-DJ14, EB3,
   EB7, EB31-EB32, EE1-EE3, EE11, EI31
   bibliographies and guides 112, DJ1, QB16
   commodity classifications 82-83
   directories EB34-EB35
   periodicals EB30
   related to output D3
Forest products EA44
Forest Service EA44
FORTUNE JA2, MA7, MA12, NB3
Freight traffic see Shipping
Fresno G9
Frost & Sullivan, Inc. JB10
FRUIT SITUATION EA23
Fuels EE1-EE3, EE20, EE22
   consumption by motor vehicles EG4
   prices, metropolitan area data EF7
FUNK AND SCOTT INDEX OF CORPORATIONS AND INDUSTRIES
   OC2

Gale Research Co. GA1, IB1, NE7, OD2, P3, QA4
Gas see Petroleum
General Services Administration C5, EJ1
Geographic area data see Local data; Census tract data; City block
    data; Congressional districts; Postal zone data; Central business
    district data; City data; County data; Metropolitan area data;
    Standard consolidated areas; State economic area data; State data;
    Economic subregion data; Federal Reserve District data; Regional
    data; and these headings as subdivisions under specific subjects
Geological Survey 125-126
Georgia (see also State data) G14-G15, R11
Gibson, Eleanor B. QA7
Gold EH11
Goldstein, Frederick A. Q2
Gordon, William C., Jr. JE4
Government agencies see Agencies
Government officials
    federal, directories of C5, M3, P9
    state and local 156
        directories of 248, FA1, FB4, P13
Governments (see also Federal government)
    area data
        local DG1 (v. 4 pt. 1; v. 5; v. 6 pt. 3; v. 7), FA15
        city DG1 (v. 1-2; v. 4 pt. 3, v. 7), DG10, JD1
        county DG1 (v. 1-2; v. 4 pt. 2, 4; v. 5, 7), DG10, DG14, JD1
        metropolitan area DG1 (v. 1, 2, 5) DG10
        state DG1 (v. 1, 2, 4; v. 6 pt. 2, 4; v. 7), DG10, DG14, FA1,
            FA15, JD1
        Puerto Rico DG1 (v. 7)
    census data DG1
    employment and payrolls DG1 (v. 3; v. 6 pt. 1, 4; v. 7) DG11
    finances DG1 (v. 4; v. 6 pt. 2-4; v. 7), DG10, DG14, FA15, JD1
Graphic statistics DA 1 (v. 5 pt. 6), DG1 (v. 6 pt. 5), EA2, EF3, H5g-h
    H7c, KA3
Griffin Publishing Co., Inc. J8
Gross national product EB20
Guam D2, DA1 (v. 1), DB5, DH1 (v. 1), DH3 (v. 1), DH12
Guides to sources see Bibliographies; Statistical series--guides to;
    and specific subjects
Gunther, Edgar Q2

HARVARD BUSINESS REVIEW 179, NB4
Harvard Economic Research Project 170, EF22
Hauser, Philip M. C4
Hawaii (see also State Data) R12
Health and medical services (see also Accidents and injuries;
    Diseases) EC1, EC5-EC6, EC22
Health, Education and Welfare, Department of 115-120
Hearst Magazines, Inc. KA1

Highways, EG4-EG5
Horticultural specialties DA1 (v. 5 pt. 1)
Hotaling, Donald O. FA2
Hotels DB1 (v. 6), DB13
Hours and earnings EC21, EF11, EF13
   area data
      metropolitan area EF12-EF13, FB9
      state EF12-EF13, EF37, FA13
      regional EF37
   farm 95, EA6, EA33
   guides to statistics EF25, FA13, FB9
House organs 233, 238, 239-240, L2-L3
Housing
   area data
      census tract DH5, EF16
      city block DH3 (v. 3)
      city BA5, DH3, (v. 1-4), DH4, EG16
      county DH3 (v. 1) ED4-ED5, JC6
      metropolitan area DH3 (v. 1-2, 4-5, 7), DH17-DH18, ED4-ED5,
         JC6
      standard consolidated area DH3 (v. 4-5)
      state 157, DH3 (v. 1, 7), DH18, ED4-ED5, JC6
      economic subregion DH3 (v. 6)
      regional DH3 (v. 1-2, 4-5), DH17
      Guam DH3 (v. 1)
      Puerto Rico DH3 (v. 1-2), DH5
      Virgin Islands DH3 (v. 1)
   census data DH3-DH5
      indexes to DH8
      methodology and manuals CA13-CA14, CA16-CA17
   characteristics DH3-DH5, DH17-DH18, DI3, ED3-ED5, JC6
   construction EB4, ED1-ED2
      alterations and repairs DI8
      area data
         city data DI1, DI5, DI7-DI8
         county data DI1, DI5
         metropolitan area data DI1-DI3, DI6-DI8, EB4
         state data DI1, DI7
         regional data DI1-DI3, DI7-DI8
      authorized DI1, DI5-DI7
      forecasts JB9
      sales DI3
      starts DI1-DI2
      value DI4
   financing ED1-ED5, EJ14
Housing and Urban Development, Department of 120-121

I

ITT Data Services JC4
Idaho (see also State data) R13
Illinois (see also State data) G16-G18, R14
Immigration EJ7-EJ8

Immigration and Naturalization Service 153
Imports see Foreign trade
Income
    consumer (see also Buying power) DH1, DH15, EF18
        census tract data EF16
        city data BA1-BA4
        county data BA1, BA4
        metropolitan area data B6, BA1-BA4, DH15
        state data BA1, BA4
    corporate see Corporations--finance
    distribution DH15
    farm EA2-EA3, EA14
        county data BA4
    forecasts, metropolitan area data BA1
    national 109, EB20, H4
    personal 109
        area data
            state EB21, NB1
            regional EB21
        guides to data
            local FB10
            county FB10
            state FB10
Indexes 272, 276-277
    geographic DH6-DH8, EF24, FA12, FB5, OD6
    subject OC2-OC8
        area data DH6-DH8, EF24, EI12, FB5, OD6, QB22
        federal publications QB3
        forecasts OA1, OA3
        marketing literature EI12, FA12, OC1, QB1
        periodicals EI12, OC2-OC8
        statistics DH6-DH8, EF24, FB5, OD1-OD12
        theses GB1-GB4, GB8
        university publications GA2, GC2
Indiana (see also State data) G19, R15
Industrial Advertising Research Institute (see also Marketing Com-
    munications Research Center) A9, H2
Industrial capacity 170, KB1
INDUSTRIAL MARKETING KC2, ND2, QC5
Industrial markets see Market studies--industrial; Markets--business
    and industrial
INDUSTRIES, FUNK AND SCOTT INDEX OF CORPORATIONS AND
    OC2
Industry
    abstracts OA1-OA7
    classifications CA2-CA3, CA11-CA12, DD5
    compendia 197, 269, BA6, JD2, KB2-KB11
    COUNTY BUSINESS PATTERNS D2
    diversification DB6 (pt. 1)
    forecasts 137, 197, 198, 269, EB2-EB3, EF20, EF22-EF23, H7b,
        KB1
    newsletters 239-240, H7c, NC7-NC12
    services H7b-c, JA1-JB9, JB12, JC1, JC7

INDUSTRY REPORTS EB3
Information centers (see also Libraries) 13, 196, 284-289, H5-H7, I3,
   JB8
   directories GA1, JE10, P3, P6-P8, P10
Information retrieval 13-20
Injuries see Accidents and injuries
Input-output 107, 170, EE4, EF22-EF23, H8-H9, JA2
Institute for Interindustry Data, Inc. H9
Institute for Social Research 171
Institute of Outdoor Advertising 196
Institutes see Research centers
Institutions, research 184-191
Insurance EJ14, OD7
Interindustry relations see Input-output
Interior, Department of the 121-127
Internal revenue collections
   federal EH5-EH7
   State 157
Internal Revenue Service 141-143
   unpublished data EH10
International Commerce, Bureau of
   publications 109-112, QA6
      catalogs 112, QB16
International trade see Foreign trade

Interstate Commerce Commission EJ10
Inventories EB3
   forecasts NB2
   manufacturers' DD1-DD2, DD10-DD11
   retail trade DB11
   syndicated services
      retail data J1-J3
      wholesale data J1, J6, J11
   wholesale trade DB14
Investments (see also Securities)
   capital see Capital expenditures
   foreign, in U. S. EB25
   U. S., abroad EB24, EB31, QA6
Iowa (see also State data) G20, R16
Irrigation DA1 (v. 3, 5 pt. 2), EE30

J

Joint Economic Committee 36
   methodology E6
   publications 92-93, C3, FB2
      catalogs E7
JOURNAL OF ADVERTISING RESEARCH H1, NA3, QC7
JOURNAL OF BUSINESS (Chicago University) 179, GB6
JOURNAL OF MARKETING GB5, NA1, O2-O3, QC6
JOURNAL OF MARKETING RESEARCH NA2, QC8
Judiciary, Committee on the DD4
Justice, Department of 153

K

Kansas (see also State data) G21, R17
Katz, Doris B. NE5
Keeping abreast of information 13, 15
Kenney, Brigitte L. FA7
Kentucky (see also State data) G22, R18
Klein (B.) & Co. MC1
Klein, Bernard MB1
Kroll (Seymour) & Associates, Inc. JB8
Kruzas, Anthony J. P3

L

Label, Maurice FA6
Labor (see also Employment; Hours and earnings; Occupations)
   EF1-EF2
  area data
    local EF1
     census tract EF16
     metropolitan area EF13
     state 156, EF1, EF13
  farm 95, EA6, EA33
  force 95, E2, EF13, EF15-EF16
  forecasts 137, EF36
  guides to data EF24-EF25, FA13, FB9
  periodicals EF2
  productivity 127
  statistical methodology and manuals CA18-CA19, CA21, EF2
  turnover EF11, EF12-EF14
Labor, Department of EF22
  publications 127-138, E2
    catalogs QB17-QB18
Labor Statistics, Bureau of
  methodology CA18, EF2
  publications 127-137, BA7
    catalogs EF24, QB19-QB21
    guides EF24-EF25, FA13, FB9
  regional offices 127, 288
Laundries DB1 (v.6)
Leased departments DB3
Legal developments in marketing, abstracts of O3
Leonard, William R. C4
Libraries 118, 284-286
  chamber of commerce 158
  depository
    Census 285
    federal P1-P2
  directories P4-P5
  governmental 286-289
  special FA11
    directories P3, P5-P8, P10

Library of Congress 286
   publications P6-P8, P10, QB22
LIFE KA3
Literature searches see Information retrieval
Livestock 95, 96, EA3, EA24
Local data (see also Agencies--state and local; Market studies--
   area; specific geographic and statistical areas (e. g.. City data))
   climate EB47
   construction DG13
   economic conditions G1-G63
   employment EF36
   fisheries and fishery products EE12
   governments DG1 (v. 4 pt. 1; v. 5; v. 6 pt. 3; v. 7)
   indexes (geographic) EF24, FB5, OD6
   indexes (subject) EF24, EI12, FB5, OD6
   labor EF1
   sources 155-168
      business firms 237
      federal agencies 146-147, DK1-DK2
      guides to EF24, F2, FA12, FA15, FB1, FB5, FB10
      services J1-J11, JA1-JA2, JB5-JB7, JB9, JB11
      universities G1-GC3
   taxes DG12, DG14, EH5-EH6
   unemployment EF36
   unpublished BA1
Louisiana (see also State data) G23-G24, R19
Lumber see forest products

M

McGraw-Hill Information Systems Co. JB7
McGraw-Hill Publications KB1
McNierney, Mary A. JE1
MACRAE'S BLUE BOOK MA1
Magazine Advertising Bureau 196, KC4-KC5
Magazine supplements see Newspaper supplements
Magazines (see also Periodicals; Media)
   advertising and marketing (see also Market research--periodicals)
      310, ND1-ND6
   business 179, 261, H5a, NB1-NB6
   consumer 196, 222-227
   farm (see also Periodicals - relating to agriculture) 227-228
   financial see Financial press
   trade 228-233, 261, 267, 268-269
      special issues 250, 267, KC6
Mailing lists (see also Directories) 258-259
   catalogs and directories MC1-MC3
   services 233, 259
Maine (see also State data) R20
Management H5d-e, H6-H7
Manley, Marion C. QA2

345

Manpower see Labor
Manpower Policy, Evaluation and Research, Office of 137
Manufactured products see Commodities
Manufacturing Industry(ies) BA6
  area data
    city DD1 (v. 3)
    county D2, DD1 (v. 3), DD3, DD10
    metropolitan area D2, DB6 (pt. 2), DD1 (v. 1, 3), DD10
    standard consolidated area DB6 (pt. 2)
    standard state economic area D2
    state 157, D2, DB6 (pt. 2), DD1, DD3, DD10, JC3
    regional DB6 (pt. 1-2), DD1 (v. 1-2), DD3, DD10
    American Samoa D2
    Guam D2, DB5
    Puerto Rico D2, DD2
    Virgin Islands D2, DB5
  capital expenditures DD1-DD2, DD10
  census data DB5, DD1-DD4
  concentration DD4
  directories 156, 248, 269, MA1-MA9
    bibliographies FA3
  forecasts EB2-EB3, NB2
  guides to statistics CA9
  inventories DD10-DD11
  materials consumed DD1
  operating ratios EI20-EI21, EI41
  plants DB6, JD1-JD2
    acquisitions and disposals DD10a
  production indexes EI1-EI2, JC3
  shipments DD4, DD10-DD11, EB2-EB3
Mapmakers 213
Maps and atlases 150, 198, 233, BA6, DA1 (v. 5. pt. 6), DK3, EA2,
  EE28, K2, K4, KA1, KA5
Maritime Administration 113
Market research
  firms
    associations I5
    directories JE5-JE7, JE9-JE11, P17-P18
  institutions H1-H3
  periodicals (see also Magazines--advertising and marketing) NA1-
    NA2
  services 218-219, 233, J1-JB12
  standards and evaluation A1-A9, I1, JE2-JE4
  university 169-172
Market research, industrial (see also Markets--business and industri-
  al) 228-233, CA1, CA23, KB1-KB3
Market Research Corporation of America J3, J9
Market Research Society O1
Market Statistics, Inc. BA1, MA8
Market studies (see also Compendia; Surveys) 241-243
  area 157, 158, 171, 179, 213, 219, 233-234, EI51, H7, K1-K4, K8
    guides to sources of FB3, FB5, Q5
  consumer 157, 169, 171, 179, 233-234

industrial 104, 105, 157, 171, 179, 198, 228-233, CA23, EI51, H7, H7b, KB1-KB3
MARKETERS AIDS, SMALL   EI52
Marketing associations I1-I5, I7-I11
MARKETING/COMMUNICATIONS   ND3, QC2
Marketing Communications Research Center H2, N1
Marketing Evaluations, Inc.   J5
MARKETING FORUM   ND4
MARKETING INFORMATION GUIDE   MB4, OC1, QB1
MARKETING INSIGHTS ND5
MARKETING MANAGEMENT, EXPERIENCES IN H5b
Marketing Research Trade Association I5
Marketing Science Institute CA1, H3
Marketing and Services, Office of 37, 104
Markets
  business and industrial 94, 107
    compendia 226-227, BA6
    services   JA1-JB5, JB7-JB9
  consumer 94, KA1
    compendia 219, 226-227, BA1-BA6, EB5, K1-K4, KA1, KA3-KA4
  farm 94
    compendia 226-227, BA4, EA1
  governmental EB1, EI50, EJ1
  home 259, KA1b
  male KA1d
  military EB1, EI50, EJ2, JB10, Q7
  negro BA4
    bibliographies and guides DH6, Q6
    compendia BA7, Q6
    National Association of Market Developers I2
  old-age DH3 (v. 7), EC22
  overseas EB1, EB31, EB33
  recreational KA1e
  style and quality 258, BA1, KA1c, KA5
Marriages EC3, EC5
  city data EC2-EC3
  county data EC2
  metropolitan area data EC2
  state data EC3
Maryland (see also State data) R21
Massachusetts (see also State data) G25-G26, R22
Mc see Mac
Mayer, Charles S. JE2
Meat EA24
Media (see also Air Media) BA2-BA4
  advisory services 218, KB1
  associations 196
  directories P16
  publications 218-236
    bibliographies and catalogs of KC1-KC5, KC7, QC3-QC5, QC7
  representatives, directories of P16

Media (Cont.)
   research 204-205, 218-236
     standards and evaluation A2-A9
   services 204-205, BA4, J4, KC6
Media Survey, Inc. 218
MEDIA/SCOPE QC4
Medical services see Health and medical services
Membership lists see Associations--directories
Memphis G53
Merchant marine 113, EG6-EG7, EJ4
Mergers and acquisitions H5c, H5i, JC5
Metals EE1-EE3, EE20
Methodology
   example of in industrial market research CA1, CA23
   keeping abreast of 262, EF2, EJ1
   primary sources for 29-30, E6
   statements and manuals, federal 29-30, 32, CA2-CA3, CA6-CA23,
     DD5, DH11, EF2, EI1
   university contributions 169
Metropolitan area data (see also Local data; Market studies--area)
   agriculture EA34
   area studies 219, 233-234, K1-K4, K8
   bank deposits EI4
   births EC2
   compendia 179, 219, B3, BA1-BA4, EB5, K1-K4, KA1
   construction EB4, DI1-DI3, DI6-DI8
   deaths EC2
   definition CA6
   department store sales DB12
   divorces EC2
   employment and payrolls D2, DG1 (v. 3), EF12-EF13, FB9
   forecasts BA1, H8
   governments DG1 (v.1, 2, 5), DG10
   guides to DH6, FB2, FB3, FB7-FB9
   hours and earnings EF12-EF13, FB9
   housing DH3 (v.1-2, 4-5, 7), DH17-DH18, ED4-ED5, JC6
   income, consumer B6, BA1-BA4, DH15
   indexes (subject) to OD6
   labor force EF13
   labor turnover EF13
   manufacturing industries D2, DB6 (pt. 2), DD1 (v.1, 3), DD10
   maps K2, K4, KA1
   marriages EC2
   mineral industries DB6 (pt. 2)
   motor vehicle registrations BA4
   population BA1-BA4, DH1, DH10, DH12, JC6
   prices, consumer EF5-EF7
   retail trade DB1 (v.1-3), DB6 (pt. 2)
   sales, retail BA1-BA4, DB11, KA2
   service trades DB1 (v. 6-7), DB6 (pt. 2)
   surveys, consumer K5-K6
   taxes, federal EH8-EH9
   transportation DF1 (v. 3 pt. 3-4)

travel EJ5
unemployment EF13
wholesale trade DB1 (v. 4-5), DB6 (pt. 2)
Miami (Ohio) G40
Michigan (see also State data) G27-G29, R23
Migration see Population--mobility; Immigration
Mineral industries
  area data
    county DE1 (v. 2), EE1-EE2
    metropolitan area DB6 (pt. 2)
    standard consolidated area DB6 (pt. 2)
    state DB6 (pt. 2), DE1 (v. 2), EE1-EE2
    regional DB6 (pt. 1-2), DE1 (v. 2)
    Guam DB5
    Virgin Islands DB5
  census data DB5, DE1
  employment and payrolls EE1-EE3
  establishments DB6
  input-output EE4
  shipments EE1-EE3
Minerals and mineral products CA23, DE1, EE1-EE3, EE20
Minerals and solid fuels, Office of EE20
Mines, Bureau of EF22
  methodology CA23
  publications 122-123
Minnesota (see also State data) R24
Minor civil divisions see City data
Mint, Bureau of the EH11
Mississippi (see also State data) FA7, G30-G31, R25-R26
Missouri (see also State data) G32, R27
Money EH4, EI1, EI3
Montana (see also State data) G33, R28
MONTHLY LABOR REVIEW EF2, EF15, EF21
Moody's Investors Service, Inc. JD1
Mooers, Calvin N. 20
Motels DB1 (v. 6), DB13
Motion picture theatres DB1 (v. 6) DB13
Motor vehicles DF1 (v. 2), EG5
  fuel consumption EG4
  registrations BA6, EG4
    city data BA4-BA5
    county data BA4
    metropolitan area data BA4
    state data 157, BA4
  statistical services JB6, NC7
MUNICIPAL YEAR BOOK FB4

N

National Accounts Marketing Association I4
National Agricultural Advertising and Marketing Association I8
National Association of Accountants 194

National Association of Business Economists IA3
National Association of Market Developers I2
National Association of Purchasing Agents 194
National Bureau of Economic Research, Inc. H4
National Bureau of Standards 114-115, EB49-EB50
National Center for Health Statistics 115
National income 109, EB20, H4
National Industrial Conference Board B9, H5, JE3, KA3
National Marketing Advisory Committee 37
National Park Service EE29
National Planning Association EF22, H8
National Referral Center for Science and Technology 286, P6-P8, P10
National Science Foundation 150-151
NATION'S BUSINESS 158
Natural resources H10
Nebraska (see also State data) G34, R29
Negro markets see Markets - negro
Nevada (see also State data) G35, R30
New Hampshire see State data
New Jersey (see also State data) G36, R31-R32
New Mexico (see also State data) G37-G38, R33
New York (see also State data) FA8-FA9, R34-R36
New York City FB6-FB8
New York Regional Statistical Center FB7
NEWS FRONT MA13, NB6
Newsletters FB1
   agricultural NC5-NC6
   business and economic 243-244, NC1-NC4
   industry 233, 239-240, H7c, NC7-NC12
Newspaper supplements 221-222
Newspapers (see also Media; Periodicals) 196, 261, 310
   publications
      area studies and statistics 219, K1-K4
      route lists 250
      surveys K5-K6
Nielsen (A. C.) Co. J1
North Carolina (see also State data) R37
North Dakota (see also State data) R38
Note taking 19-20

O

Occupations DH1, EF17
   classifications CA11-CA12, CA20
Office of _____ see next most significant term (e. g. Business
   Economics, Office of)
Ohio (see also State data) G39-G40, R39
Oil and Gas, Office of EE21
Oklahoma (see also State data) G41-G43, R40
Operating ratios 197-198, JC1, NB2
   manufacturing EI20-EI21, EI41
   retail trade 170, 197-198
   wholesale trade 197-198

Operations research OB3
Operations Research Society of America IA7
Oregon (see also State data) G44, R41
Outdoor Recreation, Bureau of EE31

P

Packaging EB3, QA4, QA13
Panama Canal Zone see Canal Zone
Paper EB3, JB3
Partnerships EH8
Passenger cars see Motor vehicles
Passport Office 152
Passports issued EJ5-EJ6
Patent Office 114, EB48
Patents EB48, EI61
Pennsylvania (see also State data) FA10, G45-G48, R42
Penton Publishing Co. KB3
Periodicals (see also Magazines; Newsletters; Newspapers) 261-262
  abstracting see Abstracts
  directories of KC6, ND2, NE1-NE3, NE5-NE7
  professional NA1-NA8
  relating to
    advertising research NA3
    agriculture EA9-EA10, EA38, EA41
    economics and statistics B6, C2, EF2, EI1; H5a, c, f; H7a,
      IA2-IA3, NA5-NA6
      local and regional 156, G1-G63
    foreign trade EB30
    labor EF2
    market research NA1-NA2
    social sciences IA5, NA4, NA7-NA8
  university G1-G63, GC1
Pesticides EA40
Petroleum (see also Fuels) DB1 (v. 4 pt. 1), EE21, NC10-NC11, OD8-
  OD9
Pipeline Research, Inc. J7
Pipelines EJ10-EJ11
Pittsburgh G47-G48
Plant and equipment expenditures see Capital expenditures
Plants, manufacturing DD3, JD1-JD2
  acquisitions and disposals DD10a
  directories of 252, JA1, KB2-KB3, MA7-MA9
Plastics EI30, JB4, OA7
Platt's Oilgram Price Service NC11
Point-of-Sale Research Co. J6
Polk (R. L.) & Co. JB6
Polls see Public opinion research
Pollution control EE24
Population EC1
  area data
    census tract DH5, EF16
    congressional district DH1 (v. 1)

city BA1, BA4-BA6, DH1 (v. 1-2), DH14, EF16, FA14
county BA1, BA4, DH1 (v. 1-2), DH14, FA14, JC6
metropolitan area BA1-BA4, DH1, DH10, DH12, JC6
standard consolidated area DH10
state economic area DH1
state BA1, BA4, DH1, DH12, EA31, EC1, FA14,JC6
economic subregion DA1 (v. 1-2)
regional DH1, DH10, DH13, EA31, FA14
American Samoa DH1 (v. 1), DH12
Canal Zone DH1 (v. 1), DH12
Guam DH1 (v. 1), DH12
Puerto Rico DH1 (v. 1), DH5, DH12
Virgin Islands SH1 (v. 1), DH1
census data DH1-DH2, DH5
characteristics DH1, DH3-DH5, DH10, DH14-DH15, EA32, EC22,
    EF15-EF16, EF18, EI6-EI7, JC6
classification manuals and methodology CA11-CA14, CA20, DH11
farm 95, BA4, DH13, EA31-EA32
forecasts BA1, BA4, DH12, FA14
guides to statistics FA14
mobility DH10, EF16
Port authorities 159
Ports EJ4
Post Office and Civil Service, Committee on QA8
Post Office Department 150
Postal zone data 150
Poultry DA2, EA25
Predicasts, Inc.   JB1-JB4, JC5, OA1-OA3, OC2
President, Executive Office of the 27, 88-90
Prices EF2-EF3
commodity EF5, EF8-EF10
    guides to OD3
consumer EF4-EF5, EF8
    city data EF5
    metropolitan area data EF5
farm EA2-EA3, EA5, EA8, EA13, EA15
forecasts NB2
retail EF7
    city data EF6
    metropolitan area data EF6-EF7
spot market EF9
wholesale EF4, EF10
PRINTERS' INK see MARKETING/ COMMUNICATIONS
Product Movement Indices, Inc. J9
Production 197
agricultural 96, EA2-EA3, EA8, EA16, EA36
foreign trade related to output D3
industrial, indexes of EI1-EI2, JC3
    methodology CA22
Productivity 127
Products see Commodities; Agricultural products; Minerals and
    mineral products; and individual products and industries
Projectron JB9

Proprietorships, sole EH8
PUBLIC AFFAIRS INFORMATION SERVICE BULLETIN MB5, OC6
Public Health Service 115-118
PUBLIC OPINION QUARTERLY NA4
Public opinion research (see also Market research) NA4
    associations IA4
Public roads, Bureau of EG4-EG5
Public utilities 157, EJ11, JD1, QA4
Publishing EB3
Puerto Rico D2
    agriculture DA1 (v.1)
    business data DB2
    governments DG1 (v.7)
    housing DH3 (v.1-2), DH5
    manufactures DD2
    population DH1 (v.1), DH5, DH12
    water supply EE27
Purchasing EB1, EI50, EJ1-EJ2
Purchasing guides see Directories
Purchasing power see Buying power

Q

Quality indexes (see also Markets - style and quality) BA1

R

Radio Advertising Bureau 196
Radio broadcasting (see also Air media) EJ12
Railroads EJ10
RAND MCNALLY COMMERCIAL ATLAS AND MARKETING GUIDE
    BA6
Real Estate QA4
Reclamation, Bureau of EE30
Recreation (see also Markets - recreational) EB41, EE29, EE31
References 16, 19, 20
Regional data (see also Local data; State economic area data; State
    data; Economic subregion data; Federal Reserve district data)
    157, 159, 237, G1-G63
    agriculture DA1 (v.2-3), DA2, EA5, EA11, EA18, EA34
    climate EB44
    compendia 171, B3, BA1
    construction DI1-DI3, DI7-DI8
    consumer expenditures, income and savings EF18
    economic conditions G1-G63
    employment and payrolls EB22, EF37
    fisheries and fishery products DC1, EE11-EE12
    forecasts 48
    guides to F1-F2, FA14
    housing DH3 (v.1-2, 4-5), DH17
    income, personal EB21
    indexes (subject) to EI12, OD6, QB22
    irrigation DA1 (v.3)

Regional data (Cont.)
    manufacturing industries DB6 (pt. 1-2), DD1 (v. 1-2), DD3, DD10
    mineral industries DB6 (pt. 1-2), DE1 (v. 2)
    population DH1, DH10, DH13, EA31, FA14
    retail trade DB1 (v. 1-2), DB6 (pt. 1-2)
    sales, retail DB11
    service trades DB1 (v. 6-7), DB6 (pt. 1-2)
    transportation DF1 (v. 1-3 pt. 2-4)
    wholesale trade DB1 (v. 4-5), DB6 (pt. 1-2), DB14
Regional plan organizations 159
Renewal Assistance Administration 121
Research see Advertising research; Economic research; Information
    retrieval; Market research; Media - research; Operations re-
    search; Public opinion research; Social sciences
Research, unpublished see Unpublished data
Research and development DB7, EI60
Research centers 170, 171, 184-191
    directories of FB2, GA1
Resources for the Future, Inc. H10
Restaurants J2
Retail trade
    advertising-merchandising activity 218, J1, J3
    area data
        central business districts DB1 (v. 3)
        city BA5, DB1 (v. 2-3)
        county DB1 (v. 2)
        metropolitan area DB1 (v. 1-3), DB6 (pt. 2)
        standard consolidated areas DB1 (v. 1-2), DB6 (pt. 2)
        state 157, DB1 (v. 1-2), DB6 (pt. 2)
        regional DB1 (v. 1-2), DB6 (pt. 1-2)
        Guam DB5
        Puerto Rico DB2
        Virgin Islands DB5
    capital expenditures DB10
    census data DB1 (v. 1-3), DB2-DB3, DB5
    establishments DB6, J2
    forecasts NB2
    inventories DB11
    operating ratios 170, 197-198
    sales DB11
Rhode Island (see also State data) R43
Rice EA26
Robinson, Patrick J. CA1
Rocq, Margaret M. OD9
Route lists 221, 250
Rural Electrification administration EA46

S

SIC see Standard Industrial Classification
Sales 197
    department store DB12
    forecasts 197, BA1, NB2

manufacturers' DD1, DD4, DD10-DD11, EB2-EB3
mineral industries DE1, EE1-EE3
retail BA6, DB1 (v. 1-3), DB3, DB11
   area data J1-J3
      central business district DB1 (v. 3)
      city BA1, BA4-BA5, DB1 (v. 2-3), DB11
      county BA1, BA4, DB1 (v. 2)
      metropolitan area BA1-BA4, DB1 (v. 1-3), DB11, KA2
      standard consolidated area DB1 (v. 1-2), DB11
      state BA1, BA4, DB1 (v. 1-2), DB11
      regional DB1 (v. 1-2), DB11
      Guam DB5
      Puerto Rico DB2
      Virgin Islands DB5
   syndicated services J1-J3, JB11
   wholesale DB1 (v. 4-5), DB2, DB14
      syndicated services J6-J11
Sales and Marketing Executives-International I3
SALES MANAGEMENT ND6, QC3
   SURVEY OF BUYING POWER BA1
   SURVEY OF NEWSPAPER MARKETS BA2
   SURVEY OF TELEVISION MARKETS BA3
Saline Water, Office of EE23
Samoa see American Samoa
Savings EF18, EI40
Savings and loan associations EJ14
Savings Institutions Marketing Society of America I11
SCAN J5
Securities EI40, JD1-JD2
Securities and Exchange Commission 149
Security Exchanges EI40
Selling Areas-Marketing, Inc. J10
Service trades
   area data
      city DB1 (v. 7)
      county DB1 (v. 7)
      metropolitan area DB1 (v. 6-7), DB6 (pt. 2)
      standard consolidated area DB1 (v. 7), DB6 (pt. 2)
      state 157, DB1 (v. 6-7), DB6 (pt. 2)
      regional DB1 (v. 6-7), DB6 (pt. 1-2)
      Guam DB5
      Puerto Rico DB2
      Virgin Islands DB5
   capital expenditures DB10
   census data DB1 (v. 6-7), DB2, DB5
   establishments DB6, J2
   receipts DB13
Services (see also Newsletters) 200-213
   abstracting see Abstracts
   business JC1, JC4-JC5
   business and industry planning 244-245, H7b-c, H8
   directories of JE1, JE5-JE8, NE7

Services (Cont.)
   economic H8, JC2-JC3, JC7
   financial JC1, JD1-JD2
   forecasting 213, H7b, H8, JB1, JB9, JC3-JC4, JC7, OA1
   indexing see Indexes (subject)
   industry H7b-c JB6-JB10, JB12
   mailing list 233, 259
   market research 218-219, 233, J1-JB12
   media 204-205, BA4, J4, KC6
   site selection 213
Sewage 116, 120, EE24
Shipping 113, DF1 (v. 3), EJ4, EJ10
   foreign trade 80, 82-83, DJ5, DJ7-DJ8, DJ11-DJ12
Shopping habits see Surveys
Silver EH11
Simmons (W.R.) & Associates Research, Inc. 205
Site selection EB40
   guides to sources on Li, Q5
   services 213
Small Business Administration
   field offices 288-289
   publications 150, GA2, MB3, MC3, QA5
Social Science Research Council 38
Social Sciences
   abstracts EI61, OB3-OB4
   associations IA4-IA6
   periodicals 262, IA5, NA4, NA7-NA8
   resources and specialists H11, JE8, P6, P10
Social security EC1, EC20-EC21
Social Security Administration 119-120
Sources
   primary 15-16, 18-19
     methodology statements in 29-30, E6
   secondary 15-16, 19
   selection 88, 296-297, 304, 305-306, 310
South Carolina (see also State data) G49-G50, R44
South Dakota (see also State data) G51, R45
Special Libraries Association I6
   publications JE1, L3, NE5, OD3, OD7, OD9, QA7, QB2
Specifications see Standards and specifications
SPEEData, Inc. J11
Sport Fisheries and Wildlife, Bureau of 123
Standard & Poor's Corp. JD2, M4
Standard consolidated areas (see also Metropolitan area data)
   definition CA6
   housing DH3 (v. 4-5)
   manufacturing industries DB6 (pt. 2)
   mineral industries DB6 (pt. 2)
   population DH10
   retail trade DB1 (v. 1-2), DB6 (pt. 2)
   sales, retail DB11-DB12
   service trades DB1 (v. 7), DB6 (pt. 2)
   wholesale trade DB1 (v. 4), DB6 (pt. 2)

Standard Industrial Classification CA1-CA2, CA4-CA5, DD5
Standard metropolitan statistical areas see Metropolitan area data
Standard Rate & Data Service BA4, KC6, MC2, P16
Standards and evaluation
  directories, industrial MB10
  research
    advertising A2-A9
    field A1-A9
    market A1-A9, I1, JE2-JE4
    media A2-A9
  selection tools 296
  sources 15-18
  statistical series 36-39, 93, C3
Standards and specifications 114, EB49-EB50, EI50, EJ1-EJ2, MA3, MA5-MA6, QA4
Stanford Research Institute H7
Starch (Daniel) & Staff 205
State, Department of 152
State data (see also Local data; State economic area data; and individual states) 146-147, 155-158
  agricultural products 96, EA8
  agriculture DA1 (v.1-5 pt. 2, 4), DA2, EA3, EA5, EA11, EA34
  births EC3
  climate EB44-EB45
  compendia 179, B3, BA1, BA4, KA4, R1-R15, R17-R57
  construction DG13, DI1, DI7
  deaths EC3
  disease EC4
  divorces EC3
  drainage DA1 (v. 4)
  economic conditions G1-G63
  education EC12-EC13
  employment and payrolls D2, DG1 (v. 3; v. 6 pt. 1, 4), DG11, EB 22, EF12-EF13, EF37, FA13
  fisheries and fishery products DC1, EE12
  forecasts H8
  governments DG1 (v.1-2, 4; v. 6 pt. 2-4; v.7), DG10, DG14, JD1
  guides to DH6, EF24, F2, FA1, FA3-FA4, FA6-FA15, FB10
  hours and earnings EF12-EF13, FA13
  housing DH3 (v.1, 7), DH18, ED4-ED5, JC6
  income
    consumer BA1, BA4
    personal EB21, NB1
      guides to FB10
  indexes (subject) to EF24, EI12, OD6, QB22
  irrigation DA1 (v.3, 5 pt. 2)
  labor EF1, EF13
  manufacturing industries D2, DB6 (pt. 2), DD1, DD3, DD10
    production indexes JC3
  marriages EC3
  mineral industries DB6 (pt. 2), DE1 (v. 2), EE1-EE2
  motor vehicle registrations BA4
  population BA1, BA4, DH1, DH12, EA31, EC1, FA14, JC6

State data (Cont.)
    retail trade DB1 (v. 1-2), DB6 (pt. 2)
    sales, retail BA1, BA4, DB11
    service trades DB1 (v. 6-7), DB6 (pt. 2)
    social security and welfare EC1
    taxes DG12, DG14
        federal EH6, EH8-EH9
    travel EJ5
    unemployment EF13
    vital statistics EC1
    wholesale trade DB1 (v. 4-5), DB6 (pt. 2)
State economic area data
    agriculture EA34
    COUNTY BUSINESS PATTERNS D2
    population DH1
STATISTICAL ABSTRACT OF THE UNITED STATES B1, OD1, QA11
    supplements B2-B4
Statistical abstracts B1-B9, JC2
    industry data 228, EB6
    state and local 156, R1-R57
STATISTICAL DIRECTORY, FEDERAL P9
Statistical Reporting Service 94
    publications 95-96
        catalogs QB8-QB9
Statistical series
    evaluation 36-39, C3
    guides to C4, EF24-EF25, FB10, OD2-OD12, Q4-Q5, QA8, QA11
        agricultural CA8
        area data FA8-FA10, FA12-FA15, FB3, FB5, FB8
        employment and labor CA18, CA21, FA13, FB9
        federal C3
        industrial CA9
        population FA14
Statistical Standards, Office of 27, 29, 37, E6
Store audits see Services - market research; Surveys
Subcommittee _____ see next most significant term
Superintendent of Documents P1-P2, QB3-QB4
SURVEY OF BUYING POWER BA1
SURVEY OF CURRENT BUSINESS 109, B6, EB21, EB23
    supplements B5, EB20, EB23, EB25
Surveys
    catalogs of KC3
    consumer H5j
        by business firms 169, 241-243
            federal agencies 94, DH16, EF18-EF19, EI6-EI7
            media 218, 225-226, 233-234, K5-K6
            services 204-205, J3-J5
            trade associations 198
            universities 169, 171
    farm 227-228
    industrial 225-226, 233, KB1
    standards and evaluation A1-A9
Syndicated services see Services

Tapia, Elizabeth W.   QA7
Tariff Commission, United States see United States Tariff Commission
Taxes
   federal   EH5-EH9, NC3
     local data   EH5-EH6
     metropolitan area data   EH8-EH9
     state data   EH6, EH8-EH9
   income, federal
     business returns   EH8
     corporation returns   DB6 (pt. 3), EH6, EH8, EH10
     individual returns   EH6, EH8-EH9
   local   DH12, DH14
   state   157, DG12, DG14
Technology   114, 137, EF20, EI61, H7
Telegraph industry   EJ12
Telephone industry   EJ12
Telephones   EA46
   directories   247-248, MB7
Television Advertising Bureau   196
Television broadcasting (see also Air media)   EJ12
Tennessee (see also State data)   G53-G54, R46
Terminology   29-30
Tesauro (S. J.) & Co.   JC6
Texas (see also State data)   G54-G59, R47
Textiles   JB12, OD12, QA4
Theses   171
   abstracts   GB1, GB8
   acquisition   GB1
   bibliographies   GB4-GB7
   indexes (subject) to   GB2-GB4
THOMAS REGISTER OF AMERICAN MANUFACTURERS   MA2
Time, Inc.   J10
Tobacco and Tobacco products   EA27, EH7
Towne-Oller & Associates, Inc.   JB11
Trade names, directories of   MA1-MA3
Trademarks   EB48, EI61
Trading areas see Metropolitan area data; Market studies - area;
   City data; County data; State economic area data; Standard con-
   solidated areas
Transit Advertising Association, Inc.   196
Transportation (see also Shipping)   JD1, QA4, QA8-QA10
   census data   DF1
   data from states   157
   home-to-work   DF1 (v. 1)
   means of travel   DF1 (v. 1), EJ5, EJ8
   urban   120
Transportation, Department of   139
Travel   114, DF1 (v. 1), EB41, EJ7-EJ9
   area data
     metropolitan area   EJ5
     state   EJ5

Travel (Cont.)
    regional DF1 (v. 1)
    forecasts EJ6
    passports issued EJ5-EJ6
Travel Service, United States see United States Travel Service
Treasury, Department of the 141-143
Truck transportation DF1 (v. 2-4), EJ10
Trucks see motor vehicles
Twentieth Century Fund H11

U

ULRICH'S INTERNATIONAL PERIODICALS DIRECTORY NE2
Unemployment EF13, EF35
    local data EF36
    census tract data EF16
    metropolitan area data EF13
    state data EF13
United States Coast Guard 140
U. S. Economics Corp. JC7
United States Tariff Commission 148-149
United States Travel Service 114
Universities see Colleges and universities; Bureaus, university
University of Michigan 171
Unpublished data (see also Experts) 158-159)
    Bureau of the Census D1, DH7-DH8, DJ1, QB15
    Internal Revenue Service EH10
    services BA1
    state and local governments 155-157
    trade associations 196
    university research centers 170, EI61
Urban places see City data; Metropolitan area data; Local data
Urban renewal ED1, ED6, FB2
Utah (see also State data) G60-G61, R48-R49
Utilities see Public utilities

V

VEGETABLE SITUATION EA28
Vermont (see also State data) R50
Virgin Islands D2, DA1 (v. 1), DB5, DH1 (v. 1), DH3 (v. 1), DH12
Virginia (see also State data) R51
Vital statistics 157, EC1- EC2

W

Warehouse withdrawals see Services - market research
Warehousing DB1 (v. 4)
Washington (state) (see also State data) FA11, G62, R52
Wasserman, Paul OD2-OD3, P18, QA3
Waste facilities see Sewage
Water P8
Water supply 116, 120, EE23-EE27

Waterways EJ4, EJ10
Weather (see also Climate) EB42-EB43
  forecasts 213, EB43
Welfare Bureau 113-114
Welfare see Social security
West Virginia (see also State data) R53-R54
Wharton School 169, 170
WHEAT SITUATION EA29
Wholesale trade
  area data
    city DB1 (v. 5)
    county DB1 (v. 4-5)
    metropolitan area DB1 (v. 4-5), DB6 (pt. 2)
    standard consolidated area (DB1 (v. 4-5), DB6 (pt. 2)
    state DB1 (v. 4-5), DB6 (pt. 2)
    regional DB1 (v. 4-5), DB6 (pt. 1-2), DB14
    Guam DB5
    Puerto Rico DB2
    Virgin Islands DB5
  capital expenditures DB10
  census data DB1 (v. 4-5), DB2, DB4-DB5
  establishments DB6
  forecasts NB2
  inventories DB14
  merchant wholesalers DB4, DB10, DB14
  operating ratios 197-198
  sales DB14
Wine EH7
Wisconsin (see also State data) R55-R56
Women's Bureau 138
WOOL SITUATION EA30
Work stoppages 127
Wyoming (see also State data) G63, R57

X Y Z

Yachts EG6-EG7
Zip code areas see Postal zone data